MASTER LIGHTING TECHNIQUES

for Outdoor and Location Digital Portrait Photography

All photographs by the author unless otherwise noted.
Diagrams designed by Terry Walker and Stephen Dantzig.

Published by:
Amherst Media®
P.O. Box 586
Buffalo, N.Y. 14226
Fax: 716-874-4508
www.AmherstMedia.com

Publisher: Craig Alesse
Senior Editor/Production Manager: Michelle Perkins
Assistant Editor: Barbara A. Lynch-Johnt

ISBN: 1-58428-185-5
Library of Congress Control Number: 2005937367
Printed in Korea.
10 9 8 7 6 5 4 3 2 1

TABLE OF CONTENTS

FOREWORD

Outdoor digital portraiture is a skill that requires the photographer to control the controllable and manage the uncontrollable to produce both usable and workable images. To do this successfully (meaning without having to spend hours using Photoshop to save every image), the photographer must possess a thorough understanding of metering, lighting, posing, his/her equipment, and the limits of their Photoshop skills. Add to this the unpredictability of weather, adults, children, and pets, and an outdoor digital portrait can turn into an outdoor disaster! Therefore, it is imperative that the digital photographer be equipped not only the proper equipment but also a set of skills that will allow him/her to create the image that he/she or the client has envisioned.

Digital photography has arrived and is here to stay—until the next great technical evolution. For some of us, the transition from film to digital was harder than for others. This new technology, while simplifying a great portion of what we do, created a dramatic change in our workflow and how we do it. A digital portrait photographer today must be able to anticipate, plan, adapt, and manage both the technical and human elements of any given photo shoot. The ability to repeatedly be able to manage all the elements of an outdoor portrait successfully under a broad range of conditions requires a tremendous technical understanding of digital photography and lighting—not to mention the ability to make both creative and technical decisions in a split second since neither the ambient light or your subjects will wait around while you figure out a solution to a lighting problem!

Stephen Dantzig, throughout the years, has become an expert digital photographer via his tireless search for a complete technical understanding of metering, lighting, and posing. His passion and creativity for photography were further elevated by all the endless possibilities and challenges that digital photography presented. This book is a culmination of Stephen's years of testing and experimenting with metering, lighting, posing, and Photoshop to obtain the repeatable techniques he used to create many of the stunning images in this book.

THIS BOOK IS A CULMINATION OF STEPHEN'S YEARS OF TESTING AND EXPERIMENTING . . .

I first met Stephen over twenty years ago while I was working at a local camera store and we were attending Rutgers University. I consider Stephen to be one of my oldest and best friends in the world and he has been an inspiration to me and everyone else that knows him. To this day, Stephen and I still laugh about some of the early images we created while trying to duplicate techniques used to create commercial images we saw in magazines. From the first day I met Stephen he was always trying to learn more about the physics, science, and art that make up photography. It is this unquenchable thirst for knowledge that to date propels Stephen forward and keeps him pushing beyond his seemingly endless limits.

In this second book by Stephen, he discusses the changes in thinking and the new skills required to make the transition from shooting film to digital. The book is written in a clear and concise easy-to-follow manner and is loaded with diagrams illustrating all the lighting scenarios used to create the images. The images are presented in a step-by-step manner that allows you to see how the image progresses from the very first shot to the final post-Photoshop image. Included is also a keystroke-by-keystroke tutorial on some of Stephen's favorite Photoshop techniques used to create these images. The information contained in this book is arranged in such a way that it can be used as a reference book when you are preparing for your next outdoor portrait or are confronted with an outdoor exposure/lighting problem.

Stephen has enclosed so much valuable information in this book that I hope you take the time to study the diagrams and the charts and begin using the techniques that Stephen has tried and tested.

I look forward to Stephen's next photographic endeavor, whatever it may be. Knowing Steve—he is just getting started.

—Al Garcia
Commercial Photographer

ACKNOWLEDGMENTS

Once again there are many people who have been a great support to me while I was photographing and writing this book. I am quite sure that I will neglect to mention some people—and I do apologize to them in advance.

First, I would like to thank Craig, Michelle, Barbara, and the crew at Amherst Media for the opportunity to write this book. The concept was challenging from several viewpoints and turned into a great learning experience. Lighting on location is a difficult undertaking, and at almost every turn was the chance to learn more. The task of explaining what worked—and what didn't work—forced me to truly understand the process of outdoor lighting and has made me a better writer, teacher, and photographer.

I was also given the task of breaking out of my customary role of commercial and fashion photographer to explore the world of portraiture. I have always felt that—for me—the two were very different worlds. While I still consider myself more of a commercial photographer, I was able to discover the challenges and joys of photographing families and children. It's a nice feeling when a mother gets goose bumps when she sees a portrait of her daughter and herself.

Teaching photography truly makes you figure it out. I have my friend and mentor Bill Higgins to thank for helping to lay the foundations from which my awareness of photography stem. I chose the word "awareness" carefully. Bill's rather unorthodox way of teaching me photography by not teaching me photography forced me to go well beyond understanding a particular technique. His approach to my apprenticeship fostered a critical ability to be aware of what factors would influence my image. To create a beautifully lit outdoor portrait you need to be constantly aware of the changes in your environment and the effects that those changes will have on how you photograph the scene. Conversely, as you change your approach to photograph the scene, you also need to be aware of how those changes will affect the image.

YOU NEED TO BE CONSTANTLY AWARE OF THE CHANGES IN YOUR ENVIRONMENT . . .

I started writing about photography for the Photoflex Web Photo School, but it was my good friend Bill Hurter at *Rangefinder* who helped to shape my skills and played an important role in turning me into a professional writer. His critiques and edits of my early work are greatly appreciated as are his continued support, advice, and friendship.

I mentioned that I see myself as more of a commercial photographer than a portrait artist. Therefore, I turned to some friends whose portrait work has always inspired me for help, and they generously agreed to be a part of this book. I am extremely proud to feature images from old and new friends. It is a feeling that defies words to include images from Al Garcia. Al and I sat "talking shop" and planning our careers over twenty years ago! Don Herzig and I leaned on each other for close to ten years in Los Angeles—of course, Don went on to win the Professional Photographers of Los Angeles County Photographer of the Year Award in 1998! Paul Gero and I struck up a fast friendship during a four-day seminar with Will Crockett—another close friend and huge supporter of mine. I continued along a commercial path while Paul ventured successfully into the realm of photojournalistic wedding photography. Stan Cox II was one of the first photographers I met when I moved to Hawaii. It seems like he and I have been friends since the day I walked into his studio. David Taylor is a Master Photographer and someone whom I respect personally and for the work he is doing with the Professional Photographers of Hawaii. Parker Pritcher is a newcomer to my "inner circle" of photo friends, but he is a welcomed addition! Harry Lang has not only been a great help to me and an even better friend, but he actually managed to take a good photograph of me! Now *that*'s a good photographer!

Then there are the people who have helped to illustrate this book. I don't know the people that my friends photographed—except the Donohers—but it was great fun working with the following people: Amy Raquel, Brooke Tanaka, Cheryl, Debbie Brown, Jenny and Aidon, Karielle, Ka'u, and Kelroy, Kathryn, Kim, Gilles, Andrew and Thomas, Ku'uipo, Manu, Ku and Paige, Monica Ivey, Nanette and Savannah, Rachael Regina, Ruthchelle Melchor, Sanna Dioso, Tanya, Teresa Bringas, Midori Every, Tianne, Tishanna, Anja Lee, Kristina Poulos, and my longtime friends, Paul and Kim Becker (and Hula!).

I LEARNED THAT YOU NEED TO BE PREPARED FOR ANYTHING WHILE ON LOCATION.

You will see that some of the techniques used in this book are very complicated. I had a great deal of help from some terrific people who were not only wonderful assistants but a lot of fun to work with. They are Ed Seid, Parker Pritcher, Marshall Hartle, John Shen, Kypo, and Claude Sable.

Of course, I owe a huge amount to my family, especially my parents, who have believed in me from day one and have watched me fly off to Los Angeles and then to Hawaii, knowing full well that my foundation will always be with them in New York.

There is one other person whose work was instrumental to this volume, but more importantly, whose friendship has been essential in my life. Terry Walker designed the icons for the diagrams in the book. Hey Ter, this is what creativity is all about. This book is dedicated to you, my friend.

INTRODUCTION

There can be no escaping it: photography has changed. Not only is digital photography here to stay, its stranglehold on the industry increases daily. Photographers are faced with a whole new set of challenges. Camera bags that were once filled with different films and filters are now filled with media cards, wires, and even laptop computers. While "ISO" is still part of the vernacular, "megapixel," "RAW," "JPEG," and "TIFF" have become common terms. "White balance" has become a way of dealing with color temperature and color balance issues. Trips to the lab have been replaced with "downloading files." Many photographers have stopped establishing a "Shirley" with their labs and are now establishing "color profiles" and calibrating their computer monitors. Debates about pulling or pushing film—or even "expose for the shadows and develop for the highlights"—are now discussions about "screen" or "multiply" layer blending modes or "masks" in Photoshop. "ROYGBIV" is now joined with "RGB" and "CMYK."

THERE CAN BE NO ESCAPING IT: PHOTOGRAPHY HAS CHANGED.

Yes, photography has changed . . . or has it? The principles that govern photography haven't changed since the earliest days of recording images. Photography is about the recording of an image on a light-sensitive material. More accurately, photography is about recording the light that is reflected off your subject on a light-sensitive material. The only constant in the ever evolving field of photography is light. It acts in extremely predictable—and generally controllable—ways. Light has a different "temperature" at different times of the day and in different situations. Light takes on a different "quality" depending on the size of the light source and its distance from the subject. A second light source will add light in a very predictable way. Different types of light sources will contain different levels of red, green, and blue light (traditional films recorded light on each of three emulsions—one each for red, green, and blue light) that will produce different color shifts in your images if the light source is "out of balance." Light continues to fall off at a rate equal to the inverse of its distance to the subject squared (if you double the distance from the light to your subject without adjusting the power output, then the quantity of light reaching your subject will be ¼ of its original exposure). These laws remain constant regardless of the capture medium.

So, if light hasn't changed, than what is all the fuss about digital capture? Why are so many portrait and wedding photographers having such a hard time making the transition to digital? While we are at it, why aren't many commercial photographers experiencing

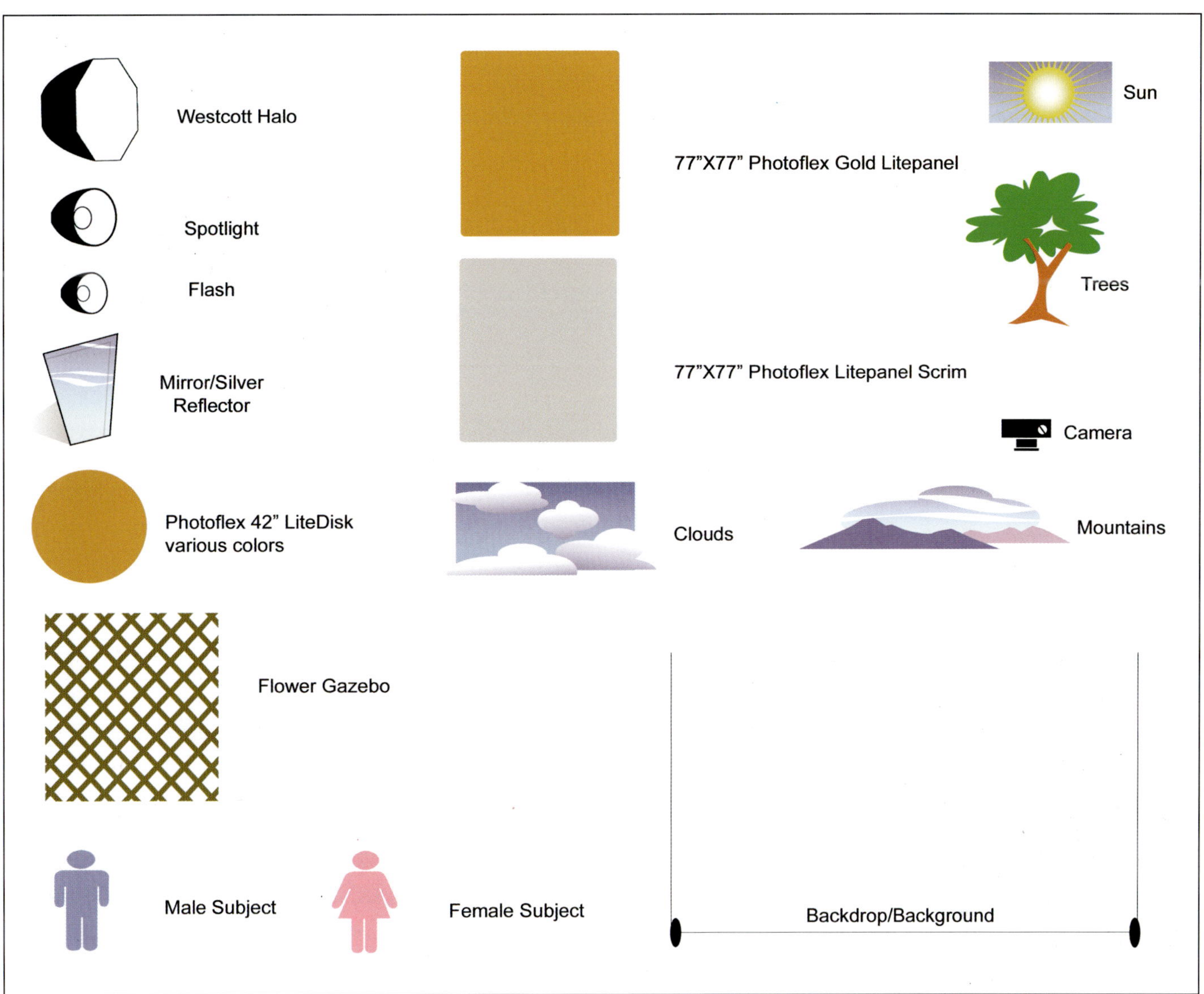

Many of the diagrams used in this book were built from the top down, rather than the customary bottom up. I chose this method to show, as accurately as possible, the position and angle of the lighting gear. All orientations are correct from the perspective of standing behind the camera.

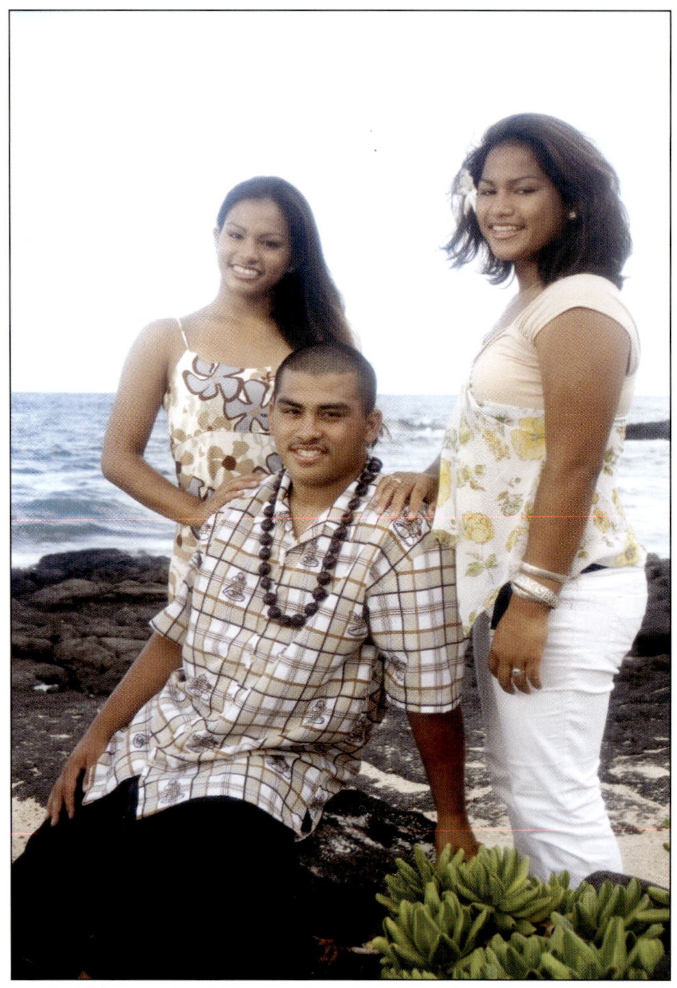

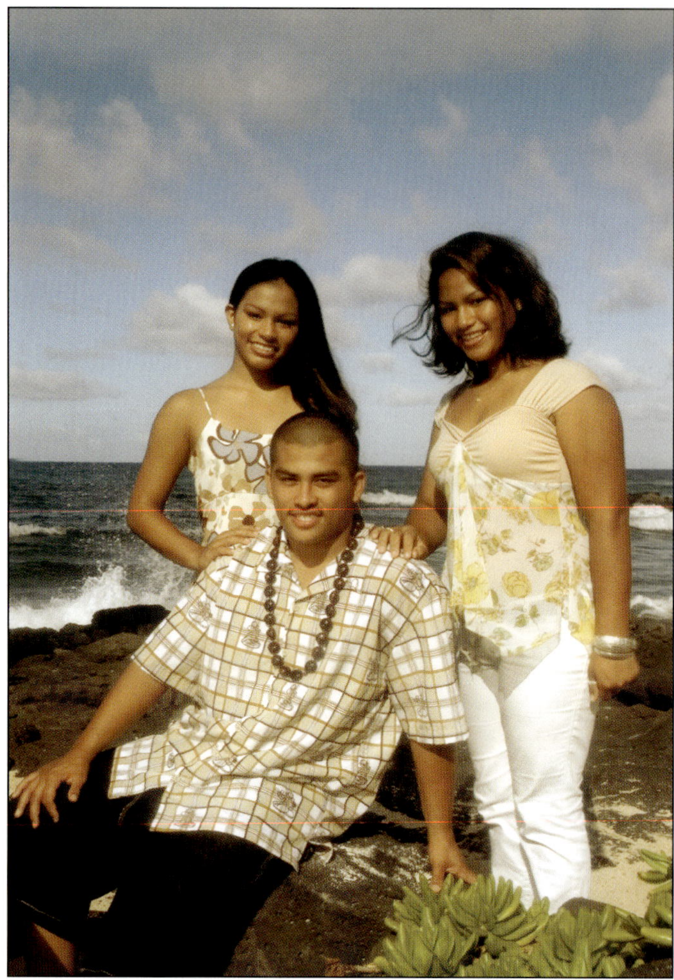

Left—The first image of Karielle, Ka'u, and Kelroy shows the effects of a thick cloud cover. Clouds do not necessarily equate to a lousy lighting situation. In fact, there are times when a thin cloud cover can create a large softbox effect while keeping some direction to the light. However, the entire scene needs to be lit by the sun sifting through the thin clouds for it to work. One situation that will be addressed in detail later is seen here: the cloud cover was localized and placed the three teenagers in relative shadow, but the background was still lit by bright sunlight (see chapter 3 for more information). The light was metered for their skin tones, so the background was overexposed, and we lost the details that define the beautiful location. **Right—**The situation changed within minutes as the sun came out from behind the clouds. The sun was still fairly high in the sky, so I had to choose whether to have my assistant use a reflector to bounce light into the three faces or try to bounce light to illuminate the left side of our subjects to create a rim/hair light effect. I chose the hair light, which, in hindsight was the wrong choice. **Facing Page—**There weren't many images that showed my poor judgment because the light changed once again! This image was captured as the sun began to hide behind a new set of clouds. The light was changing so fast that by the time Karielle, Ka'u, and Kelroy's mother stepped out of the scene after providing another meter reading, the setting was incorrect and actually underexposed the trio. However, the values were not that far off, so this image was one that could be "saved" in Photoshop. See page 12.

as much trouble transitioning to digital? It has nothing to do with talent or knowledge. Right now, digital capture acts more like transparency film—the workhorse of traditional commercial shooters—than negative film—the old standby in the portrait/wedding game. Negative film has a much wider exposure latitude than transparency film—and even wider than digital. The "rule" when I was learning to shoot negative film was to routinely overexpose the film by 1 stop—you'd get richer colors that way. Over time film manufacturers developed "truer" films, and overexposing film became more of an option than a requirement. However, neg-

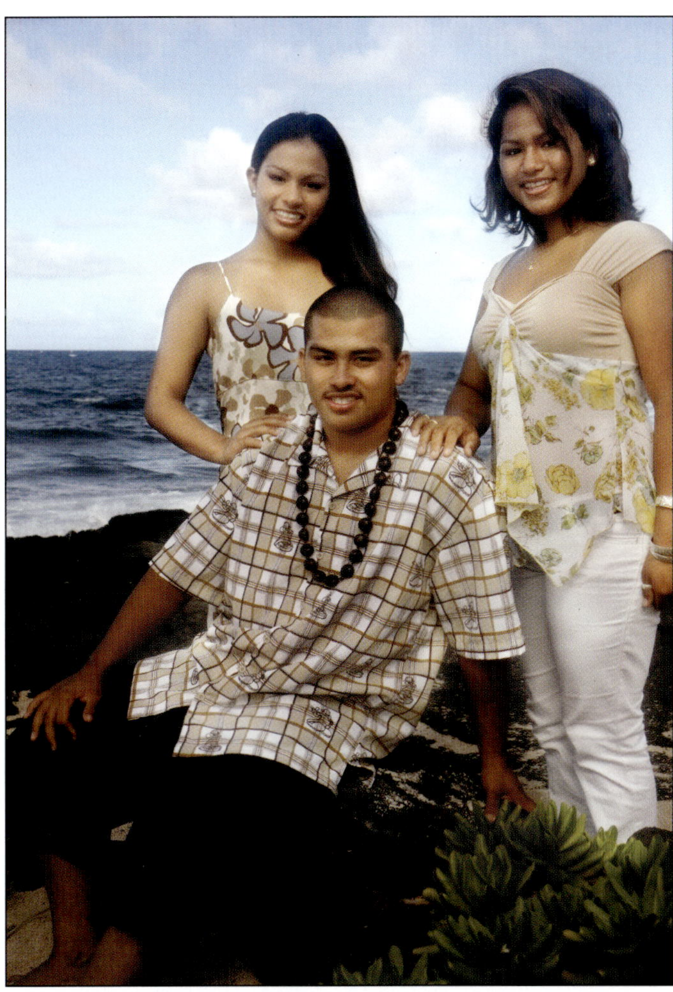

ative film could still "hold" enough information to make a saleable print if the image was overexposed by $1^1/_2$ to 2 stops or underexposed by 1 stop.

There are no such luxuries with transparency film and especially with digital capture. You begin to lose data at ⅓ stop over and ½ stop underexposure; your whites are gone at 1½ stops over, and your shadows begin to clog up at 1 stop under. Commercial shooters are used to strict exposure parameters and have had to tighten the reigns only slightly to "fit" into the world of digital. Portrait and wedding photographers have had to completely reevaluate their method of exposure control to work within the digital realm.

What has changed with the proliferation of digital photography is the need for control—of your lights and of your lighting. A narrower exposure latitude will also necessarily yield a higher-contrast image. One of the first things that all photographers learn about is f-stops. Somewhere along the line portrait photographers started talking about lighting "ratios" and which ratios created a pleasing portrait and which ones could be used for a more "dramatic" portrait. It seems that a funny thing happened on the way to "ratio land." We forgot that ratios are based on f-stops! The world of digital photography requires us to revisit that simple, yet painfully complex notion of f-stops. You simply do not have as many to work with in the digital realm.

The transition to the constraints of digital photography for portrait photographers has been easier in the studio than outdoors. Light in the studio is infinitely controllable. Light in the studio stays put until you decide to change it. Creating digital portraits outdoors is much trickier: light outdoors is constantly changing. A large part of this book was photographed on the beautiful islands of Hawaii. It turns out that playing in one of nature's most spectacular playgrounds is a double-edged sword. The results can be breathtaking, but the process of creating the images is extremely difficult. I would guess that there are few places where the light changes as rapidly and as dramatically as it does in Hawaii. Remember that there are no subtle changes with digital capture. Your image shows drastic changes with small changes in the lighting. The increased contrast of digital capture, coupled with the changing conditions, can wreak havoc on your image. What was once an interesting highlight strategically placed on a piece of film is now a blown-out blotch of white that is devoid of pixel information. The "subtle" shadows are now at best black without detail, or worse, black with tiny specs of digital "noise."

The above three images were taken within a less than five-minute time span. Each image was metered carefully, but the conditions were changing so fast that they were sometimes different by the time I changed the settings on the camera! While it is true that almost every digital image will require some manipulation (that's just part of the "new" workflow), there will be times when you may need to rely on your post-production skills to make an image work. Photo manipulation programs can help in many situations, but the "fix-it" range is frighteningly narrow.

I have mentioned many times that I love photography because it is a field within which there is no end to

USING MULTIPLE CURVES ADJUSTMENT LAYERS AND LAYER MASKS

The last image in the series of portraits on page 10–11 was created under difficult lighting conditions. Though we were as critical as we could have been with the metering, the light simply changed too quickly to nail a perfect exposure. The resulting image was flat and lifeless but held most of the necessary information needed to create a well-balanced and pleasing portrait. The vast majority of digital images need a little color and contrast manipulation in post-production. This one (image 1) needed a little more! The first step in creating a saleable portrait was to create a curves adjustment layer in Photoshop.

1. Open the layers palette and click the adjustment layer icon at the bottom of the palette. Choose Curves.
2. Use the eyedropper tools to conduct your basic color correction. The white eyedropper tool was set for 245, 245, and 245 in RGB mode; the black eyedropper tool was set for 10, 10, and 10; and the gray eyedropper was set at 128, 128, and 128. Find the darkest spot in your image (use the information palette to judge the darkest spot) and the lightest spot, and use the respective eyedroppers to reset the values. The gray eyedropper can be used to correct any remaining color cast by setting an appropriate spot in your image to neutral gray.

The color correction technique just described will provide a quick fix for most of your images, but it just made this image worse. (See image 2.)

3. To create a new layer, I selected the background layer and hit ctrl/cmd + J.[1] Then I created a new curves adjustment layer, this time using the curves grid to make my adjustments. I wanted the curves adjustment layer to affect only the new layer, so I grouped the new adjustment layer with this layer by clicking ctrl/cmd + G. This creates a "clipping mask" and is done using a different technique in Photoshop CS2. In the CS2 layers palette, you place your cursor between the layers to be masked and, while holding the alt/opt key, click.

The result of this adjustment was pretty bad (see image 3)! We had nice skin tones but lost the beautiful sky and ocean behind the family. The next steps were the key to enhancing this image:

4. I activated the second layer and went to the layers drop-down menu and selected Add Layer Mask>Hide All.
5. I chose the brush tool and set the foreground color to white. I painted in the new curves adjustment by moving the brush tool over Karielle, Ka'u, and Kelroy—leaving Kelroy's arms and legs in shadow.

I was originally pleased with the image at this point, but the more I looked at it, the more I realized that the clothes were too bright. Modifying your changes is simple with layer masks.

6. I switched the foreground color to black, set the brush opacity to 50%, and painted the clothes back in to 50% of their original darkness (page 14).

---

1. Note that in the keystroke ctrl/cmd + G, the first key (ctrl) before the slash is for PC users. The second key (cmd) is for Mac users.

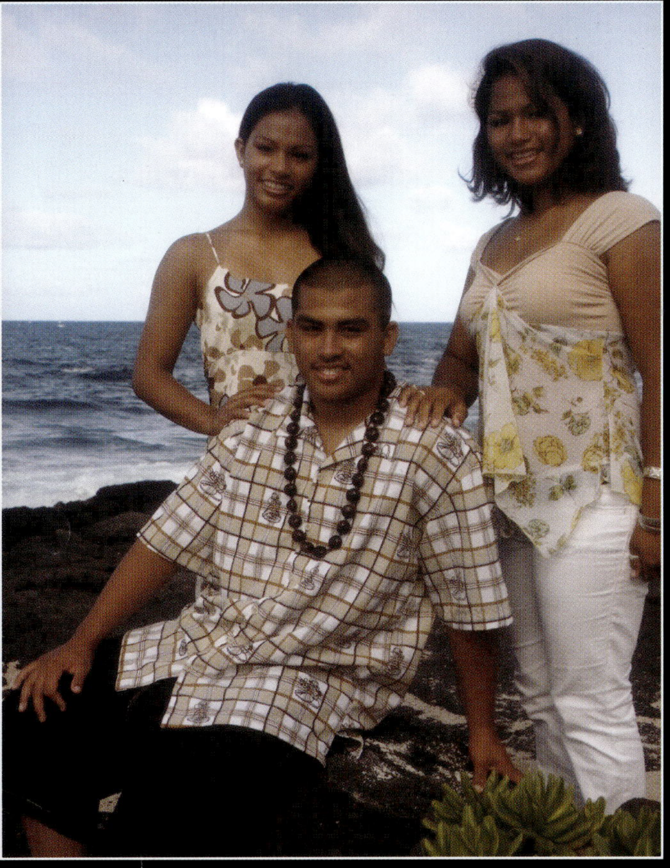
Image 1

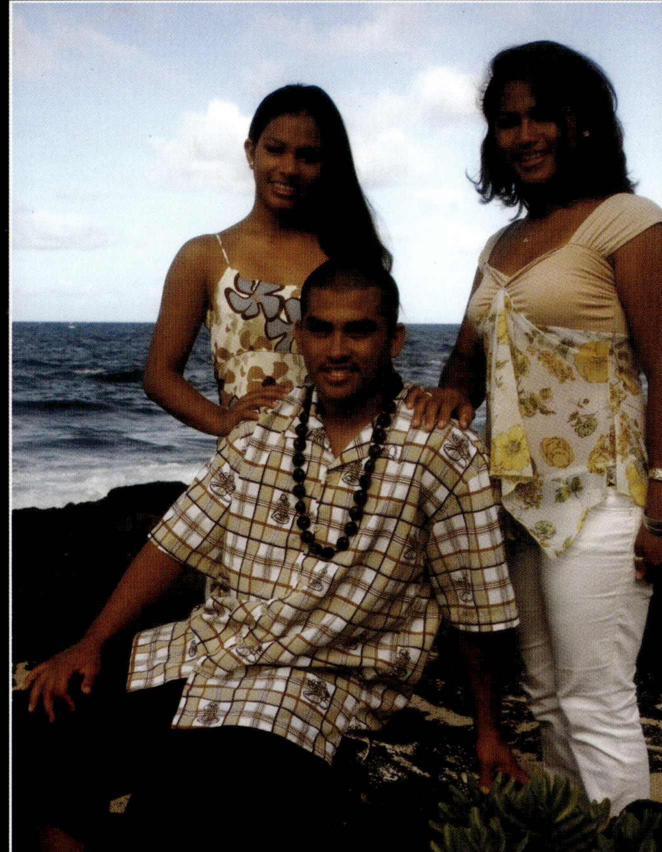
Image 2

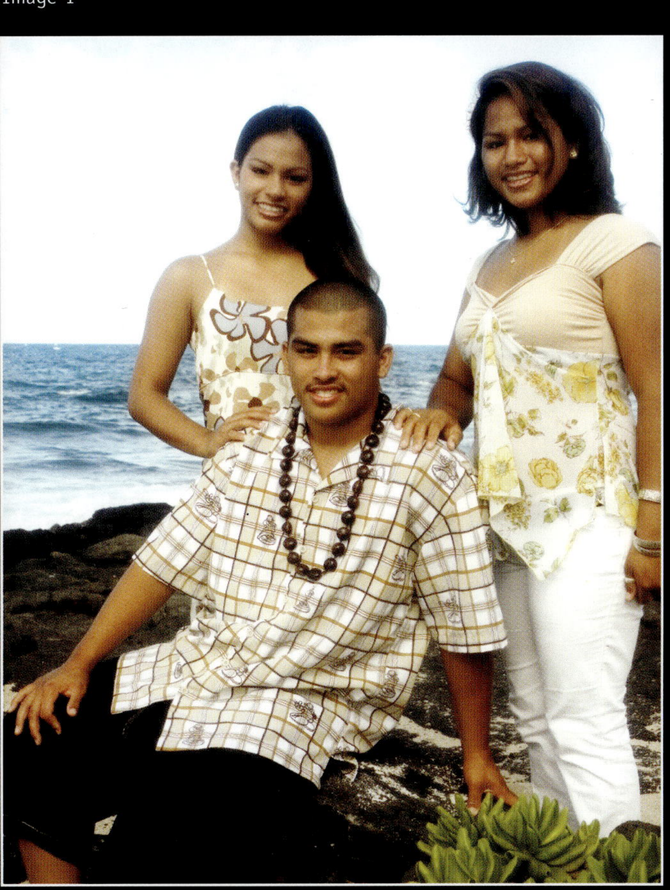
Image 3

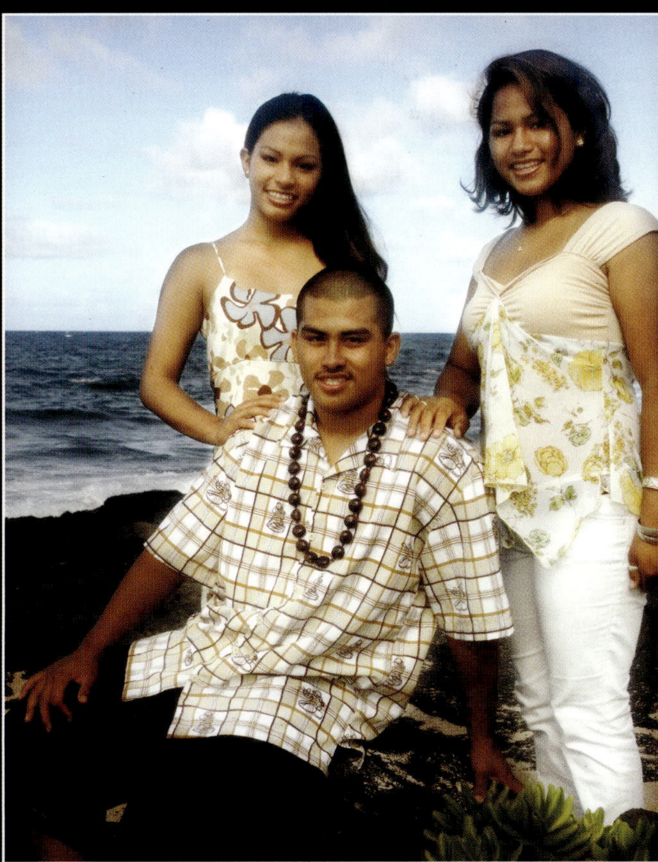
Image 4

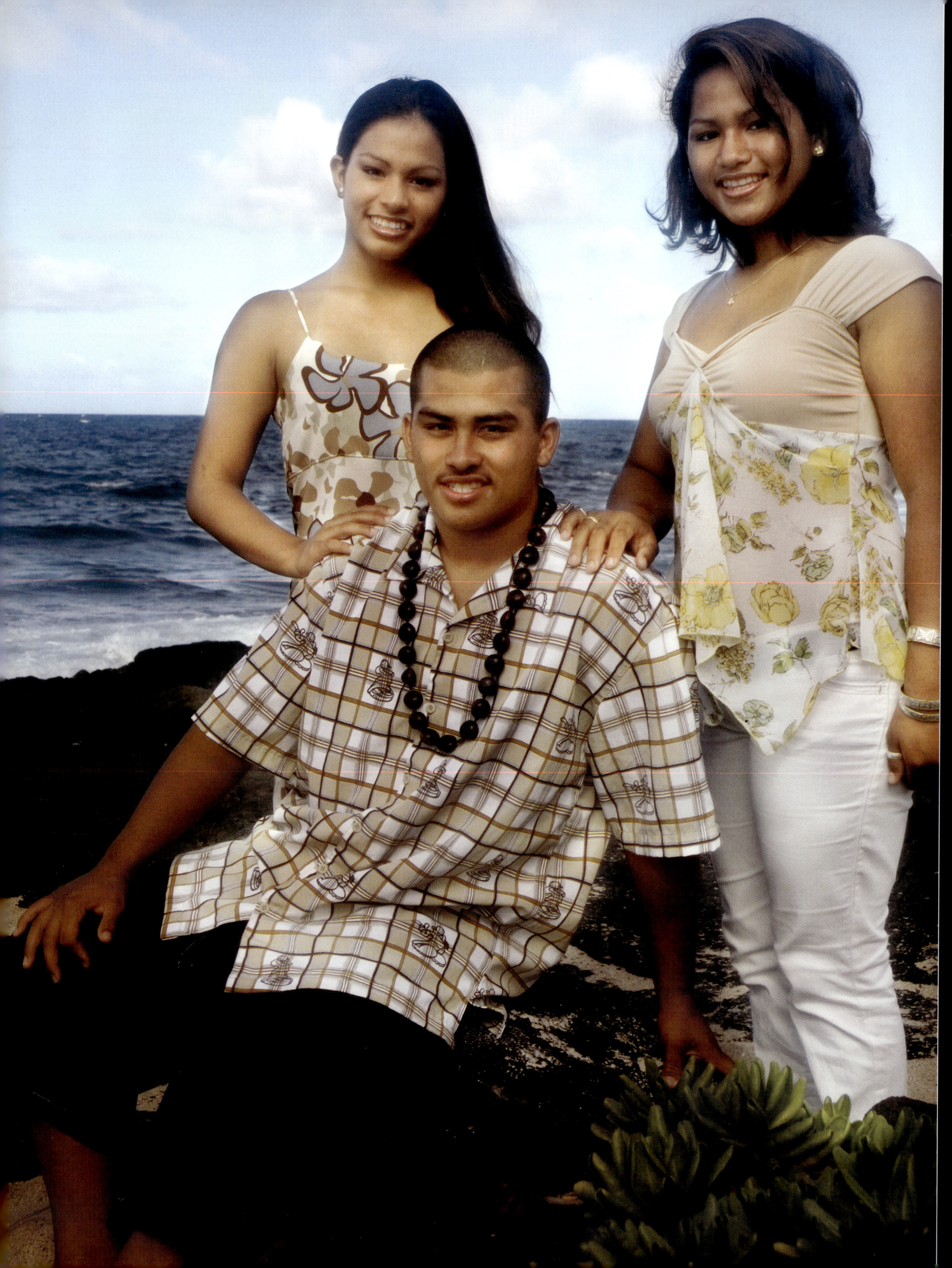

the learning. I learned a phenomenal amount about outdoor lighting while writing this book. It has been a great, albeit at times frustrating, experience. I learned that you need to be prepared for anything while on location. I tried several new techniques for this book—some worked, some didn't. I had a choice to make while writing this book: I could include only the images that worked and describe how they were created or I could include the duds and talk about what I learned from the experience. I chose to "swallow my pride" and include the images that I created that were not quite what I had anticipated because the mistakes helped me to solidify my understanding of the laws that govern how light works. In some ways it is my responsibility to share my blunders with you because they made me think about the process of creating outdoor images within the digital realm. So, I will show you what worked as well as what didn't work, and I will also show you what I did to make the technique work better the next time. I have included technical data for as many images as I could, but sometimes the conditions changed too rapidly and I had to work with what I was given in order to create images for the people I was photographing. I have also included images and insights from some terrific photographers and good friends.

THE MISTAKES HELPED ME TO SOLIDIFY MY UNDERSTANDING OF HOW LIGHT WORKS.

This book is about lighting. It will, however, offer some insights for photographers who are looking for a successful transition from film to digital (or serve as a reference for those who are starting in the field with digital capture). We will also briefly discuss the different types of portraiture and how they differ from fashion and beauty photography. In addition, we will explore basic digital retouching techniques and finish up with some tips for running a successful digital portrait business.

CHAPTER 1

OVERVIEW: LIGHTING FOR PORTRAITURE

How you light your portraits will depend greatly on the type of portrait that you want to create. In many ways, the term "portrait" is—or has been—defined by the lighting. "Classic" portraiture is heavily influenced by the lighting styles used by the old Masters of the canvas. Rembrandt, for example, has his name attached to a commonly used lighting technique relied upon by many formal portrait artists. Lighting ratios for formal portraits tend to be soft and subtle with large light sources providing the quality of light reminiscent of the window light used by the Masters. Classic, or formal, portraits tend to be meticulously posed, with the lighting and backdrop carefully choreographed to match the subject's wardrobe.

Portraiture can also be a way to capture the essence of the person(s) and tell a story about who he, she, or they are. While this can be accomplished via the formal approach, a more free-form photojournalistic approach is often used to create an "informal" character study of the people photographed. The lighting styles and ratios can vary dramatically depending upon the desired image.

These two divergent means of creating a portrait overlap in "environmental" portraiture. Environmental portraiture differs from classic studio-based portraiture because it emphasizes the person's surroundings to help tell their story. Environmental portraits can still be "formal" or photojournalistic and are often used for executive portraits.

Portraiture, as described above, is often used to create images for commercial or advertising applications. Beauty and fashion portraits are often created using a whole different set of rules.

The common feature that underlies all these styles of portraiture is light—and for the purposes of this book, *outdoor* light. Light has a number of distinct and intractable laws that govern how it looks. As noted earlier, photography is simply the recording of the light reflected off of a subject onto a light-sensitive material. Photographers need to understand the principles of light in order to manipulate it into the form with which they want to record an image. Controlling these principles is relatively easy in the studio where the photographer is in complete control over every light illuminating the set. Outdoor photography involves applying these principles to a set where one major light source is ever present. The sun is subject to the same laws as strobe lights but can be more difficult to control.

The other factor that this book will address is the need to force all of the invariable laws of light into a currently unforgiving image-capture medium. There is a gross misconception that digital photography is easier and faster than traditional film photography. In fact, it is not unusual for a photographer who is well versed

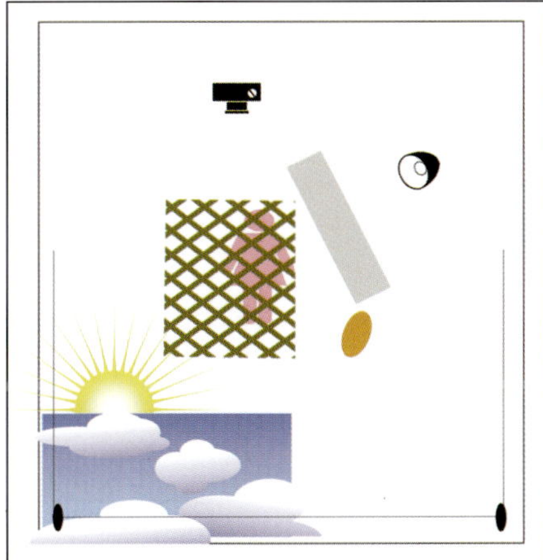

"Classic" or formal portraiture relies on a meticulous interplay of light and pose. The lighting is generally soft or diffused, with a subtle ratio from highlight to shadow. We created the lighting for this beautiful portrait of Monica Ivey by adding light to the scene. Bright sun surrounded a flower-covered gazebo, but the sun was beginning to set behind Monica, placing the front of the gazebo in shadow. We set up a 77x77-inch scrim to the left of the camera position and fired a monohead strobe through the scrim to create a large, soft light source. We used a gold reflector to bounce some sunlight into the gazebo behind her to keep it from going black without detail. We shot the image at 1/500 second at around f8. The fast shutter speed keeps the light highlights in the sky behind Monica from becoming too bright. See the above diagram.

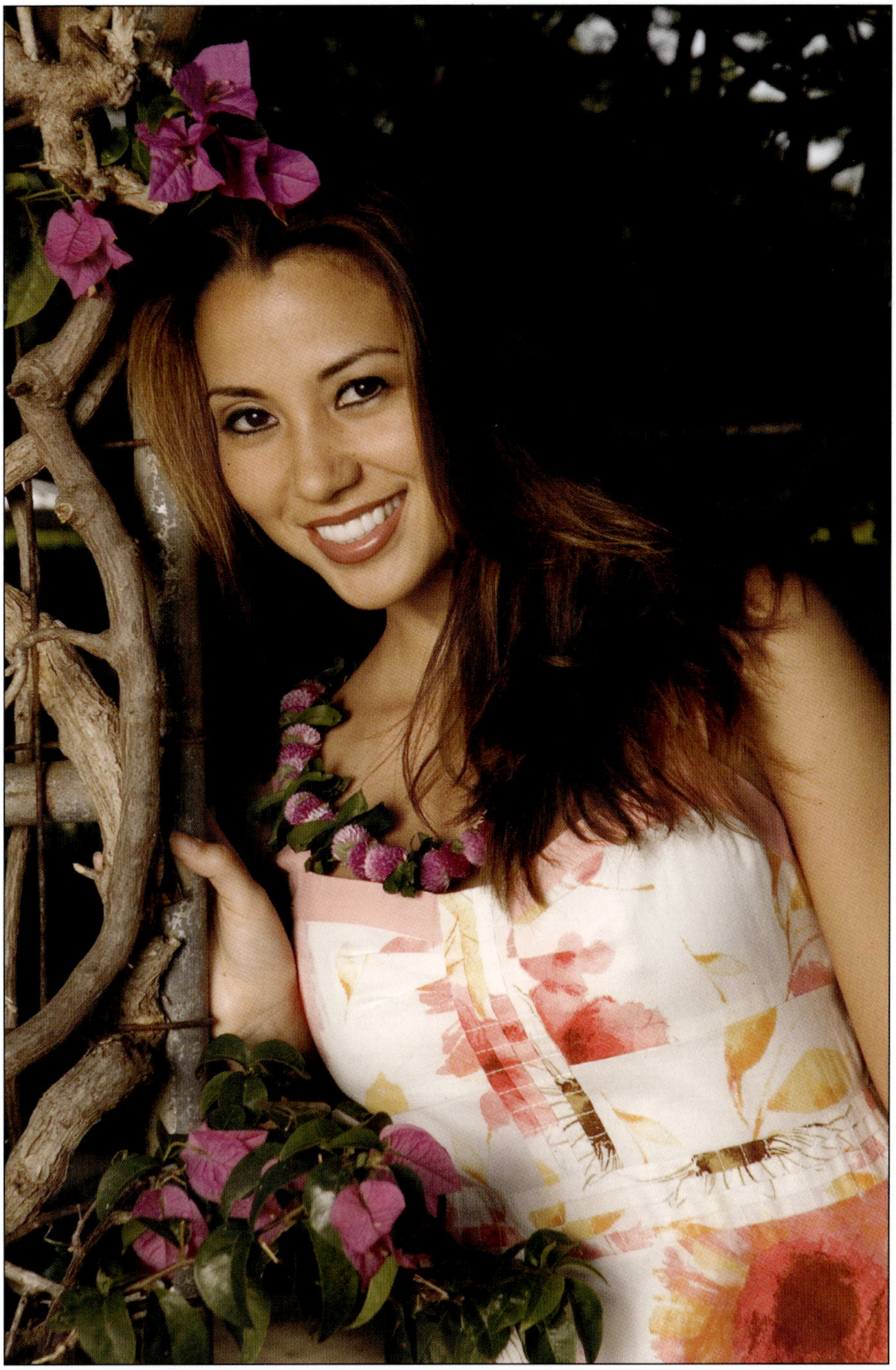

in the nuances of negative film photography to experience a great deal of difficulty when making the switch to digital capture.

Controlling light outdoors also means knowing your tools and understanding the limits of your equipment. The wonderful image of a happy bride on page 18 was taken on a bright, hazy day in Southern California. The bride had just stepped out of a taxi (!) and was behind the restaurant where the reception was held. The building provided enough open shade to create a soft light effect while rays of sunlight streaming through some trees created relative highlights around her forehead.

Paul Gero shot the image using the camera's through-the-lens metering system. While the reflective meter system works in many situations, Paul relies on his experience to constantly check the scene in his viewfinder and continually asks himself whether the

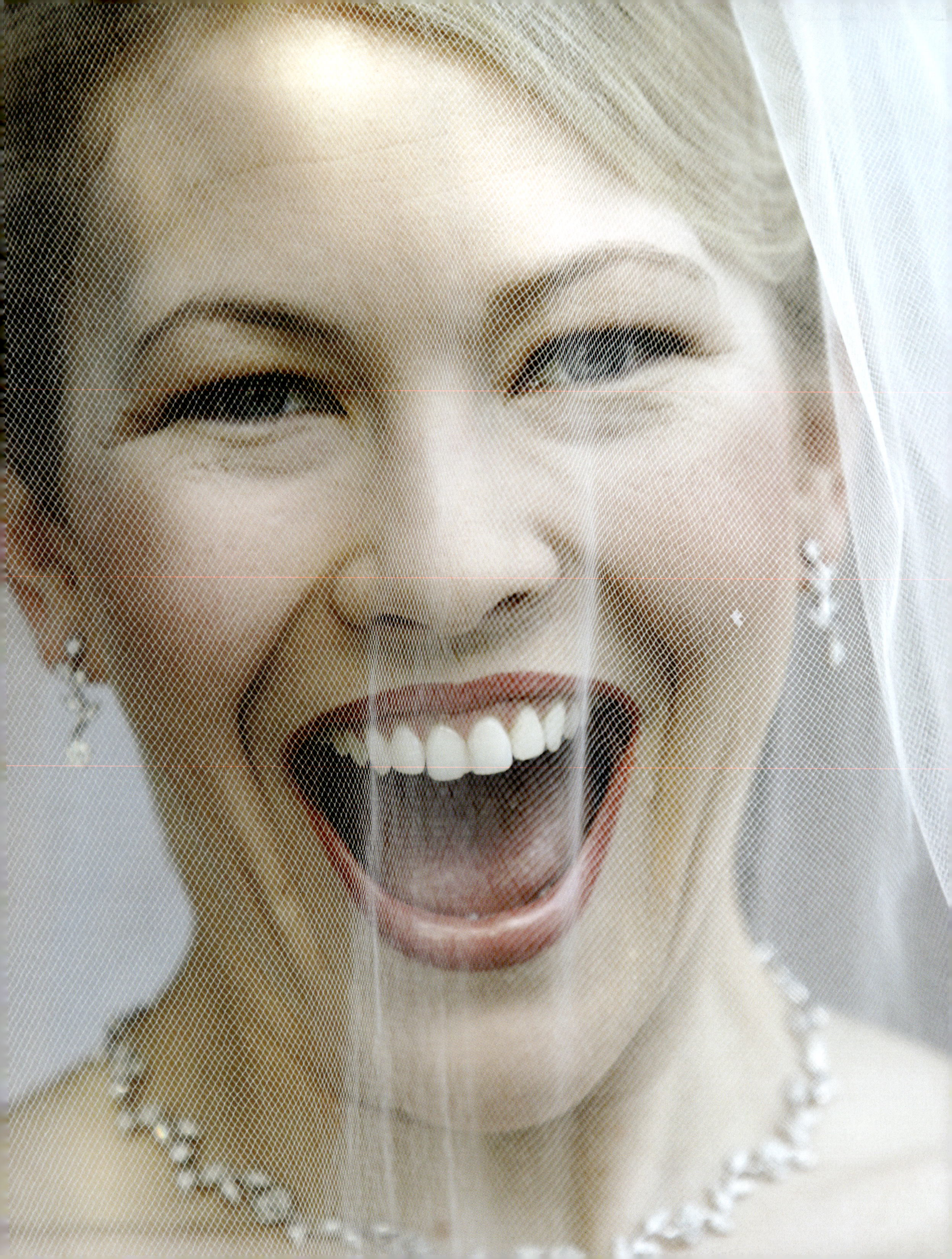

Facing Page—Photojournalistic portraiture tends to be influenced more by the story than the lighting. Many wedding photographers are offering a photojournalistic approach to capturing the big day. The documentary approach has become as popular as—and in some cases more popular than—the traditional or formal wedding style. A wedding photographer who is operating in photojournalistic mode is constantly aware of what is happening around him/her and has to be able to almost predict what will happen next. With a finger ever ready on the shutter release, the photojournalistic wedding photographer mingles, capturing images as the event unfolds. The task of creating great portraits "on the fly" is extremely challenging because as the events change, so often do the lighting conditions. The successful photojournalistic wedding photographer must also be a master of taking photographs in whatever lighting conditions present themselves and creating consistently pleasing images. Paul Gero handled both critical aspects of photojournalistic wedding photography beautifully in this image of an ecstatic bride. A photojournalistic portrait is supposed to tell a story about the subject within the context of what is happening around them. Paul's portrait certainly fits the bill. Note also that the "rules" of cropping and framing are also much looser in a photojournalistic portrait than in a formal one. Tight cropping can sometimes tell the story more effectively than backing up from your subject. **Right**—"Environmental" portraiture combines aspects of both of these styles; the lighting is fully controlled but the environment plays a role in the portrait. Teresa Bringas' outfit, pose, and the proximity of the beach combine to show an important influence in her life.

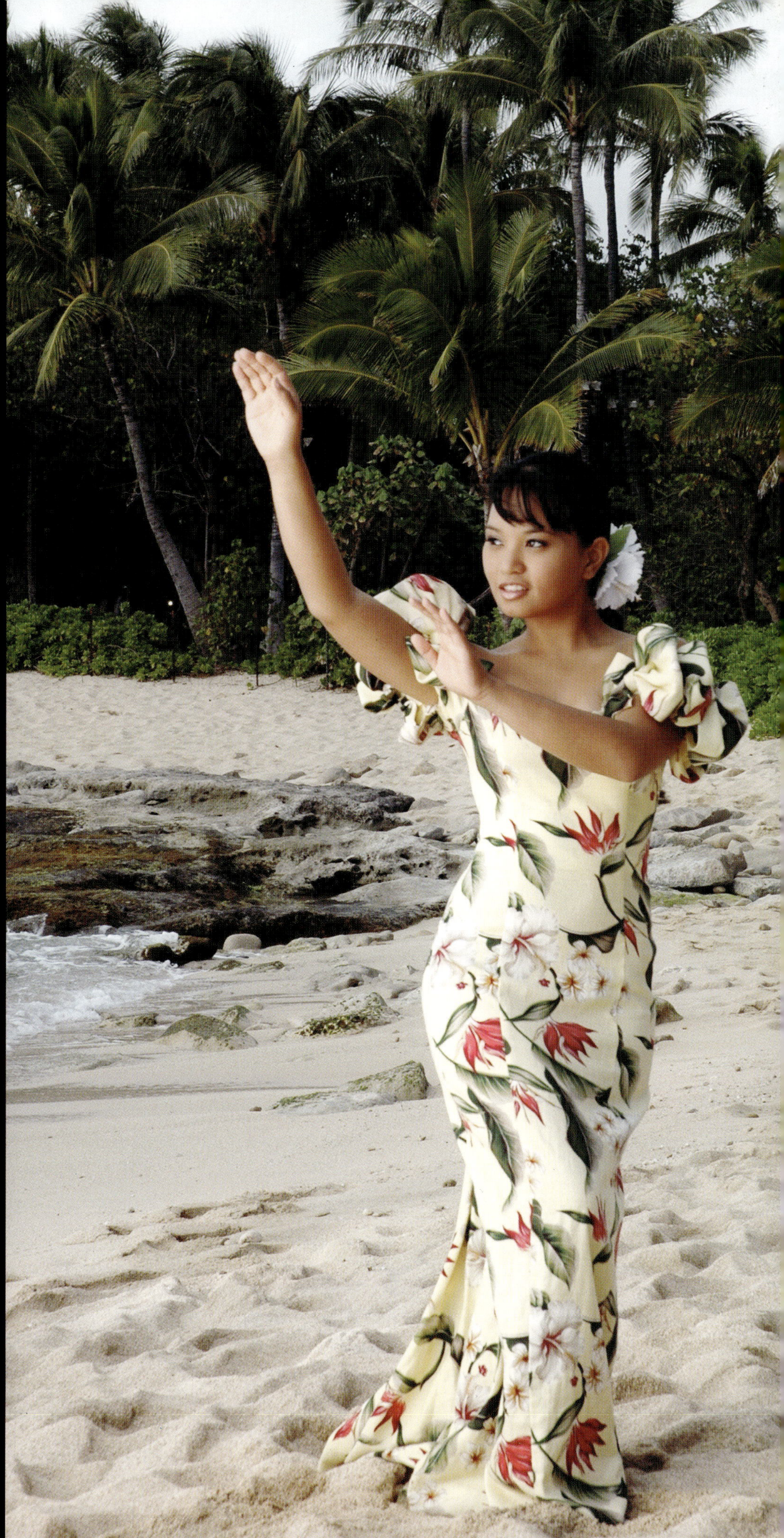

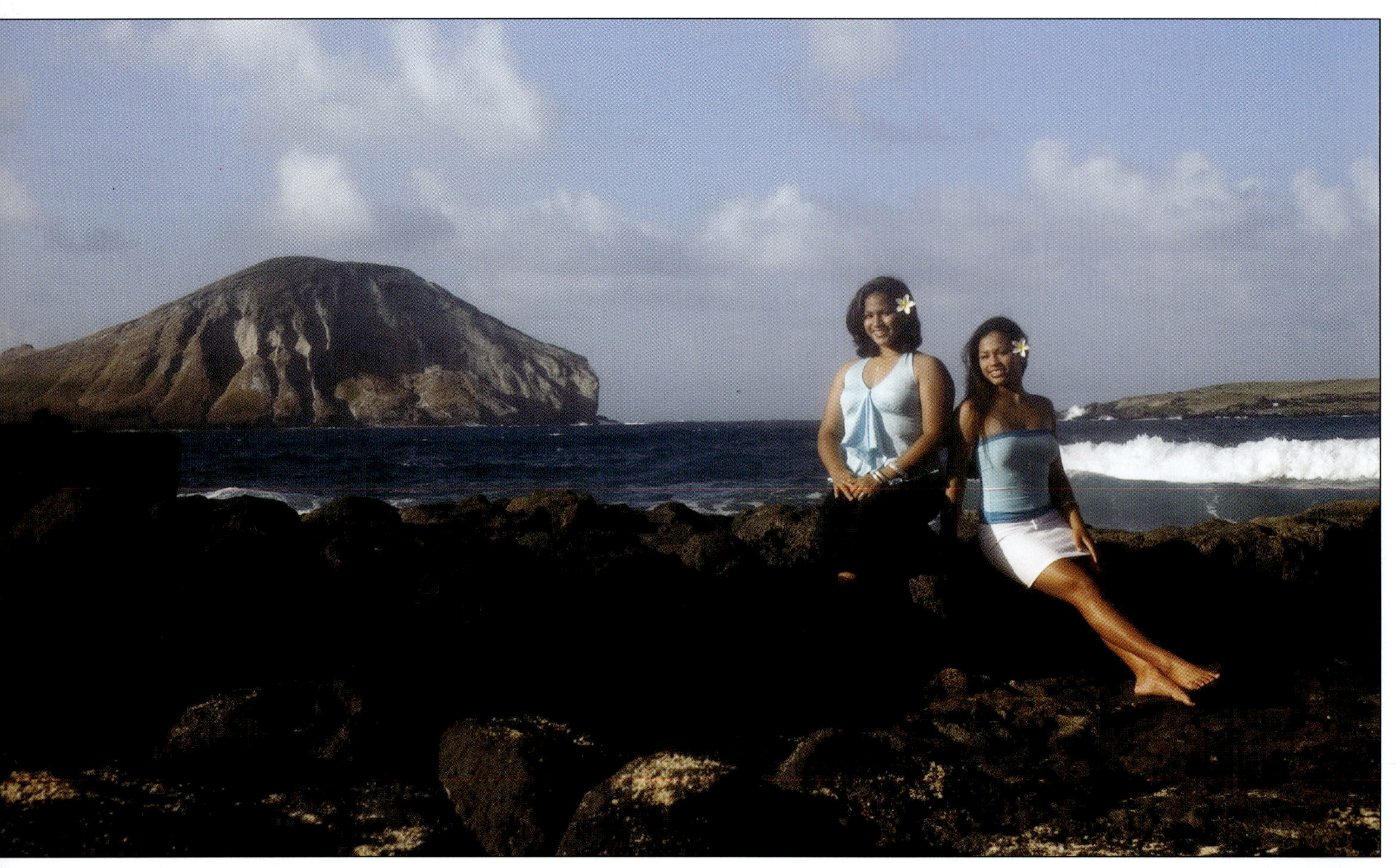

Late-afternoon light was used to create this location portrait of Ka'u and Karielle, and a gold fabric was used camera right as a fill. The sun was constantly in and out of a cloud cover, so the girls' mother was on hand to meter the light as it changed. I had to grab this shot during the rare times on this day when the sun was out and lit the girls and the backdrop evenly. The image has the full range of color values available with digital capture, from the whitecaps of the ocean to the black lava rocks. It also highlights one of the advantages of shooting portraits outdoors—sometimes the location is stunning. Don't be afraid to back up and include the location in your portrait.

information provided by the meter is correct. A reflective meter reads the light bounced back from your subject and places that value in the midtone range of your image. Reflective meters can be "fooled" by an overly light or dark scene. Paul lets his equipment do its job but then takes control by making the final determination about whether he needs to adjust the "suggested" exposure. His world is capturing one-time moments on the fly, so his success is truly based on his knowledge of his equipment and his understanding of light to make snap judgments about the accuracy of the information presented.

Paul now shoots all of his images in RAW mode and feels that it gives him the most information possible. He likens the JPEG/RAW comparison to that of an original transparency versus a high-quality duplicate slide: you've got the availability of more information, why not capture it? He says that shooting RAW also expands the exposure range of the capture but is quick to caution against being sloppy with your exposures: RAW is not a fix-all for bad exposures; you still need to be as tight as you can. However, RAW does give Paul a little extra leeway to work in conditions that are not 100 percent controllable. He also likes the way RAW images render colors more than the algorithm used to compress many JPEGs. Having more control over the color temperature of the image after the fact, if needed, is an added bonus of shooting RAW.

There are a multitude of decisions to be made when creating portraits on location. One choice that has to

Although some retouching was done in Photoshop, the main impact of this fun portrait was real. We all got wet! The retouching was limited to removing people from the background. Although this was a setup portrait, it had some components of a photojournalistic approach where you have to make the best of what the situation provides. For obvious reasons I was not able to bring a lot of lighting gear to balance the side light from the sun, so I positioned the couple to get the most from the sun without creating a harsh side lighting effect and relied on the built-in flash to add some fill and bring the exposure up to an acceptable ratio of highlights to shadows. The whites on the side of the Paul's jacket are just about blown out, but the rest of the image makes it worth the sacrifice. Throughout this book, we will discuss ways to keep the tonal range in your image within the limits of digital capture.

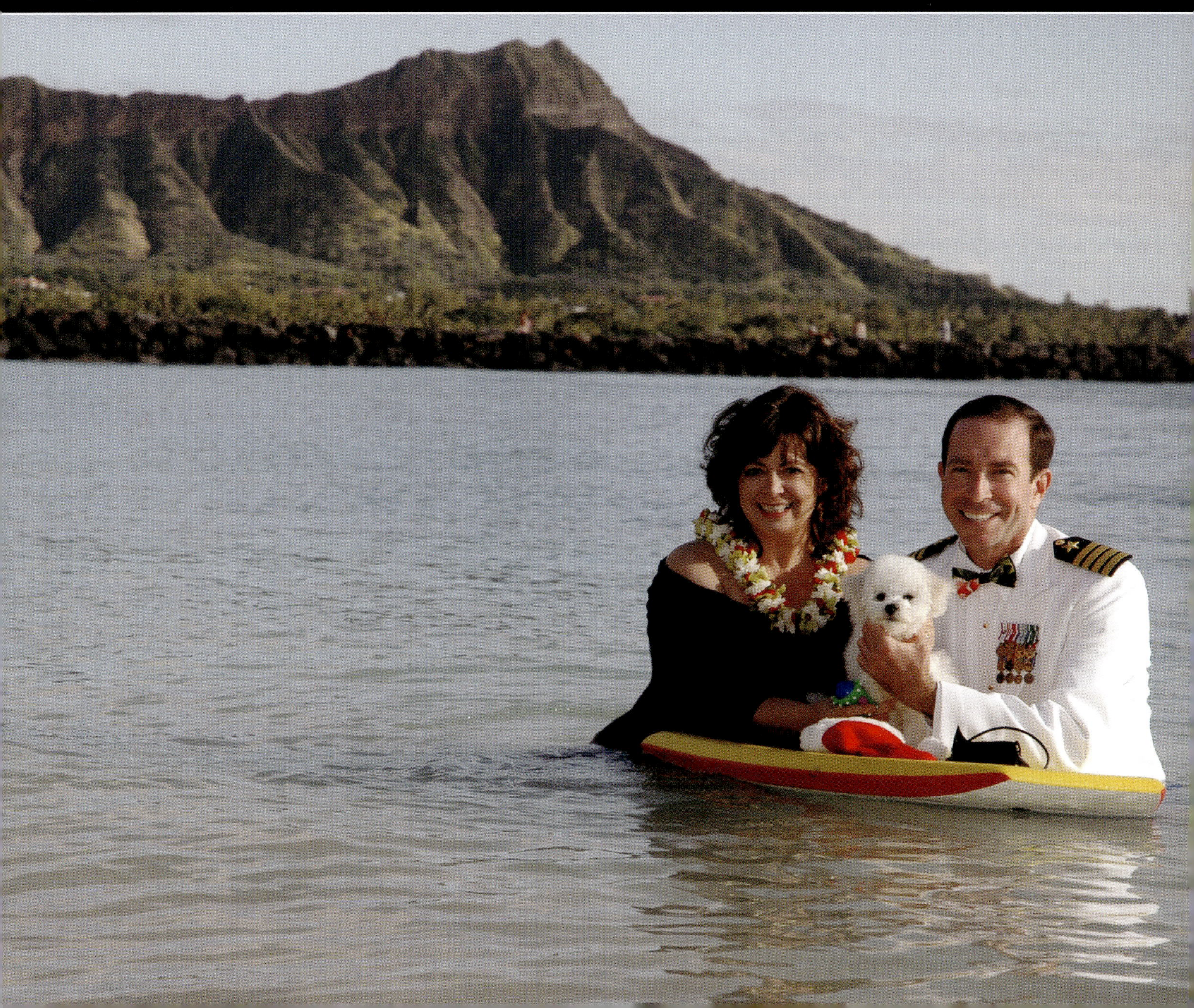

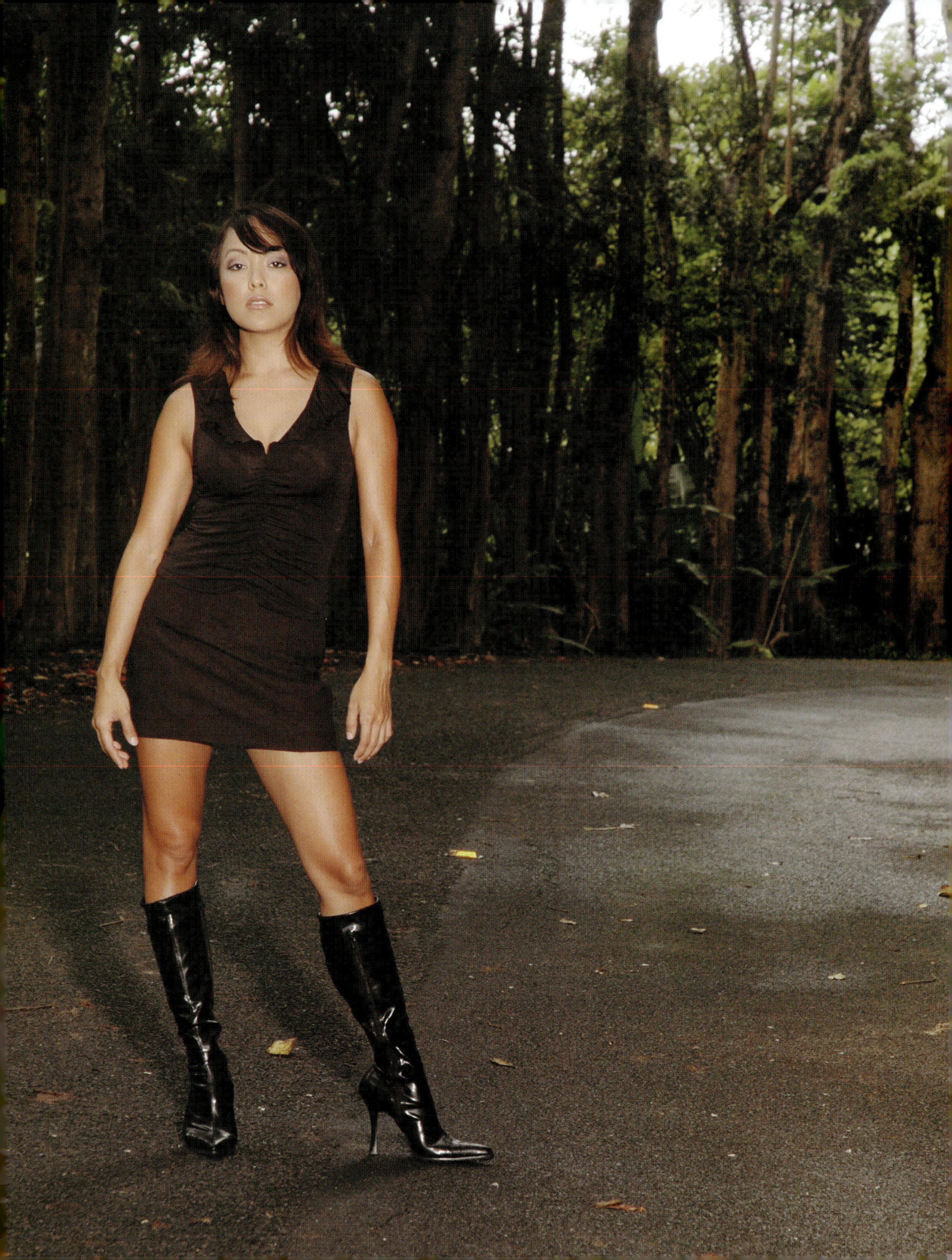

be considered is whether to shoot tight and emphasize the subjects or to allow your subjects to become part of the scene around them. Shooting close is fine, but sometimes taking the opposite approach can produce breathtaking result.

Fashion images may use smaller light sources than traditional portraits. Smaller light sources have more contrast than larger lights and can test the limits of the digital medium faster. However, the smaller light sources can create very dramatic images when used properly.

A good portrait will also show the personality of your subject. Sometimes a sense of adventure (and a sense of humor!) adds to the impact of the portrait. Paul and Kim (page 21) helped create a very different take on a common scene in Waikiki.

Facing Page—Kathryn was photographed on a winding road on the east coast of Oahu. The Koolau mountain range was just in front of her. Clouds form over these mountains almost every day, so the ambient light was soft and somewhat flat. The trees that form part of this tropical rain forest further diffused and lessened the ambient exposure. I used a monohead strobe fitted with a grid spot to create a harsher lighting scheme for this fashion image. The spotlight was more intense and had more contrast than the ambient light. The exposure was primarily set by the strobe because the forest surrounding us was so dark. I could have slowed the shutter speed more to further lighten the backdrop, but I was already at 1/60 second and I didn't want to risk motion blur. I wanted the dramatic effect of a dark backdrop but lightened part of it in Photoshop by creating a duplicate layer and using the screen blending mode. I then applied a gradient mask to the screened layer to keep most of the image dark.

CHAPTER 2

THE LAWS OF LIGHT

CAPTURE RANGE OF FILM VERSUS DIGITAL

Perhaps the most fundamental difference between photographing an image on negative film and digital capture is the amount of information that each medium can hold. Color negative shooters are used to working with about 9–10 stops of information, yielding an effective range of your midtone exposure plus or minus 4½–5 stops. The range for black & white films is even greater. The result of this latitude is a relatively low-contrast image showing the subtle gradations from white to black. The popular 3:1 ratio produces beautiful tones, while the photographer still has plenty of room to play with more "dramatic" ratios and still hold detail in the whites and blacks. Furthermore, negative film has a great deal of "error range" built in. A color negative can be overexposed by 2 stops or underexposed by 1 stop and still yield a saleable print. In fact, for many years it was common practice to purposefully overexpose negative film by 1 stop. Prints from negative films, especially wall portraits, were beautiful illustrations of the photographer's ability to use and control a wide range of light.

Transparency shooters played by a whole different set of rules. The end product for commercial photographers was rarely prints. Instead, images created in the commercial world were destined for the offset printer. Transparency films have a much narrower exposure latitude with 7–7½ stops representing the limits of the films' ability to hold information. The numbers don't sound very drastic, but the difference of 3 stops of recordable data is huge. The whites and blacks that a negative film shooter banks on to fill out the tonal range of an image—of a bride and groom, for example—can be gone when shooting transparency film. A photographer shooting transparency film needed to be in much tighter control of his/her metering and had to closely monitor and modify the light at the extremes of the film's tolerance because the resulting image had much more contrast than the same image photographed on negative film. The added contrast was needed because a good deal of that contrast is lost in the printing process. For most commercial purposes, the exposure had to be within about ½ stop either way of dead-on before valuable information was lost (the notable exception to this is fashion photography, where transparency films are sometimes wildly overexposed for the effect).

Neither method nor photographer was better than the other—they were simply different tools for different jobs. A negative shooter whose image looks terrific over the fireplace might find the image too "flat" for a publication. On the other hand, a commercial photographer might have difficulty producing a family portrait with all the tones—he or she may not expose for the full range and may inadvertently lose a great deal of information.

Digital photography has brought these two divergent worlds together, but it is the commercial photographer who has had the easier time with the transition. Digital capture—at least thus far—has exposure latitude that is as tight—or tighter—than transparency films. Shooting in RAW format helps expand the latitude, but both negative and transparency photographers have had to make some adjustments. However, the tight reigns of digital capture are much closer to the commercial photographer's comfort zone.

As a commercial photographer, Al Garcia is often faced with shooting in high-contrast situations where it is not feasible to modify all of the light affecting his scene. He has taken what he knows from the commercial photography world and has applied it successfully to portraiture. He states, "[With] digital [it] is harder to nail a dead-on exposure. It is difficult to keep detail in the highlights. If your exposure is over by about a stop, your highlights will lose their detail and require manipulating in Photoshop. However, if your exposure is under, and you are not working in a very broad EV range, digital is extremely forgiving, and an image that on film or transparency would be totally unusable can be restored to a great shot. So, basically, in high-contrast scenarios, when shooting digital and it is not possible to modify the light (e.g., architectural photography), I tend to expose for the highlights and print (manipulate or correct) for the shadows. Sounds familiar and backwards, doesn't it? Does anyone remember shooting and printing their own black & white images?"[2]

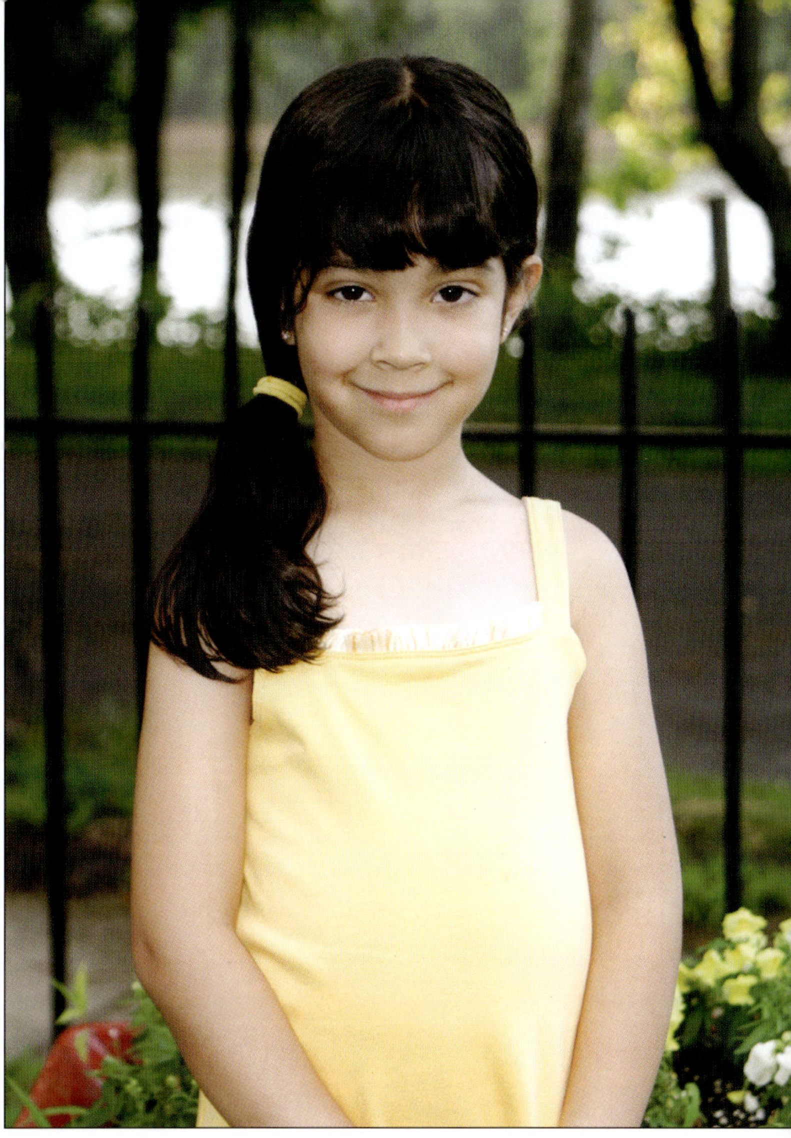

Al Garcia described how the portrait of Katie was made: "This image was created using the camera's built-in flash with the camera set on shutter priority. I varied the ISO and shutter speed to control my background. I placed Katie in a shallow EV-range scene to avoid the sun 'peeking through' and burning in highlights. It was late afternoon, and the magic light was fading fast."

Al recognizes the narrow exposure range of digital capture but knows that there is more latitude within the shadows than the highlights. For the shot above, he chose a scene with lower contrast and used the relatively greater shadow range to his benefit. "Because of digital, this setup allowed me to work quickly with the confidence that I was creating usable and/or workable images. If I were shooting chromes, I would not have been able to shoot at the speed that I was shooting without constantly spot metering." Al also used a very shallow depth of field to keep the fence from becoming a distraction and positioned Katie very carefully—the trees behind her frame her head, and the repeated yellows form a second frame for her. We will examine

2. "EV range" refers to the range of exposure values that are within the scene. Al is describing a technique that can be effective in pushing the boundaries of digital capture when you are forced to make a choice between losing highlights or losing detail. He suggests that you will have more success in exposing for the highlights and bringing up the shadow values in post-production. However, it still needs to be emphasized that Al is talking about a fairly shallow exposure range. You do have more room on the shadow side than in the highlights with digital capture, but beyond a certain point all you will add to your image is noise.

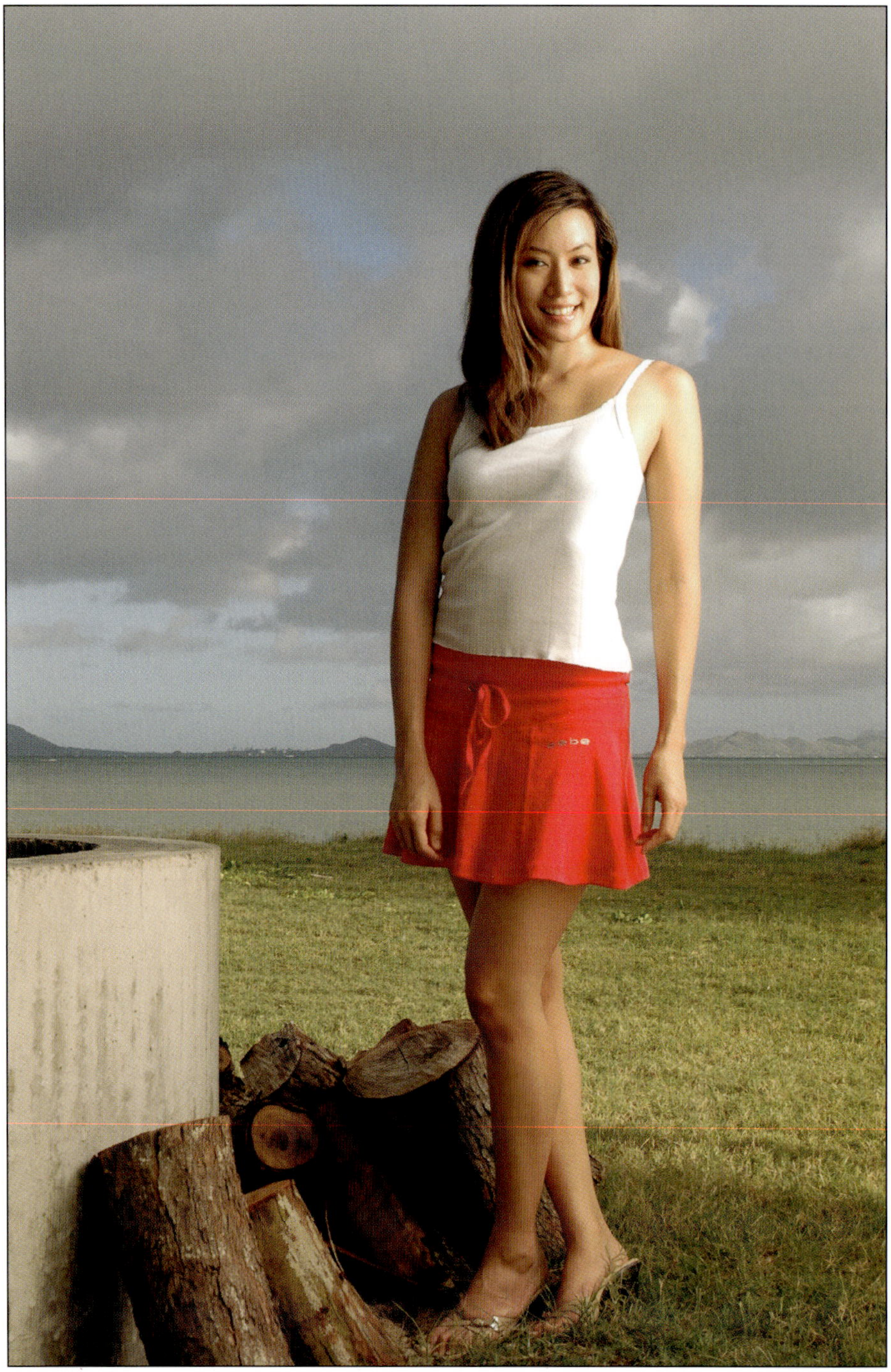

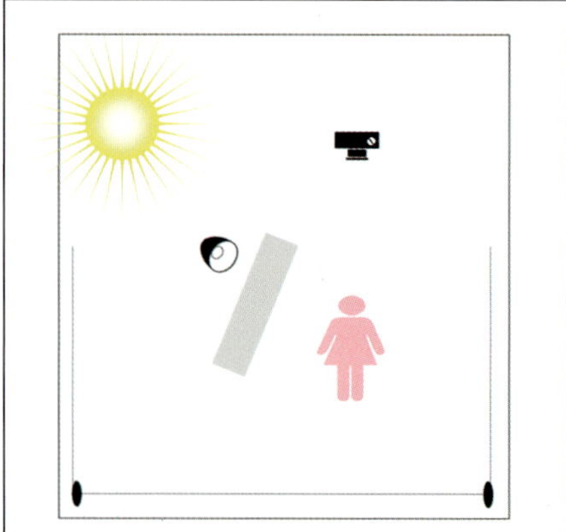

This image of Brooke Tanaka shows one of the dangers of digital capture. The image was created by placing a strobe behind a scrim to balance the harsh side light from the sun. The scrim was intended to expand and soften the sunlight and act as a softbox for the strobe. It was placed very close to Brooke, which would generally create a beautiful, soft effect. However, the main problem with this setup was the distance between the strobe and the scrim. The strobe was placed too close to the scrim, effectively becoming a modified spotlight, negating the effects of the scrim. The combined exposure on Brooke's face was correct, but the strobe shot through the scrim was still too harsh, creating parts of her white shirt that were without pixel information. The light on her face also had too much contrast for this image. See the above diagram.

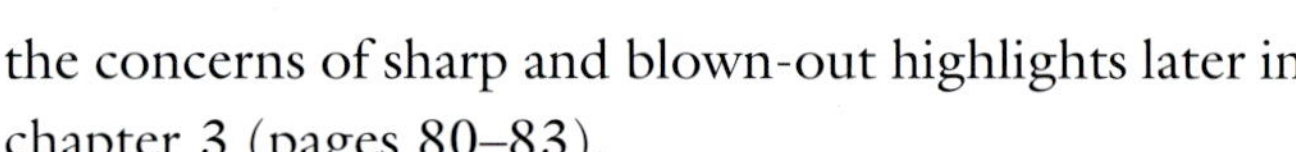

the concerns of sharp and blown-out highlights later in chapter 3 (pages 80–83).

The key to creating successful digital images, either for a portrait client or for a commercial enterprise, is to understand how the various laws of light interact with each other in conjunction with the narrow exposure range. The interplay of these laws can initially be quite confusing, but the starting point is actually very simple. The starting point of any quality image is its exposure—or, more accurately, the properly metered exposure. What you do with the properly metered exposure is part of the creative portion of photography: do you want to shoot the portrait as metered for a perfect exposure, or do you want to purposely under- or overexpose your image for a certain effect? The choice, once you know where to start, is yours.

METERING

The image that you want to create starts with proper metering. The idea of a narrow exposure range in digital capture has already been mentioned a couple of times—and will likely be discussed again—because there can be no guesswork in digital photography. While it is true that RAW capture can expand the exposure latitude of digital photography, you run the risk of dramatically increasing the noise in the image, especially when trying to fix an underexposed image. You are still much better off nailing a proper exposure from the start.

Fortunately, there is a tool available that takes the guesswork out of calculating a proper exposure. The light meter is an invaluable tool. This device captures incident light or reflected light, measures the amount of light (in units of light called foot-candles, the amount of light given off by a lit candle at a distance of one foot) using a series of light-sensitive components, and translates that information into language that the photographer can understand (e.g., f-stops).

Incident light meters read the light that falls on your scene, and reflective meters read the light that bounces back from the subject. Light meters are calibrated to what is known as 18 percent gray (an estimate of the midrange between black and white) and will yield an exposure reading to record what is metered in the middle grays. For example, take an 18 percent gray card

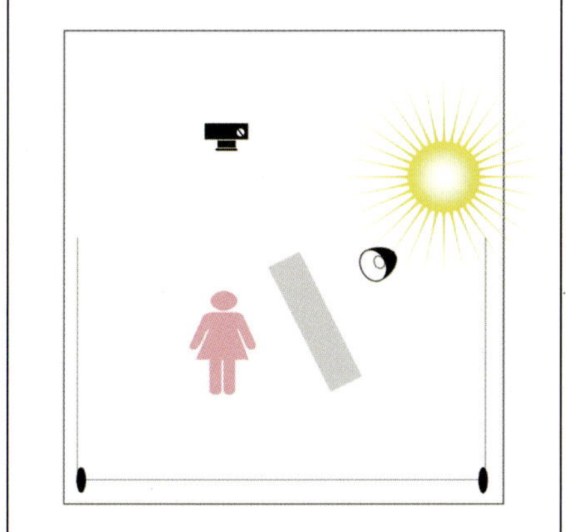

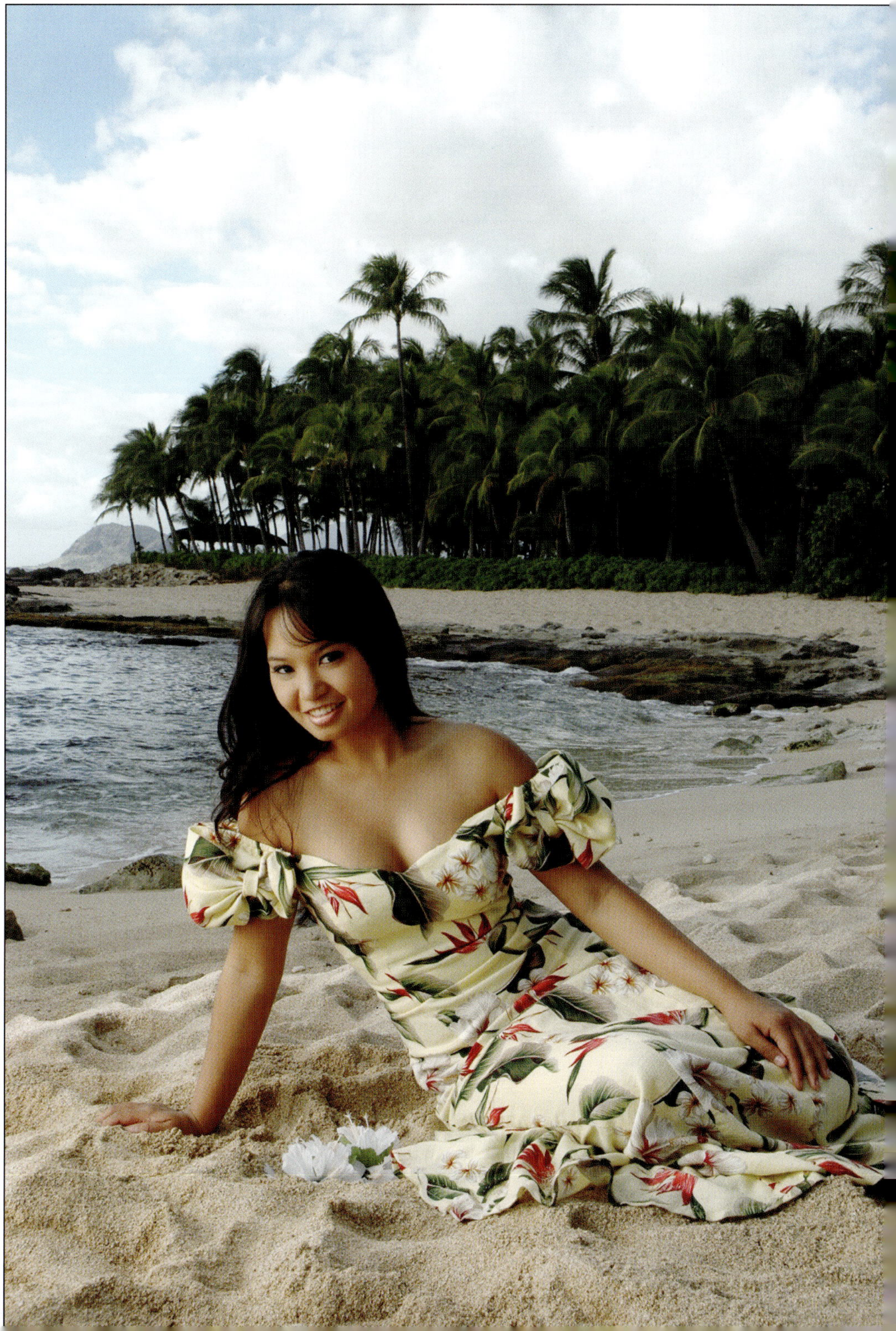

This image of Teresa Bringas shows a much more effective use of the same technique. The strobe and scrim setup were backed farther away from her to allow the scrim to do its job of softening the light from the spotlight. The ambient exposure was about f8 at 1/250 second, and the combined strobe-ambient exposure was f11 and 1/250, creating a nice balance between the strobe and ambient light. As we will see later, you can adjust the impact of the strobe-ambient ratio simply by moving the strobe. Teresa was positioned lower in the frame to balance the composition and to show the beautiful location. See the above diagram.

that is evenly lit. Place an incident meter right next to the card with the dome of the meter pointed toward the camera and take a meter reading. Take a reflective meter reading by holding the meter at the camera position and aiming the meter at the gray card. Both techniques should yield the same reading.

In other words, your meter understands only midtone gray. It is up to the photographer to accurately interpret this information for the particular scene. The area of a scene to be metered is the area that the photographer decides to render neutrally. In portraiture, the most important element of your scene is the subject's skin tones. A "neutral" rendering simply means that the skin tones are representative of how the person actually looks. In other words, a dark-skinned person should have dark skin in the portrait while the

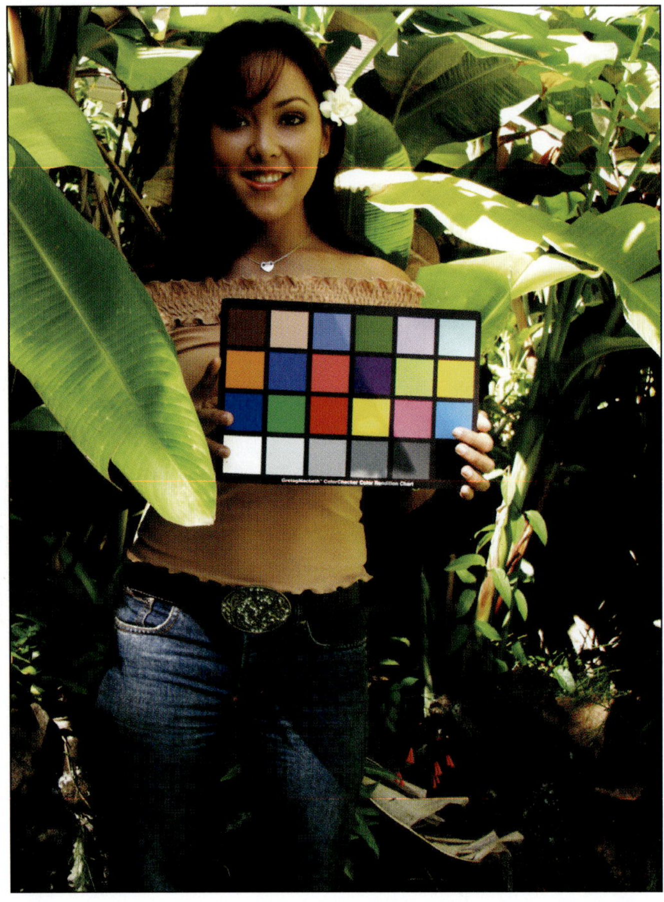

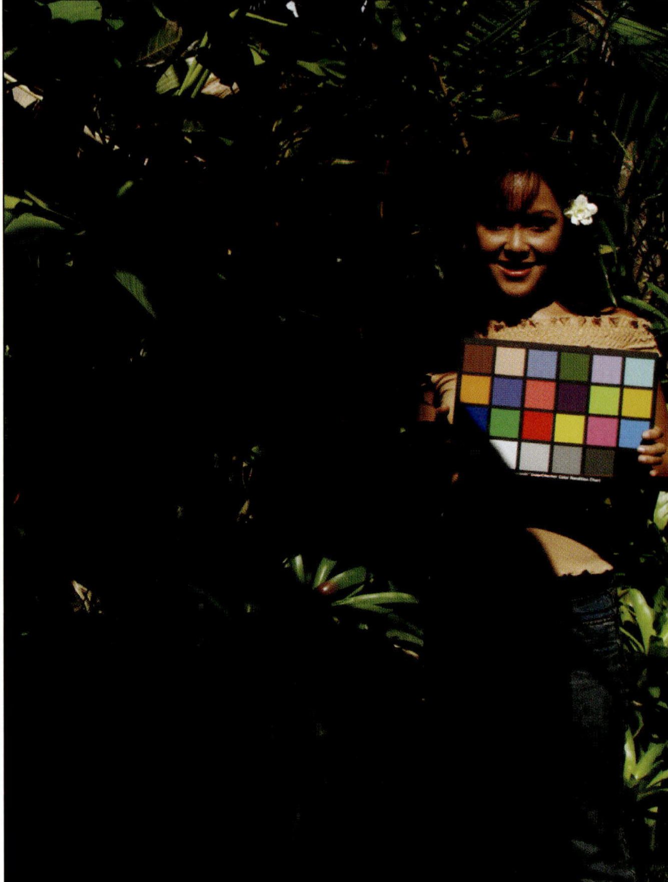

Above—Your meter will take a reading of the light that either falls on or is reflected from a given spot in your scene. It is important to meter the correct spot because the device will take that information and turn it into 18 percent gray—everything darker will record darker and everything in your scene that is lighter will be rendered lighter. It is absolutely critical to understand that with digital capture, you've only got a range of midtone gray plus or minus about 3 stops of recordable data. You will likely lose data in high-contrast settings, so you'll need to decide what the important parts of the scenes are and expose for those areas. Both of the examples above are exposed properly. One shows a color card exposed in the shade. The highlights behind Kathryn are blown out because the light under the shade is much less than the bright areas lit by direct sunlight. The overall appearance of the image seems to be overexposed. Similarly the image exposed in direct sun appears to be underexposed because the details in the shadows were lost. However, the color card is perfectly exposed in both photographs. These are the exact concerns that you will need to balance and control to create images showing the range of tonal values while maintaining detail in the highlights and shadows. **Facing Page—**Here is an example of a beautifully exposed portrait showing details in the whites as well as the shadows. Karielle's white shirt has detail, and the blacks of her hair and the lava rocks are rich and not "blocked up." The image was created on a day when the light changed dramatically and frequently. At this particular moment, however, the sun was only partially hidden behind the clouds, providing a soft but directional light that was accentuated by a silver/gold reflector.

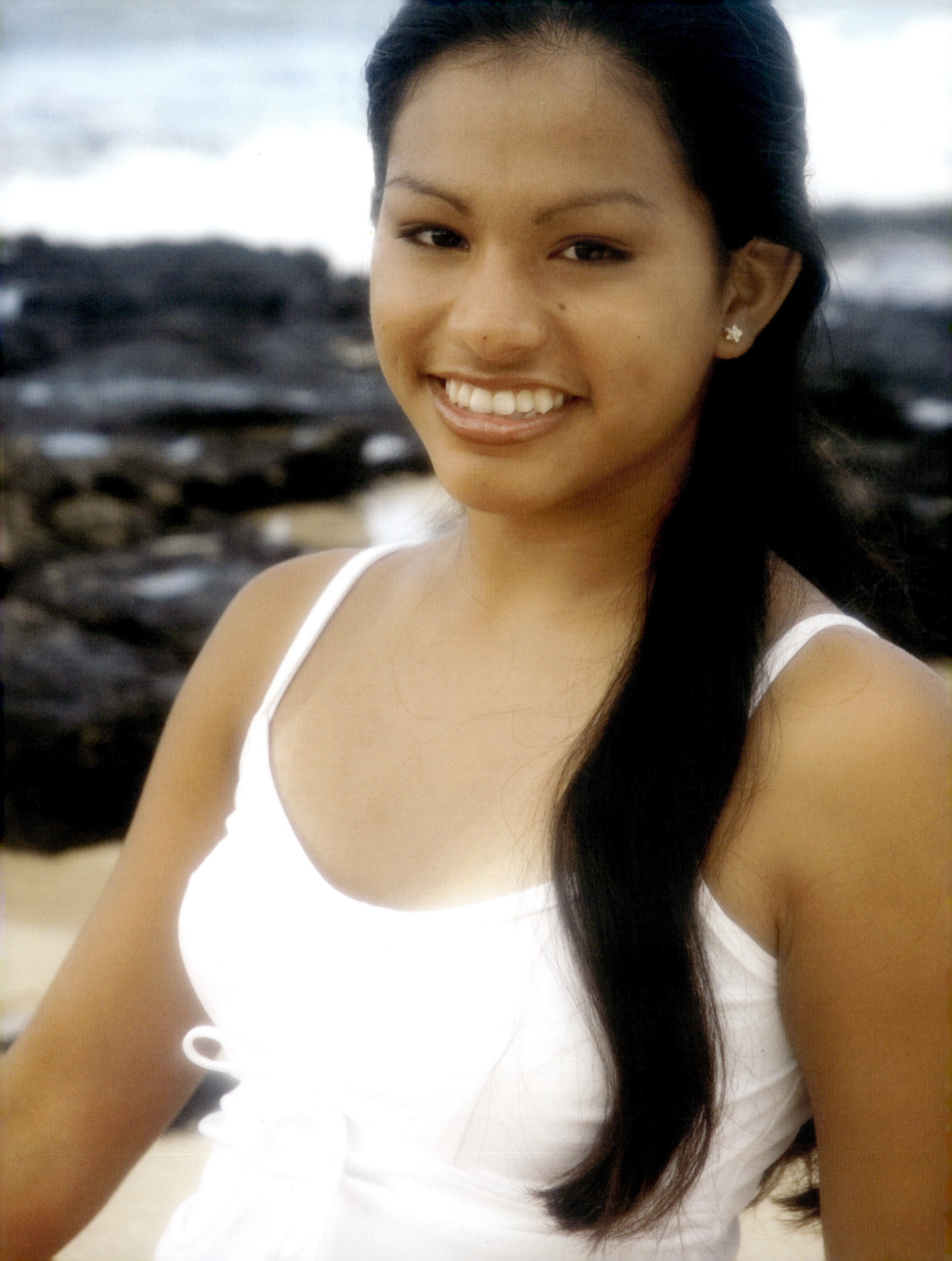

reverse is true for a light-skinned person. Incident and reflective meters will each do the job, but each has benefits and drawbacks. Reflective light meter readings can be used effectively, but it requires the photographer to be extremely accurate in aiming the meter. For example, you had better not slip with the meter if your subject is wearing a black outfit! What you think is a properly exposed face may turn into a gray shirt and wildly overexposed skin tones.

A second potential drawback to using a reflective meter to gauge the exposure in a portrait session has to do with the nature of light meters. Your meter is not going to know if you are taking a reading off of a light- or dark-skinned person—it will translate the data obtained into 18 percent gray. Subsequently, you will

BACKLIT SITUATIONS CAN ALSO BE PROBLEMATIC FOR REFLECTIVE METERS . . .

record overexposed, washed-out skin tones on a dark-skinned subject or underexposed, "muddy" skin tones on a light-skinned person. You would need to make the proper exposure compensation and, in our example, underexpose the first image and overexpose the second photograph. This is, in fact, the opposite of the old wives' tale of "stopping down" to shoot a dark-skinned person and "opening up" to photograph a light-skinned subject.

Backlit situations can also be problematic for the kind of reflective meters that average the light from the entire scene. In this case the meter will record the backlit areas as 18 percent gray and will subsequently underexpose the foreground—including your subject. "Center-weighted" reflective meters can help, but they also have trouble. A center-weighted meter simply reads the light being reflected off of the middle of your scene. These meters are better in backlit situations because the odds are better that more of your subject will be within the metered section. However, a center-weighted meter can still be fooled when its target is different than the surrounding scene (e.g., a brightly lit patch of a beach in the middle of a group of trees). Backlit situations present particular difficulties that extend beyond metering concerns. These situations will be discussed in chapter 3.

Spot meters come in several diameters and measure the light that is reflected off specific areas of the image. A reflective spot meter is usually considered to be an auxiliary or "special use" meter but can be very useful in tricky lighting situations such as those just described. The best use for a spot reflective meter might be in conjunction with an incident meter reading. Use the incident meter to assign midtone gray to the desired section of the scene, then use the spot meter to determine whether the remaining areas of your composition will fit into the exposure latitude of digital capture.

Incident meters read the light that falls on the subject and record the specific area as midtone gray. Everything that is darker than the meter reading will record darker, and everything lighter will record lighter. In other words, everything in your scene will be recorded in a natural relationship to what you have metered. I prefer to use incident meter readings for portrait and fashion work because it is easy. I don't have to think about making exposure compensations to record my subject's skin tones neutrally. The main drawback to using an incident meter is proximity: you need to be close enough to your subject to easily walk up and place the meter next to his/her cheek.

Light meters, like everything else in photography, vary greatly in quality and accuracy. The first meter I used measured light in ⅓-stop increments and used a rotating dial to approximate the exposure. This meter worked fine when I was shooting negative film because the intense need for accuracy doesn't exist with that medium. However, I was told in no uncertain terms that I needed a new meter when I shifted to transparency films and digital capture! The better meters on the market are accurate to within 1/10 stop and meter ambient, strobe, and combined lighting schemes.

How to Use the Incident Light Meter. Assuming accuracy, the use of a reflective meter is easy: aim the meter at your subject from the camera position and push the button! There is, however, considerable debate about the best way to use your incident light meter. The meter is held at the point of interest in the scene. Where you aim the meter depends on who you ask: some photographers say to point the dome of the meter at the light source. Other photographers state that the dome of the meter must be aimed at the camera. I have always been in the camp that says to point the dome down the lens of the camera. However, I have modified my viewpoints because metering your scene is not as simple as it sounds—especially when capturing images digitally.

Light surrounds your subject. Some light will illuminate the front of your subject. If you decide that this light is to provide the basis for your exposure, then it will become your main light. Your main light is simply the light (or lights) that provides the base illumination for your portrait. The main light also determines the direction of your light and the foundation for your lighting ratios. We will examine these concepts in greater detail later in this chapter, but for now we'll

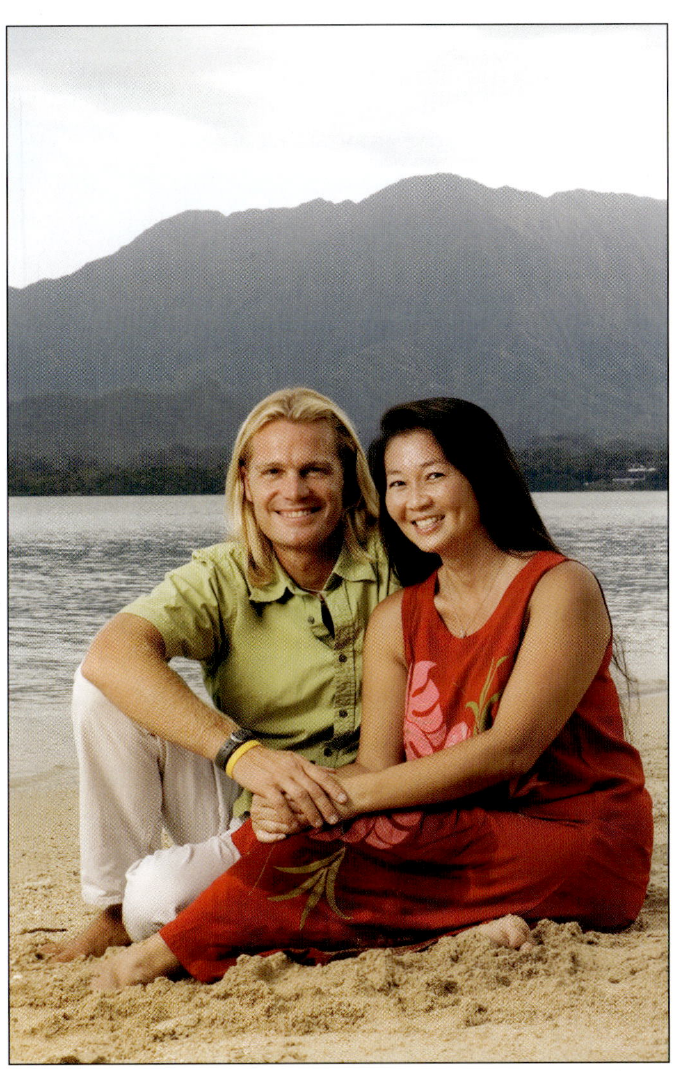

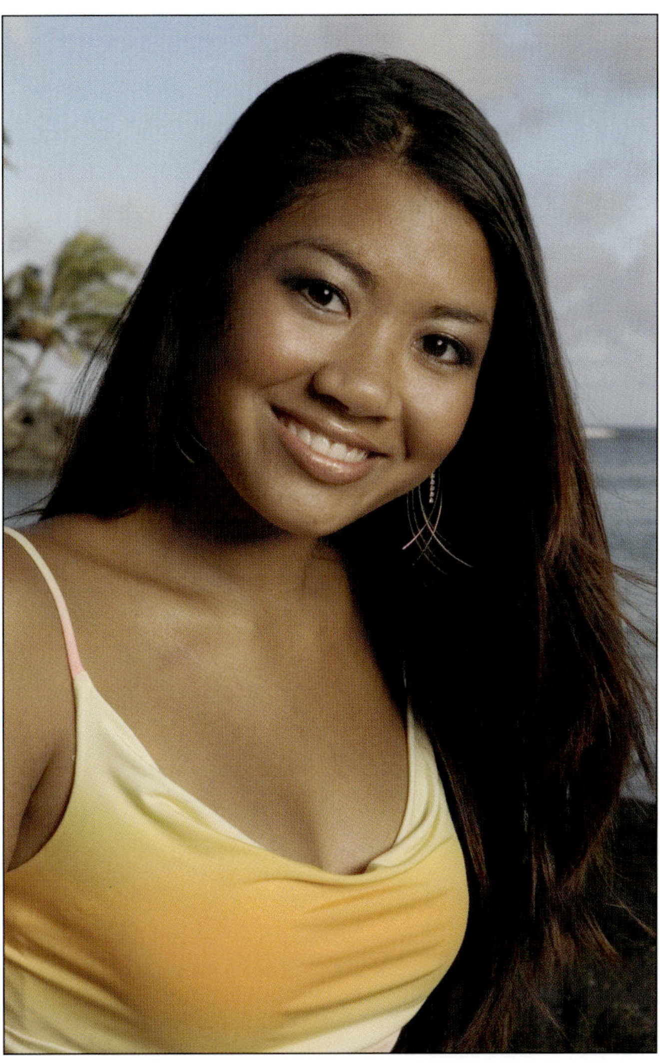

Left—Kim and Gilles have distinctly different hair colors and subtly different skin tones. An incident meter reading taken at their faces makes it extremely easy to render their respective hair and skin tones naturally. **Right—**Rachael Regina is a beautiful young lady with rich, dark skin tones. Nailing down a proper exposure was easy with an incident light meter. However, specular highlights (the reflections from your light sources) tend to be more apparent with a subject with dark skin than someone with lighter skin. A bigger light source will result in a broader, more spread-out highlight. Here we tucked a strobe head inside a halo-style softbox but aimed the strobe at the silver lining inside the halo rather than shooting straight through the front fabric. The bounced light that passed through the diffusion material was broader than it would have been if the strobe was simply fired through the front of the halo, resulting in a softer light source and beautiful specular highlights on Rachael's face. The exposure of the strobe was balanced to the background.

focus on metering the amount of light that illuminates your subject.

Light will also strike the sides and top of your subject, adding depth and dimension to your image. The use of these lights in relation to your main light is what will take a two-dimensional medium and create an illusion of three dimensions. It becomes important to think of your set as being lit by two types of lights: front lights and non–front lights. Front lights are any lights that illuminate the front (from camera position) of any part of the set. Lights that illuminate the backdrop are front lights because the front of the backdrop is lit. Any other lights, including lights that illuminate the hair or provide an edge or rim along your subject's body, are non–front lights. Hair and rim lights help to "lift" and separate your subject from the backdrop.

THERE WILL COME A POINT WHEN MOTION BLUR WILL BECOME A FACTOR . . .

The two types of lights are metered differently. Therefore, two kinds of metering are necessary: metering for exposure and metering for balance. Metering for exposure involves measuring the amount of light falling on the front of the set. Front lights are involved in metering for exposure. To meter the front lights, stand in the position of importance (e.g., the subject's position) and point the dome of the meter down the lens of the camera.

Metering for balance involves setting the values of the non–front lights in relation to the main exposure. These lights "balance" the scene by helping to determine the highlights that add visual interest to the photograph. To meter these lights, position the meter at the point of importance with the dome aimed at the light source.

Exposure is determined by the interplay of three factors: the ISO set on your camera, the size of your lens opening, and your shutter speed. The ISO is what we used to call the "film speed." Higher ISO numbers mean that less light is needed to create a properly exposed image. The "faster" settings always had a tradeoff. In the film world a faster ISO meant that you could shoot without a strobe in lower light conditions but you risked creating an image with more grain than you would get with a slower speed. In the digital world a faster ISO can mean increased digital noise.

There is actually a fourth factor to consider when determining proper digital exposures: your camera's rated ISO might not be correct! I've heard of many instances in which a photographer's camera was off by as much as a full stop. Run tests to calibrate your meter, then, dial *that* ISO into your meter and shoot accordingly.

Once the ISO is set, the photographer needs to determine the relative importance of the f-stop versus shutter speed in determining the starting point of your exposure. The aperture is generally known to control the depth of field in an image while the shutter speed determines how much motion is depicted. Generally speaking, it is the depth of field that is the overriding concern of the portrait photographer, so the first decision to be made is: "What will the working aperture be?" The "working aperture" is what the camera is set to, and it may differ from the metered aperture—that is part of the creative process. Studio photographers have an easier time than outdoor shooters because for most applications the aperture is the only exposure setting that matters when shooting in a dark studio with strobes. Shutter speeds that are not extremely slow will not record any of the ambient light in most studios; however, the shutter speed does need to be set at, or slower than, the camera's sync speed. The light meter will read the light from the strobe and will indicate the appropriate aperture at a preset ISO.

Outdoor photographers (and photographers who shoot in the studio with flood lights) do need to consider the shutter speed when controlling the exposure because you are recording the ambient light instead of (or in addition to) the light from a strobe. There will be times when the amount of ambient light available will become a factor in choosing a working aperture. For example, the amount of light decreases dramatically as the sun sets. You will have to keep slowing down the shutter speed to maintain your working aperture. There will come a point when motion blur will become a factor, and you will need to start changing your f-stop in order to keep shooting without creating blurry images. Of course, you sacrifice depth of field as you open the lens.

The actual exposure recorded is a factor of the metered exposure in relation to the working aperture. Part of the creative flow in photography is the decision of how your image will be rendered. If you choose to match the metered aperture to the working aperture (keeping the shutter speed and ISO constant), then your image will be "neutral" or "proper." If your metered aperture is greater than the working aperture, then your image will be overexposed. The reverse is true for a metered aperture that is less than the working aperture. Photographers who are used to overexposing their images may be in for a surprise: while there is a bit of room to play with your exposures, it is very limited with digital capture.

Many digital photographers use the preview mode in the camera to check the exposure. This is a potentially dangerous method for checking your exposure because your camera might not be correctly calibrated to your meter. Also, the density of your image

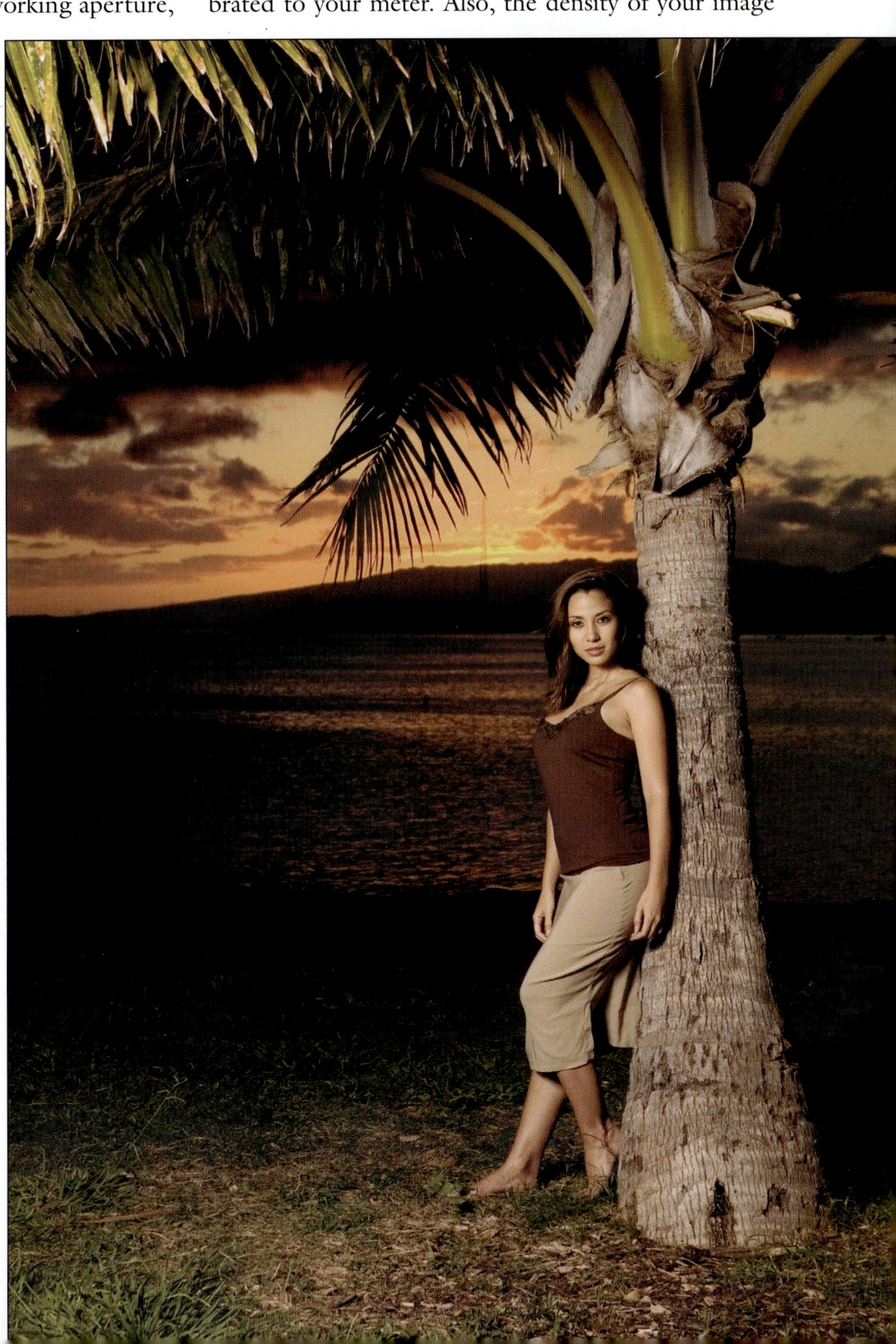

Though the preview screens on the backs of most digital cameras are lousy exposure guides, they can be useful to judge general lighting and composition concerns. They can also be used in specific situations like photographing sunsets to see if you are in the ballpark. Monica Ivey was lit with a monohead strobe in a halo-type softbox. The richness of the sunset behind her was controlled with the shutter speed and was generally monitored by viewing the preview screen on the camera. However, the main exposure was still determined by using a good incident light meter. The exposure was f5.6 at $^{1}/_{320}$ second. We will examine the techniques used to create sunset portraits in chapter 3.

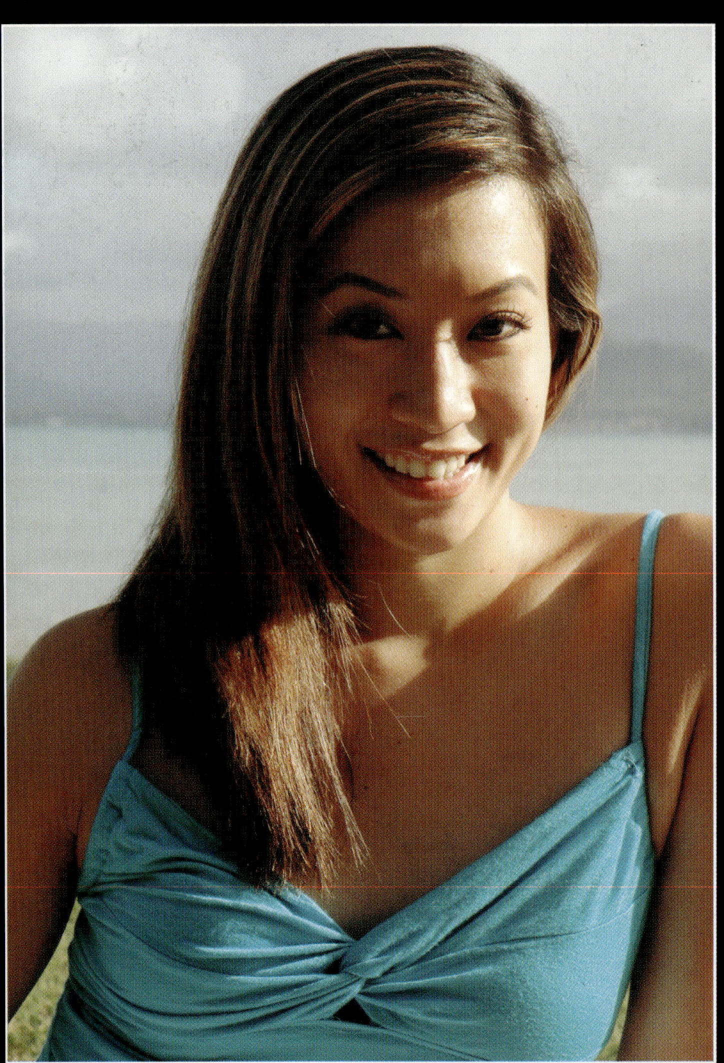

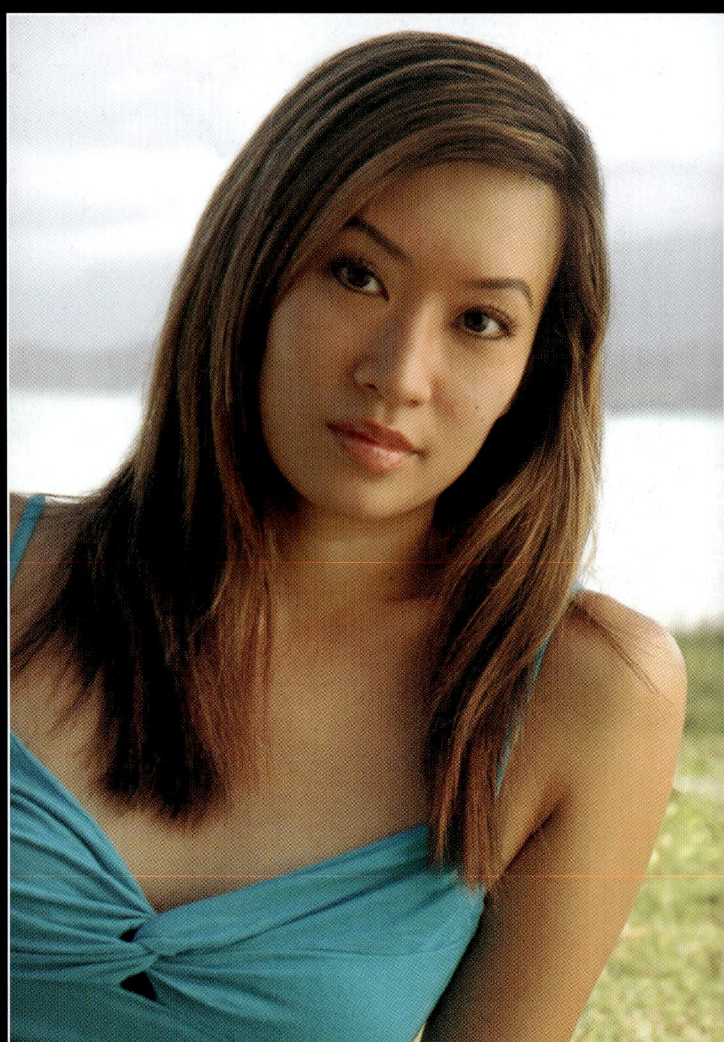

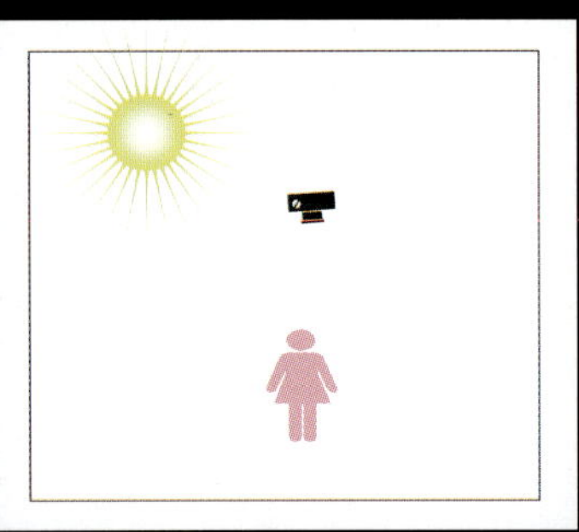

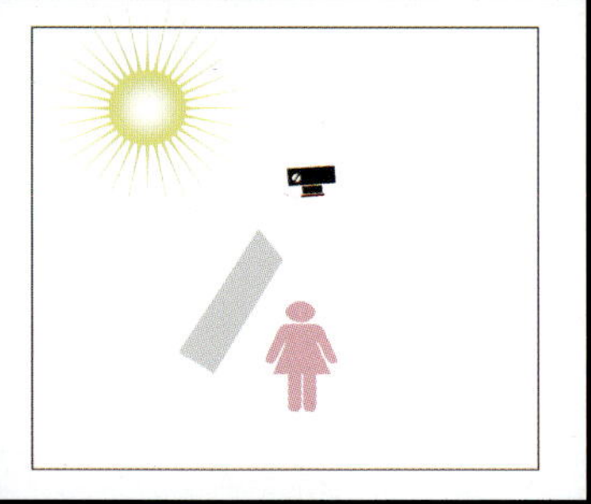

One of the major factors involved in outdoor lighting is the size of the light source in relation to your subject. The other is the distance from the light to your subject. Larger lights will produce a softer quality of light. However, the distance from the light to the subject also plays a critical role. A light source that is far from the subject creates a harsh lighting effect. The sun is a perfect example of this interplay. The sun is the largest light source available, so by definition it should create beautifully soft images. This, as we see from the first image of Brooke Tanaka (left), is not the case. The extreme distance between the sun and the earth turns the huge ball of light into a pinpoint light source, yielding harsh, deep shadows and bright specular highlights throughout most of the day. You will need to modify the effects of direct sun to produce professional (and saleable) portraits. One such modifier, a scrim, is a translucent sheet stretched over a frame. The sunlight passes through the fabric on its way to your subject, and the scrim itself becomes the light source. In the case of the second image of Brooke (right), the light source is no longer the pinpoint sunlight, it is a 77x77-inch Litepanel that is brought in close to the subject. The panel is positioned so that the back edge of the scrim is just beyond her shoulder. This technique is much like feathering a softbox in the studio—it allows the whole scrim to provide soft, beautiful light that wraps around the subject. The second image of Brooke also has a warmer feel to it than the image lit with direct sunlight. This has to do with color temperature concerns (which will be explained later in this chapter). Notice also that the background is lighter in the image with the scrim.

Left (Top and Bottom)—Barebulb flash can be a very effective fill light. Unfortunately, this image doesn't illustrate that fact. There are a couple of problems with the lighting. The portrait was captured on a day when the sun was continually going in and out of a cloud cover. The idea was to have an easily changeable system with a reflector handy for when the sun was out and the strobe set up for when the clouds blocked the sun. The strobes were set so the exposure would be the same with the reflector or strobe. The cloud cover created a very soft but flat light that, with the strobe, acted as a fill source. The amount of light added by the strobe was about the same as the ambient light, so we essentially had two main lights. The size of the light sources then became evident, with the harsh quality of the small light overpowering the soft light from the cloud cover. Dragging the shutter would have allowed me to show more of the detail in the mountains behind my subjects and would have shifted the ratio between the ambient and strobe light in a more favorable direction. The only thing that does work in this shot is the interaction between Nanette and Savannah. **Right (Top and Bottom)**—The ratio between the strobe and the ambient light was close in this photograph of Paige and Kuheleaumoku; however, the strobe was placed in a halo-style softbox. In this case the sun is the harsher of the two light sources and creates a nice edge light, providing some needed contrast in the image.

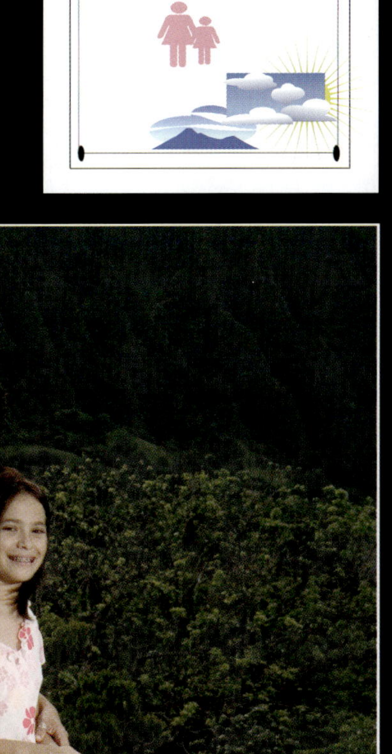

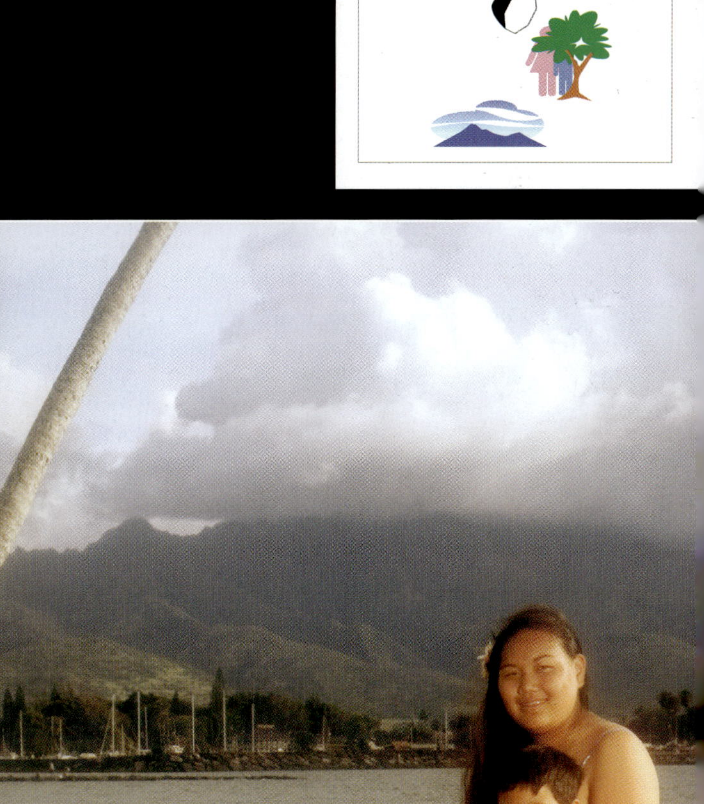

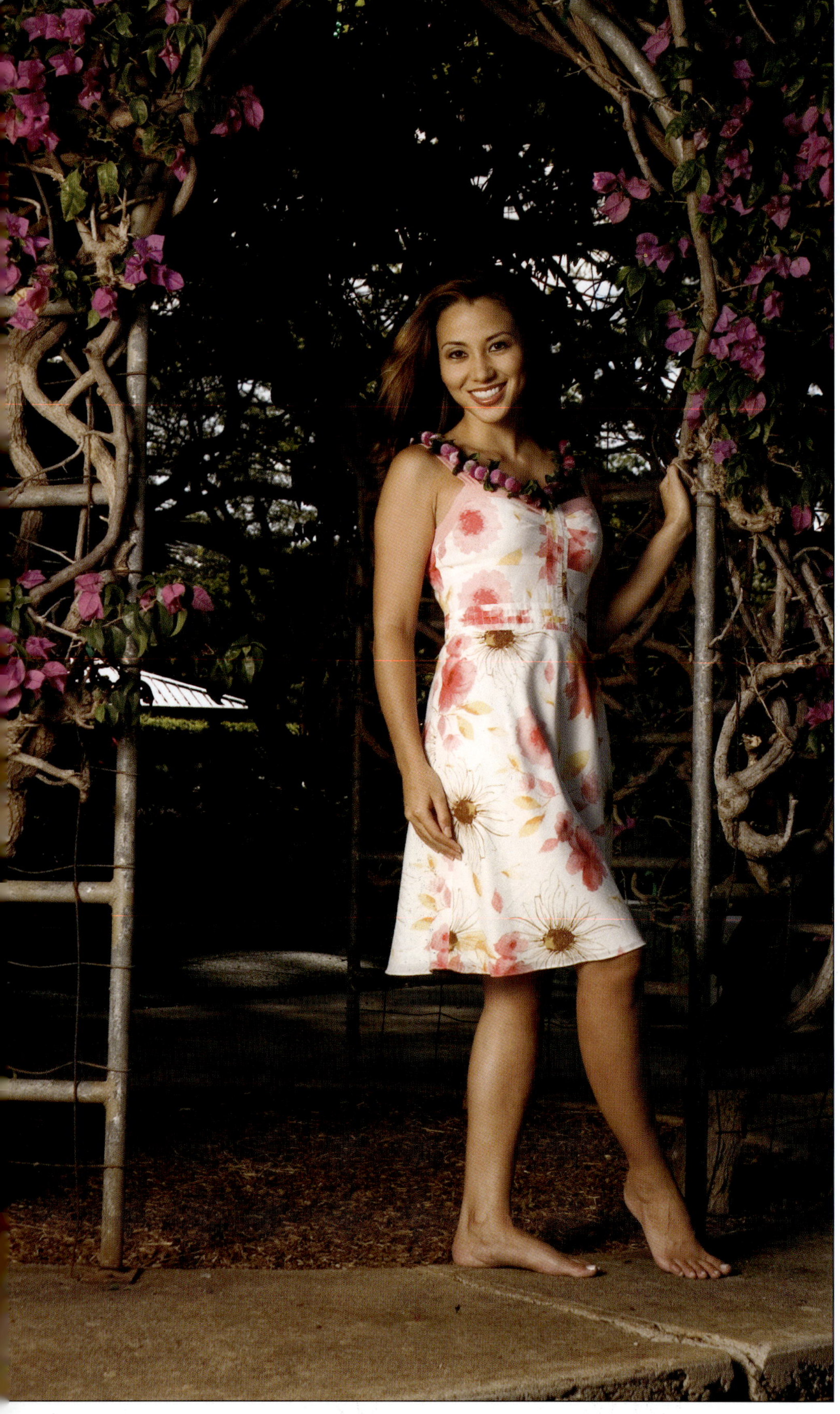

For most portrait work, you'll get the most out of the setup by backing the strobe away from the scrim. The light coming from the strobe will expand as the strobe is backed away, so it will illuminate more of the scrim, and more of the light will be diffused by the scrim. This does not create harsher light because the *scrim* is the light source that is illuminating your subject, and that has not moved. The scrim was placed just out of camera range, and the strobe was backed up a few feet from the scrim. A gold reflector bounced some light into the gazebo behind Monica Ivey.

will change depending on the angle at which you are holding the camera (this same concern holds true for many laptop computers). Digital previews, like Polaroids in the "old days," are great for checking composition and general lighting, but they are lousy critical exposure guides.

Histograms provide a numerical exposure check that provides more accurate data about the information actually captured. Histograms take the data collected and graph it in a range from highlights to shadows and show whether an image is under, over, or properly exposed. However, there are several techniques that the portrait photographer uses that can fool a histogram. A "low key" portrait is one where the subject is wearing dark clothing against a dark backdrop, and the lightest portion of the image is the face. A histogram will read the information and load it toward the shadows portion of the graph, indicating an underexposed image. The reverse will be true for a "high key" portrait, like a white-on-white set.

Will Crockett has come up with a solution he calls the "face histogram." Simply use the elliptical selection tool in Photoshop and select the mask of your subject's face (include a hint of the hairline and some of the chin in your selection) and run a histogram on the selected portion of the image. Most of the data should now bunch up in the middle of the graph with gradual extensions reaching out toward the highlight and shadow areas. Results will, of course, vary depending on the actual skin tones of your subjects: data for darker-skinned subjects will load toward the shadows while data for light-skinned people will load toward the highlights.

QUALITY OF LIGHT

Controlling and manipulating light is the technical key to creating a pleasing and saleable professional portrait. Outdoor portraiture involves the use and control of one constant light source: the sun. Other light sources may be brought in to accent or even override the sunlight, but its presence is always a factor. One of the first things we learn as amateur shutterbugs, unfortunately, is that the sun is a lousy light source! Sure it provides us with awesome images at sunrise and sunset, but for the rest of the day it produces awful images!

OUTDOOR PORTRAITURE INVOLVES THE USE AND CONTROL OF THE SUN.

Direct overhead sunlight produces images that are extremely contrasty with bright highlights and deep, dark shadows. The results are ugly at best with negative film and are just about useless with digital capture because the range from highlight to shadow is beyond what can currently be captured with digital technology. The issue here has to do with the quality of the light. Direct sunlight has an extremely harsh quality. The characteristics of a harsh light source are:

- A rapid transition from highlight to midtone to shadow
- A sharp and distinct edge between highlight, midtone, and shadow
- Deep and dark shadows
- Bright and sharp highlights or "hot spots" (also known as "specular highlights")

A light source with a soft quality has the following characteristics:

- A slow and gradual transition from highlight to midtone to shadow
- Soft and blended edge transfers across the tonal ranges
- Subtle and light shadow areas
- Broad, smooth, and light highlights or "hot spots"

Portrait photographers are usually interested in creating images with a softer quality of light, so by definition, the sun is a lousy choice for a light source. However, portrait photographers are not relegated to the studio all day because the sun won't cooperate! Understanding what makes a light source harsh or soft allows the photographer to manipulate the sunlight to create the images that he or she wants.

The size of the light source relative to the subject is one factor that determines its quality. For example, a strobe with a 7-inch reflector would be a harsh light source for a person but would be a relatively soft source for insects! The sun is a huge light source, but it still creates a harsh quality of light.

The distance between the light source and your subject is the second variable in the quality of light equation. The farther the light is from your subject, the harsher the quality of light. Therefore, the sun, due to its extreme distance from your subject, becomes a pinpoint light source. Expanding the size of the light source and bringing it in closer to your subject are two ways to soften the quality of light falling on your subject. We will discuss some of the ways to modify direct sunlight in chapter 3.

Quality of light issues pertain to all light sources, not just the sun. The image of Brooke Tanaka on page 26 shows the effects of placing a spotlight too close to a scrim. While the scrim did in fact soften the impact of the strobe, the close proximity of the strobe to the scrim still created a harsher than desired highlight. We will explore the interplay of the distance between the strobe and the scrim as well as the distance between the scrim and your subject in chapter 3.

Quality of light issues are also apparent when you use strobes outdoors. Your choice of strobes will also affect the quality of the light illuminating your subject. Barebulb flash can be a very effective fill light but needs to be used carefully because it is an extremely small light source and can easily create a harsh quality of light. Softboxes and scrims can be used to modify and soften the light from strobes (see pages 34–35).

COLOR OF LIGHT

Light has different colors. The human eye does a remarkable job of translating these variations into what we see as "white" light. In fact, light is a series of wavelengths of electromagnetic energy. Visible light is actually an extremely narrow band of these waves falling somewhere on the continuum between microwaves and sound waves. The light that we see is comprised of seven distinct colors, each determined by the distance between the crests of each wave. The colors are red, orange, yellow, green, blue, indigo, and violet.

FLUORESCENT LIGHTS RESULT IN A GHASTLY GREEN CAST THAT NEEDS TO BE CORRECTED.

Outdoor photographers need to be keenly aware of the interactive role that these seven colors play because they change depending on the time of day and the surroundings. Technically, the issue has to do with the color temperature of light. Color balance concerns appear when the degree of red, green, and blue light emitted from a light source are not consistent with each other. An example of this is shooting indoors under fluorescent lights. Fluorescent lights tend to spit out more light along the green wavelengths and result in a ghastly green cast that needs to be corrected. The color of outdoor light does change, but not because of a shift in the balance between the light waves. Sunlight is always "in balance," but that does not mean that your digital sensor will "see" white light all the time. The only time that all the colors combine to produce what is considered "white light" is around noon. The sun is highest in the sky, and the light waves travel the shortest distance to reach the Earth. The shorter light waves (the blue end) are not diffracted by atmospheric interference as much as at sunrise and sunset. The sun is closer to the horizon at sunrise and sunset, and the light travels a greater distance. Therefore, more of the longer light waves (the reds and oranges) reach the Earth, resulting in light that appears amber or "warm."

Color temperature issues were not a major concern to portrait photographers shooting negative film because prints were fairly easily modified at a professional photo lab. Transparency shooters had to be much more aware of the temperature of light, and now digital photographers need to understand the dynamics involved. While digital images are correctable to a degree as well, it is much more critical to be aware of how the light is acting at the time of image capture.

Light has a temperature that is measured on the Kelvin scale. "White" light is considered to be the starting point for color temperature and measures 5500K. In actuality, high noon, which is the standard for white light, is closer to 6000K, but 5500K has become the temperature around which most modern daylight-balanced films were based and now seems to be a standard choice for white balance in digital capture. As the sun rises or sets its color temperature gets "cooler," and this paradoxically results in a "warmer" image. A "higher" color temperature results in a "cool" or bluish image.

A "neutral" image is one where the capture medium matches the color temperature of the light. In the language of a film shooter, this meant choosing a daylight-balanced film for outdoor photography and modifying the color temperature with filters as needed. The color temperature of light at sunrise or sunset comes close to a tungsten level, so a photographer could shoot tungsten film and choose a different set of filters to neutralize the color shifts.

In the world of digital photography, color issues are controlled by using the white balance setting on your camera. The white balance setting tells the camera what type of light you are shooting under and adjusts the color accordingly. Many cameras have preset white balance values that are measured in degrees Kelvin. These preset values are similar to choosing a daylight-balanced film or a tungsten film. The advantages of using these presets lie in the creative control afforded the photographer. Just as with the film counterparts, the photographer may selectively change the color temperature of some of the lights on the set to create a variety of effects. The drawbacks to using preset white balance values are also similar to transparency films: your image will change as the color temperature of the light changes. The changing color temperature of light is especially critical when shooting outdoors.

How far from neutral you want to render your image is a creative choice. Many portraits have a "cozier" feel when photographed on the warm side—that is, at a lower color temperature than neutral. However, in order to control the color temperature of the light illuminating your subject, you must first know what factors affect color temperature.

Three factors that affect color temperature are particularly inherent to outdoor lighting. They are:

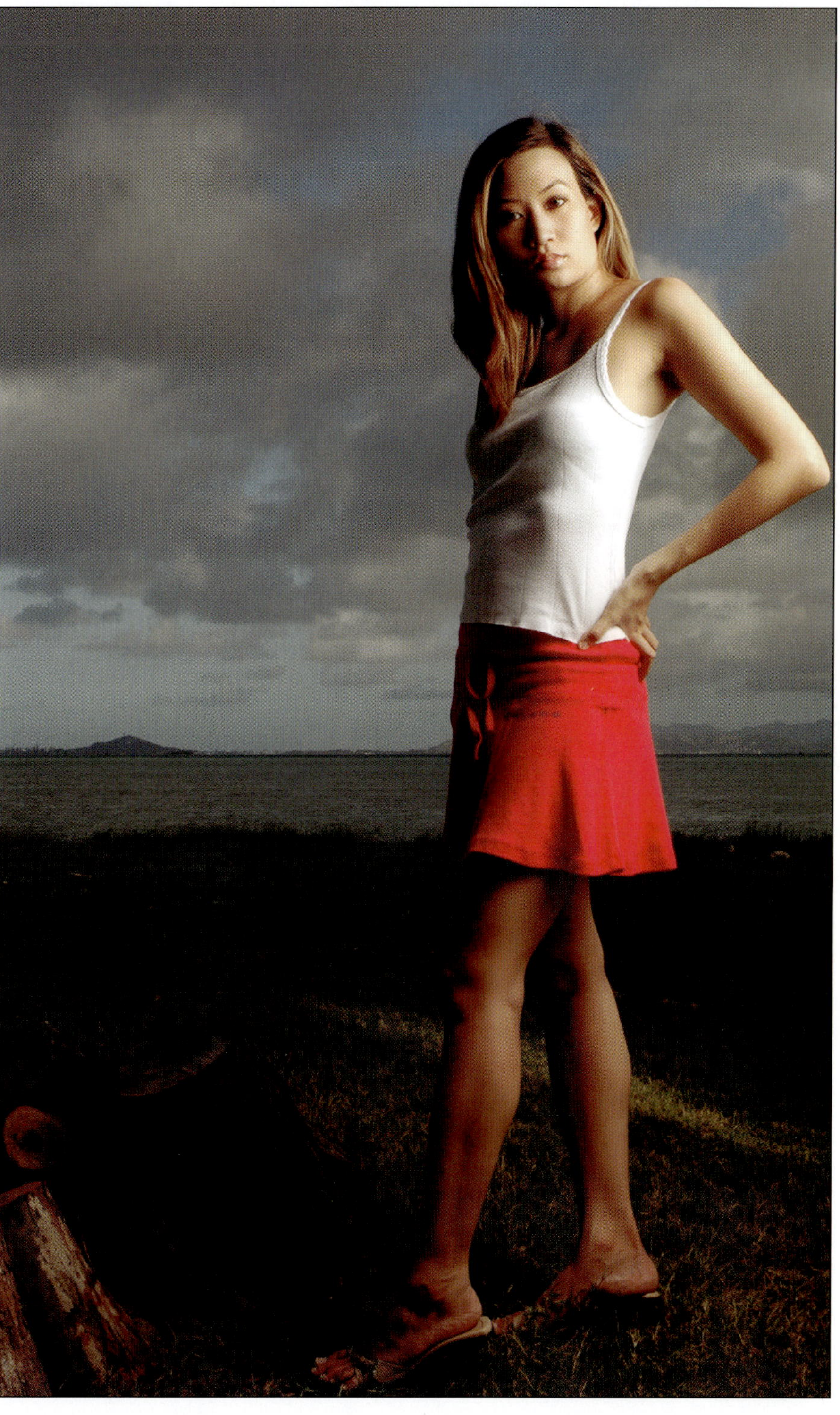

Placing a scrim between the strobe and your subject increases the size of the light source and softens the quality of light. There are two factors that will affect the look of the image produced. The scrim does become the light source, so it will produce a softer look when brought in close to your subject. However, the distance between the strobe and the scrim will also have an effect. If the strobe is placed very close to the scrim, then you will have the effect of a diffused spotlight, almost nullifying the effect of the scrim. However, as this image of Brooke Tanaka shows, you can use this technique to create dramatic portraits. This is the same setup as the photograph that didn't work (page 26). This image works better because it was shot at a faster shutter speed. Shutter speed is critical role when combining strobes with ambient light. The relationship between shutter speeds and the strobe–ambient combination is detailed in chapter 3.

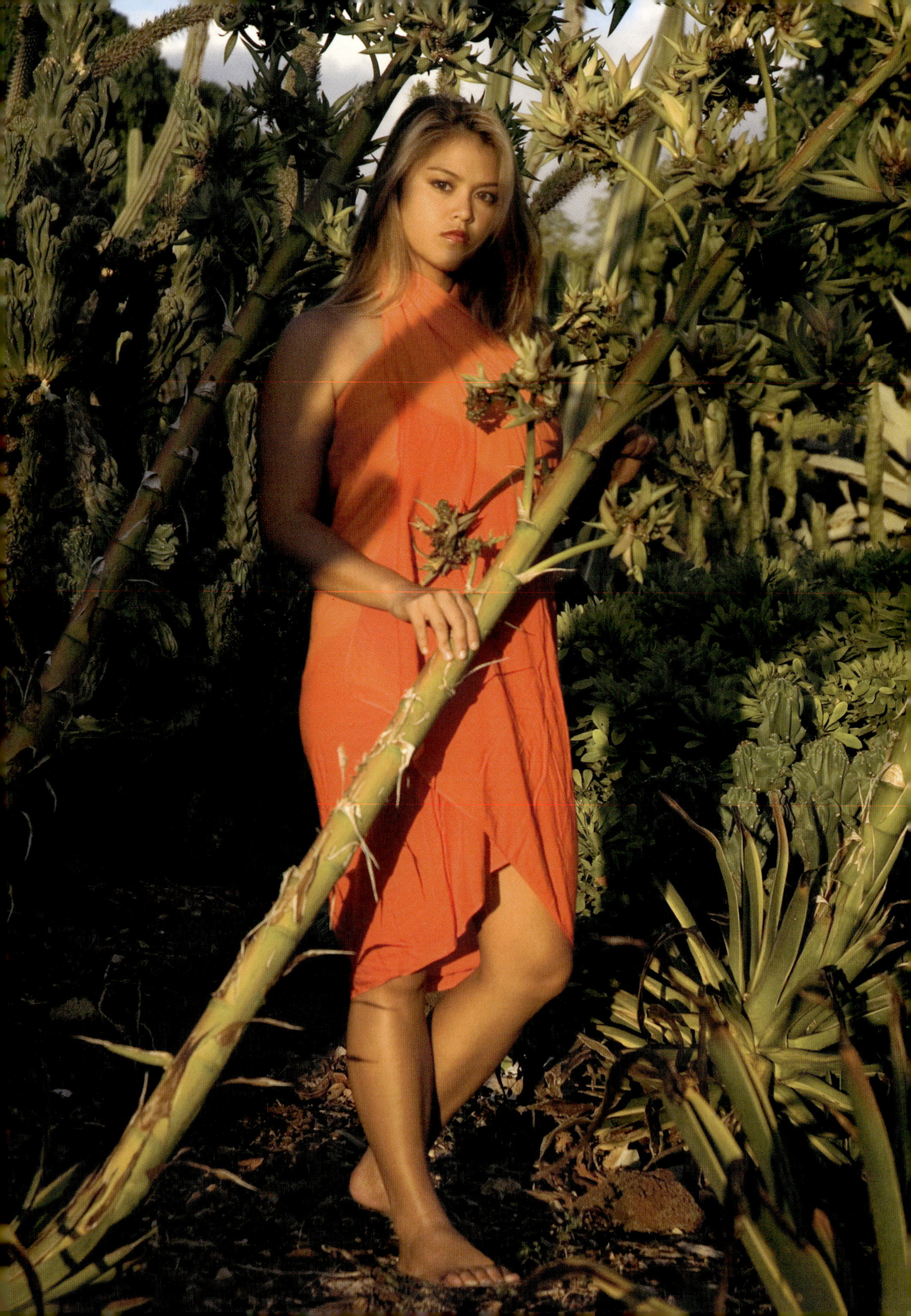

- **Time of Day.** As mentioned above, the temperature of the sunlight changes as the sun rises in the sky and sets again. The color temperature of the light is much lower at sunrise and increases steadily until high noon when it begins to lower again as the sun approaches the horizon toward sunset. The effect on your image—if your capture medium is balanced to daylight—will be very warm or amber through neutral and then warm again.
- **Clear Skies versus Cloudy Skies/Direct Sunlight versus Open Shade.** The statement that sunlight at high noon is considered white light is dependent upon a cloudless day. Clouds will raise the color temperature of sunlight and will result in a cool or bluish hue. The same rule and effect apply to photographing your subject in open shade. An example of how these factors affect your image—and a technique to "fix" it—will be shown later in the book (page 70).
- **The Way Your Light is Modified.** With very few exceptions, outdoor light needs to be modified to produce the results you want. Your choice of light modifier will alter the color temperature of the sun (or any light source). Bouncing light off a silver reflector will raise the color temperature of the light. Placing white translucent materials between the sun and your subject or bouncing light off a white surface will lower the color temperature.

There will be times when you will use a strobe as part of your outdoor lighting scheme. The age of the flash tube will affect the color temperature of the light coming from the strobe: older tubes tend to have a lower color temperature than do new ones. Similarly, the power setting on some units will alter the actual color temperature of the strobe. The final effect that these factors have on your image will depend upon whether the strobe is used as a main light or a fill source.

Facing Page—The time of day will affect the color temperature of natural light. Late-afternoon sunlight produces an amber color shift to your images that is paradoxically due to the cooler color temperature of the sunlight. The light travels farther as the sun approaches the horizon, so the shorter wavelengths—the blues and the greens—are more subject to defraction than the longer orange and red wavelengths. Ku'uipo was photographed as the last rays of direct sunlight lit the scene. The camera was set on daylight white balance, so the image has a deep amber cast because of the lower color temperature of sunset light.

COLOR BALANCE ISSUES

While visible light contains seven colors, color photography is mostly concerned with the red, green, and blue spectrums. Light sources like the sun or controlled strobes emit light fairly evenly across the three spectrums. In other words, these light sources are in balance even when the color temperature shifts. Color balance refers to a different set of problems that are mostly related to shooting indoors under mixed lighting conditions where one (or more) light source emits more light along one of the spectrums and is therefore out of balance. The most common situation is shooting under fluorescent lights or when fluorescent lights are used as a fill source. We have all seen photographs with a ghastly green shift. The green shift is due to the overabundance of green light coming from the light source.

Color balance issues are not often a great concern when photographing outdoors because you generally bring your light modifiers with you (e.g., additional strobes, scrims, etc.) and could solve the problem by not bringing an out-of-balance light source with you. However, there may be rare times when color balance becomes a problem in an environmental or executive portrait. For example, you may be photographing an executive in front of a factory, and fluorescent lights may be illuminating the background. Color temperature issues are a matter of creative judgment, but color balance problems need to be fixed.

Solutions. The solutions to color issues—either playing creatively with color temperature or fixing color balance problems—have become much easier in the digital world. In conventional photography, both issues were addressed by using filters and gels to fit your needs. The use of a preset white balance still enables the photographer to use these tools—and therefore still maintains the creative aspects of color temperature. However, many of the better digital cameras have a custom white balance setting that allows you to automatically set the white balance according to whatever lighting situation you find. The custom white balance is set by placing a white card under the same lighting scheme as your subject, filling the viewfinder with the card, and pushing a button. Simply set the custom white balance each time your light changes. Check the manual for your camera for details about how to set a custom white balance.

I am one of the many digital photographers who are comfortable with the "old" way of thinking in terms of daylight balance versus tungsten balance. As noted above, many of the better digital cameras have several white balance presets in addition to the opportunity to set a custom white balance. One way to work in this mode is to consider digital capture along the same lines as shooting transparency film—your choices are to balance the capture mode to either daylight or tungsten and make the necessary adjustments (if needed) using filters or gels. Gels are more common in studio situations where you want to control the color temperature (or balance) of specific lights. In these cases particular gels are placed over specific light sources, thereby altering the look of that light.

I PERSONALLY LIKE MY AFTERNOON IMAGES TO BE RENDERED ON THE AMBER SIDE . . .

However, filters can still be placed on your lens to correct for color temperature concerns at a preset white balance. The #80 series of filters are used to convert tungsten light to daylight. The #85-series filters convert daylight to tungsten light. The #81- and #82-series also lower and raise a light's color temperature respectively but do so at much more subtle degrees. For example, a #81A filter could be used when photographing someone in open shade to slightly lower the color temperature of the shade. Similarly, the light on the beach at sunset might be too amber. A #82-series filter could be used to raise the color temperature of the sunset to a level where the skin tones are still more amber than neutral, but not reddish-orange.

It was mentioned earlier that color issues were easier to deal with in the realm of digital capture. Choosing the correct filter on location does seem like a throwback to the "old days" when a valuable tool like custom white balance is available. However, there may be times when you don't want a perfectly neutral image. I personally like my afternoon images to be rendered on the amber side of neutral. I will shoot early morning or evening images with my white balance preset to 5500K and let the image go amber.

This techniques works for most of my images, but I do have to admit that sometimes the color temperature drops too much and the image turns out too red or orange. Fortunately, many color "problems" may now be addressed after the fact. Adobe has added a set of "photo filters" to Photoshop. Photoshop CS includes a set of filters that act as warming, cooling, and specific colors (like magenta to counteract a green cast). Furthermore, they can be used as adjustment layers. Between the adjustment layer and layer masks, the digital photographer now has total control over color issues! This may be the first (and only) time when it is okay to think, "I'll fix it in Photoshop!" The technique is demonstrated in chapter 3. Capturing your image in RAW allows you to alter the color temperature after the fact as well.

INVERSE SQUARE LAW AND OUTDOOR APPLICATIONS

The inverse square law states that light will "fall off" rapidly as the light source is moved farther from the subject. The spread of light expands as its source is pulled back from the subject. Its power decreases by the same factor. The reverse is true as the light source is brought in closer to the subject. A discussion of the inverse square law may seem out of place when talking about outdoor lighting where the sun will be involved with most images. However, the major challenge for the outdoor digital portraitist is to force a scene with over twenty possible "stops" of information into a medium that can capture about seven of those stops. You are going to have to selectively add and subtract light from certain parts of the scene to record an acceptable amount of information. The inverse square law will not be a factor in metering direct sunlight

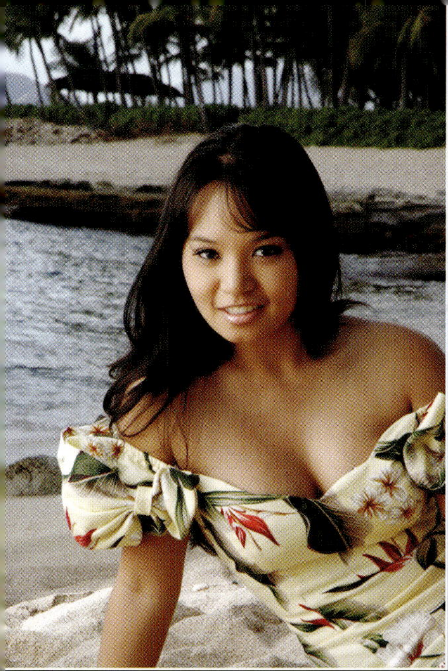

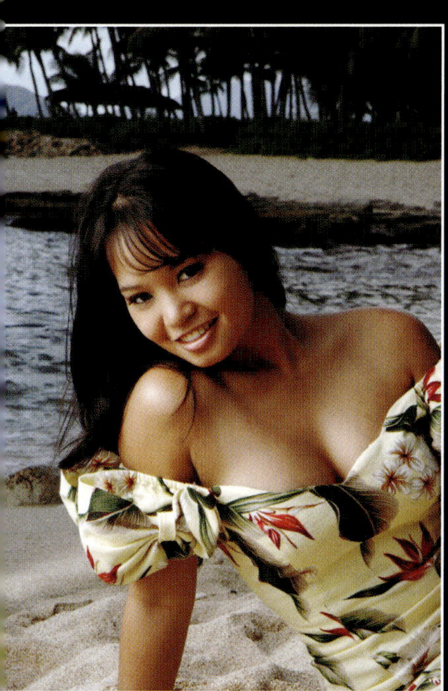

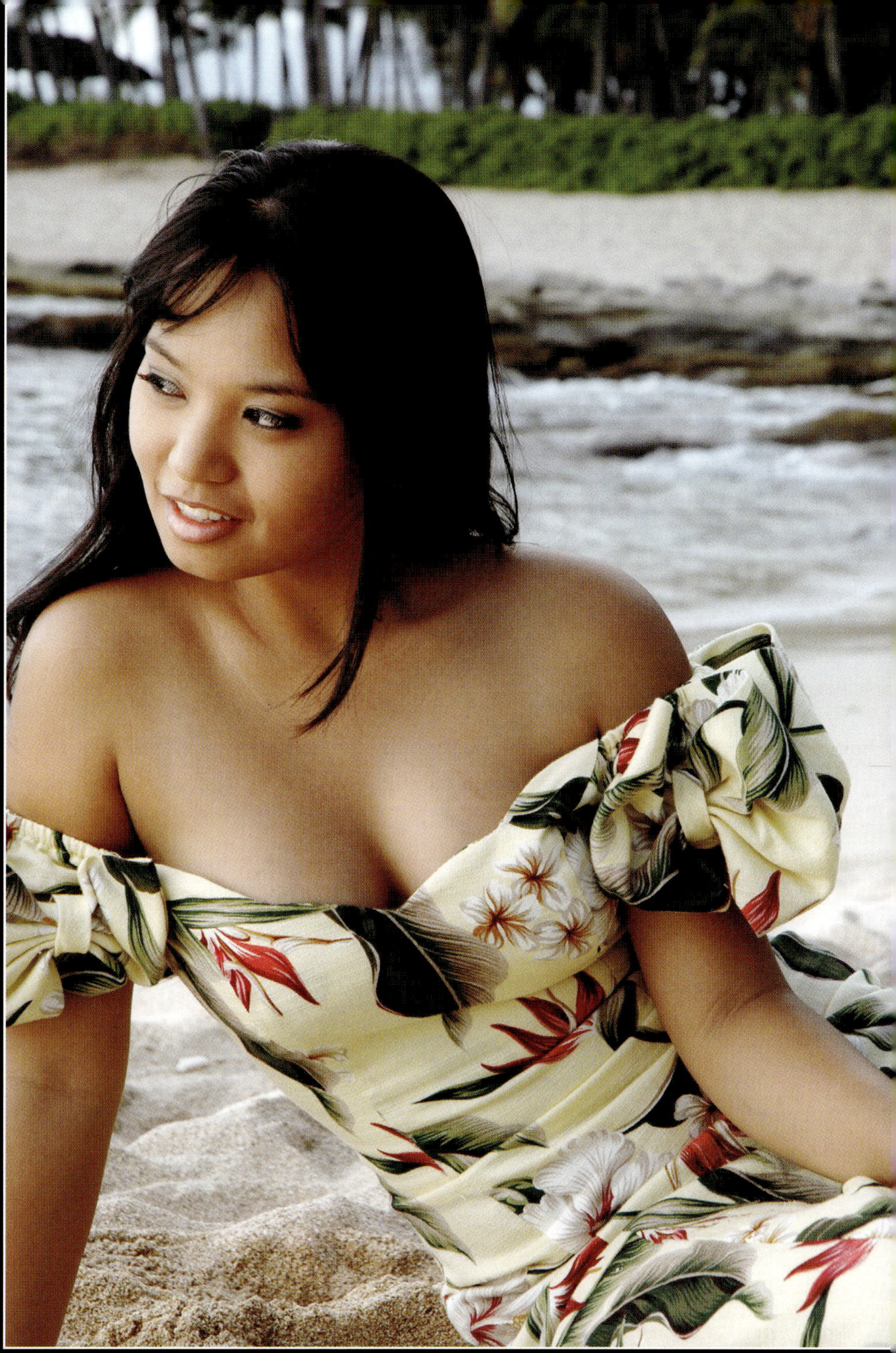

Top Left—Teresa Bringas was photographed in a beautiful cove on the southwest coast of Oahu, Hawaii. The sun was beginning to set over the ocean but was still too high in the sky to use as an unmodified main light. The sun was also peeking in and out of a cloud cover, which complicated the situation. We set up a 77x77-inch Litepanel scrim and used a strobe to shoot through the scrim, in effect turning it into a softbox. Teresa was positioned where she would not be shielded by the shade of the scrim. The goal of using artificial light on location is usually to make it look as natural as possible, so we placed the strobe and scrim along the same axis as the sun to create natural-looking shadow patterns. **Bottom Left—**You can use the inverse square law to modify your lighting ratios and alter the background exposure without moving your scrim or changing the settings on your strobe. **Above—**The impact of the strobe is negligible in this image because of the falloff due to the increased distance between the strobe and the scrim. The strobe–scrim combination acts as very mild fill light.

because the light has already traveled such an extreme distance. However, direct sun will rarely be used by itself to light your portrait. You will be bouncing, diffusing, or in some other way using indirect sunlight to illuminate your subject, and the inverse square law will come into play, especially if you add strobes to the equation or use the light streaming through a window as your main light.

THE INVERSE SQUARE LAW WILL BE A FACTOR IN YOUR OUTDOOR PORTRAITS . . .

The inverse square law states that light falls off at a rate that is inversely proportionate to the square of the distance from the light to the subject. All that really means is that the metered exposure for a light source will change as the light is moved closer to or farther away from the subject. The important aspect is that the changes in exposure are consistent and predictable because they are based on a law of physics. For example (using arbitrary numbers that actually double the distances), say a light meter takes a reading of f16 from a light that is 1 foot away. The same light placed 2 feet from the meter will read f8 (½ squared, or ¼ the power). The same light placed 4 feet away will register f4 because it is now at 1⁄16 the power. It is the predictability involved that allows you to control the effect of moving the light sources and to know what needs to be done to bring a scene into balance. Remember that moving a light source also has an effect on its quality of light, so juggling these two laws can get tricky.

As a general rule, the inverse square law will not affect the exposure of direct ambient light. The inverse square law will be a factor in your outdoor portraits when your main light source is diffused or reflected and when combining strobes with the ambient light surrounding your subject. The mathematics required to figure out the exposure compensation involved in moving your light strobe can be maddening—even without factoring in the interplay of the ambient light. However, the inverse square law has a direct relationship to f-stops. Let's say for simplicity's sake that we place a light source 8 feet from our subject and meter it at f8. If we then move that light to a distance of 11 feet and do not change the power setting, we will have an exposure of f5.6. The same light at 5.6 feet away would yield an exposure of f11!

The inverse square law will have several effects on the exposure of your strobes—which will then affect the overall exposure of the scene. The simplest effect will be seen when using a strobe in isolation or in a softbox/umbrella situation where the distance between the strobe and the diffusion material/reflector is constant. Moving the strobe closer or farther from your subject without changing its power will have an impact on the overall exposure and look of the scene because of the way in which strobe light interacts with ambient light to create the final exposure. Moving your strobe light without making other adjustments may change the whole relationship between strobe and ambient light. Consider the following examples:

There was an example earlier in this book (page 39, far right image) where a strobe was placed very close to a scrim. The scrim essentially acted as a diffuser for a spotlight. While the image created was dramatic, it did not make the best use of the scrim. The inverse square law tells us that we can make better use of the scrim by backing the strobe up and letting its light disperse farther. The broader spread of light will illuminate more of the scrim, which will in turn create a beautifully soft light for an engaging portrait. Remember though that backing the strobe up will have an impact on the exposure.

The first of the series of images of Teresa Bringas (previous page) was exposed at f11 at 1⁄125 second. The strobe was set about 6 feet from the scrim. The ambient exposure at Teresa's cheek was f8 at 1⁄125, so the strobe was also f8. The combination resulted in a 2:1 ratio on Tee's face and allowed the background, lit by ambient light only, to be underexposed by 1 stop.

You can also use the inverse square law to modify the lighting ratios and alter the effect of the strobe as well as modify the background illumination without moving the scrim or changing the setting on the strobe. This would come in handy when you have found your optimal distance from the scrim to your subject and if you did not have an adjustable strobe.

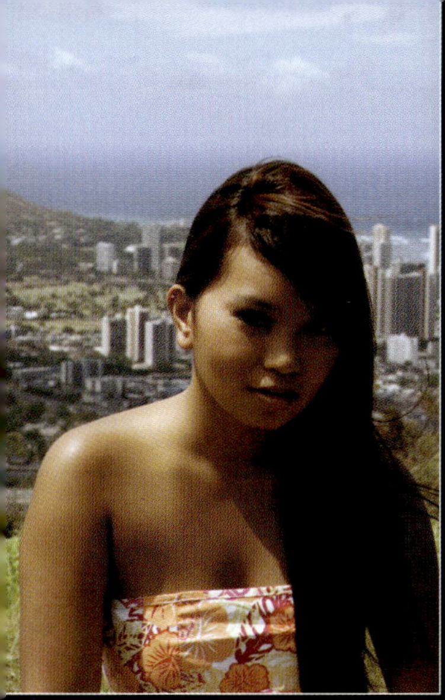

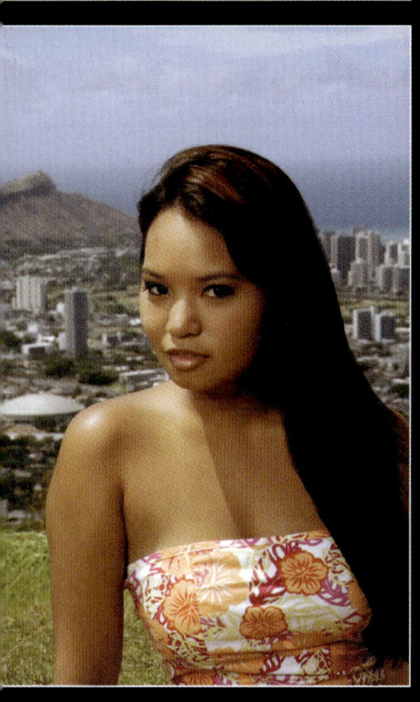

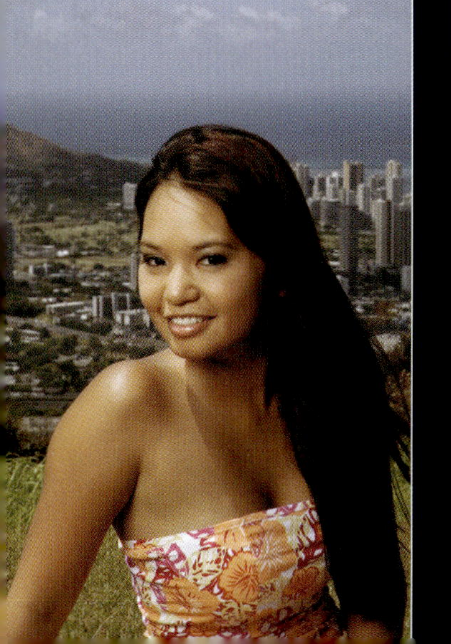

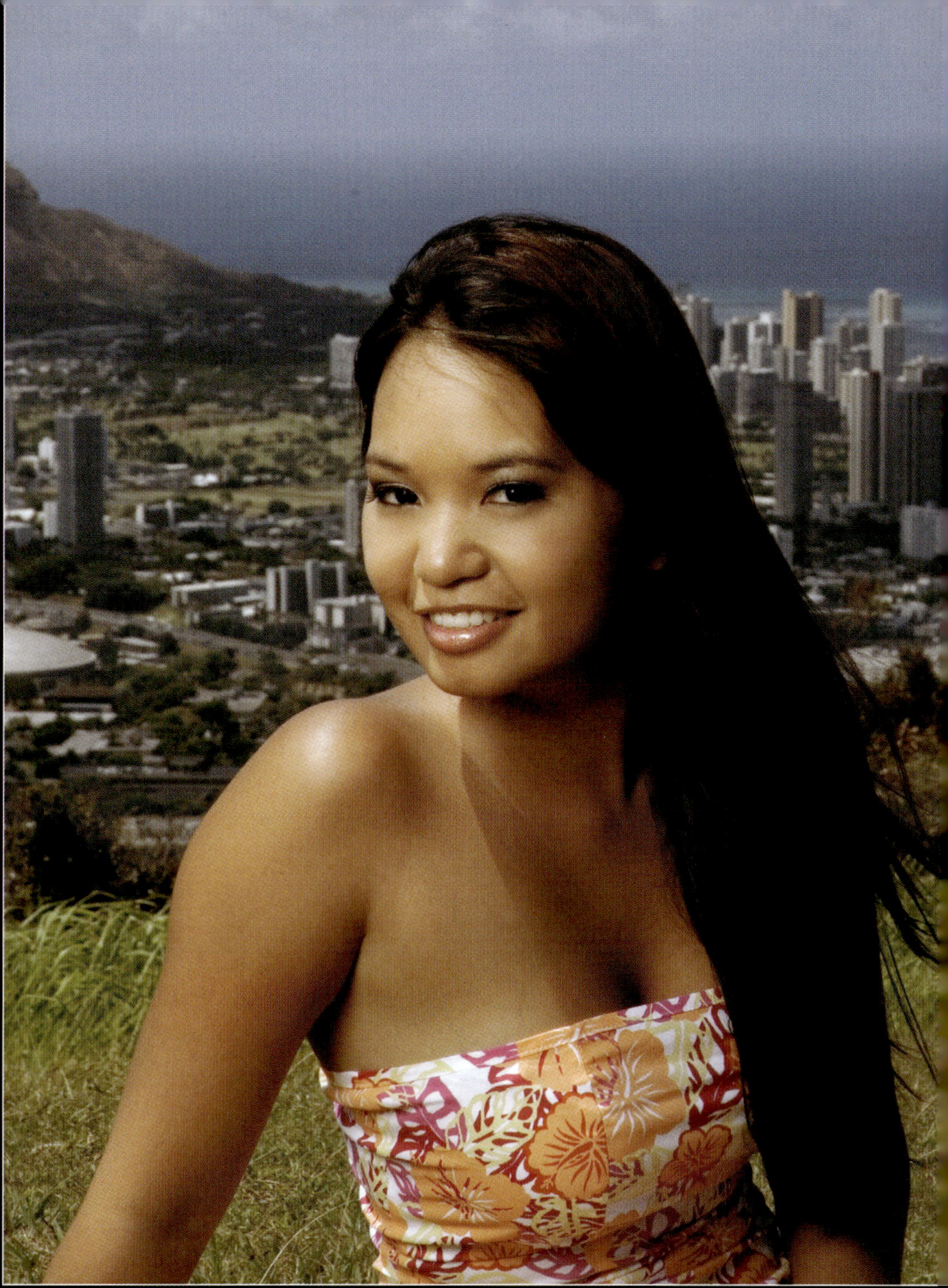

Top Left—Once again overhead sunlight created ugly, harsh shadows that are anything but flattering. There are several ways to "fix" this problem. For this series we will see what we can do by adding a strobe to the scene. The exposure for this image was f11 $^{5}/_{10}$ at $^{1}/_{250}$ second (shot slightly underexposed at f14 [11 $^{6}/_{10}$]). Moving your strobe without making other adjustments will alter the exposure of your strobe and the overall scene. Moving your strobe in this manner can also alter its relationship to the ambient light. **Center Left—**The addition of a strobe helps the image dramatically. However, there are still shadows that are distracting because, with the current setup, the strobe is acting as a fill source. **Bottom Left—**The strobe was moved in about 4 feet and now adds about a full stop to the exposure. The strobe and the ambient exposure were about equal, and the effect of the strobe is much more apparent. The shadows from the sun have become much less offensive. Note also that the backdrop has gotten darker with each image because the strobe is adding more light, but the falloff is dramatic so it doesn't affect the backdrop. **Above—**Moving the strobe in 4 feet eliminated the harsh shadows to the point where I was able to finish the job with a few strokes of the healing brush in Photoshop.

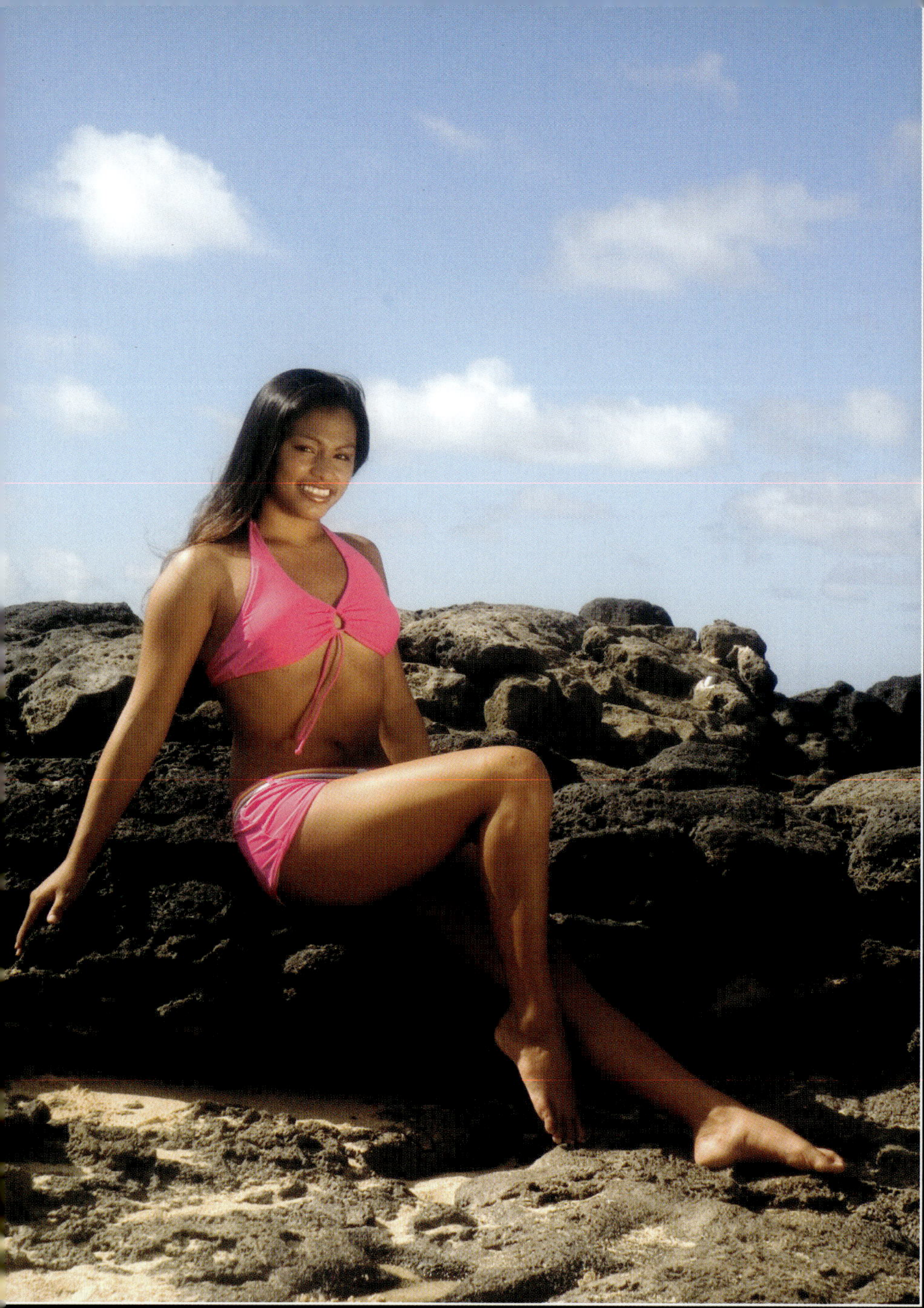

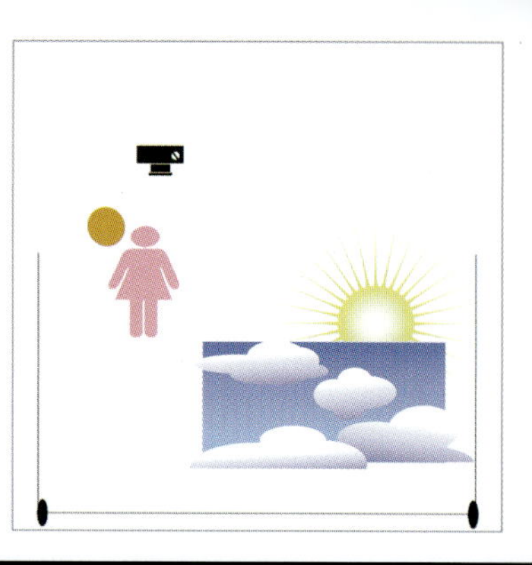

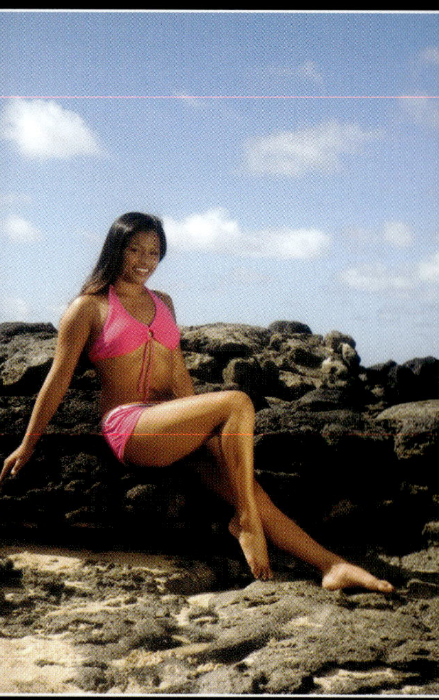

Swimwear is a popular wardrobe item for creating teen portraits. Locations like the beach provide natural environments for these photographs. Beaches also usu ally require some kind of modification of the light—in this case we used a reflector to catch the light that was streaming over Karielle's shoulder and bounced it back into her face. The reflector is most effective when it is placed at the same angle as the main light but opposite that light. The sun was coming from ove the model's right shoulder, so the reflector was placed to her left. A common error is to place the fill card too far behind the subject; this will work beautifully if you want to add an accent to your subject's hair or body, but it won't be very effective to fill in the shadows created by the main light. The light will be reflected back at the exact angle that it strikes the reflective surface, so the angle at which the reflector is held is critical. Place the reflector opposite the main light but in front of your subject. Find the spot that will catch the light from the main light that passes your subject and will bounce the light back in at the same angle. There may be times when the reflector is almost perpendicular to the main light. Note that slight movements can produce dramatic differences in where the bounced light falls. Here we see an example in which the reflector lights Karielle's face beautifully and another where the angle was slightly off.

The second image of Teresa was created by bringing the strobe in to about 3 feet from the scrim. The overall exposure was now f14, so with the ambient light unchanged, the strobe added $^{2}/_{3}$ stop more light to her face. Several things happened by making this change: the strobe–scrim became more of a main light, changing the lighting ratio to about 4:1; the strobe now defined the shadows of Teresa's face more dramatically; and the background was underexposed by 1$^{2}/_{3}$ stops (compare the brightness of the sand behind Teresa).

Backing the strobe up creates the opposite effect: now the strobe–scrim becomes the fill light because of the dramatic falloff of light. We put the strobe about 12 feet from the scrim for the third photograph in this series (the distances are approximate—we didn't have a tape measure, but we tried to estimate a doubling and halving of the distance to show how the inverse square law works). Doubling the distance (from where the strobe was originally set up) drops the power of the strobe to $^{1}/_{4}$ of its original strength. The ambient light was still f8, so the strobe adds $^{1}/_{4}$ stop of light. The actual exposure fell between f8 and f9, so the choice was to slightly overexpose the image by setting the camera at f8 or slightly underexposing it by setting the camera at f9. We chose f8. The background is lighter than in the previous two images because it is properly exposed rather than underexposed.

You can obtain similar effects without using a scrim to shoot through. The images on page 45 were created at about 10:30 in the morning with high overhead sunlight. The first image shows the disastrous results of shooting the scene without modifying the light. This was the best of the photographs using unmodified light: Teresa wasn't able to turn her face to the right because the shadows were terrible!

A strobe was tucked inside a Westcott halo-style softbox and placed about 8 feet away from Teresa. The ambient exposure at $^{1}/_{250}$ second was now f11$^{3}/_{10}$. The strobe added $^{6}/_{10}$ stop for a final exposure of f11$^{9}/_{10}$ (slightly underexposed at f16—we will examine how to determine the final exposure of a scene that combines strobes with ambient light later in this book (chapter 3). Here the strobe acts as a fill light, adding slightly more than $^{1}/_{2}$ stop of light.

The strobe was already at full power so we had to move it closer to Teresa to downplay the harsh light.

ANGLE OF INCIDENCE=ANGLE OF REFLECTANCE

The angle of incidence=angle of reflectance law will help you create highlights in your image while staying within the exposure latitude of digital. In fact, you can set up hair and rim lights with an exposure value close to your main light exposure. Light bounces off a surface (angle of reflectance) at the same angle that it strikes the surface (angle of incidence). We are recording the light that reflects off of our subject. Lights—or reflectors that bounce light—are often placed at sharp-

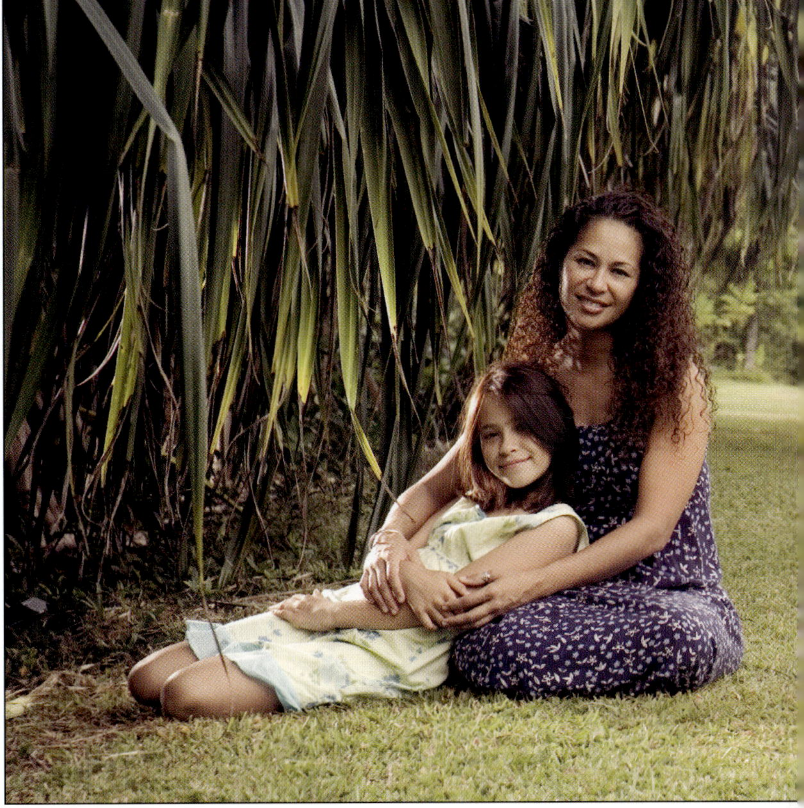

A hair light that is balanced to the main light will appear brighter than the main exposure partially because of the angle of incidence=angle of reflectance law. In this case the ambient light read f5.6 at $^{1}/_{60}$ second. A strobe with a 20-degree grid spot was hidden behind the trees and was used as a rim/hair light. The strobe was metered at f5.6$^{1}/_{10}$ but appears brighter due in part to the sharper angle at which the light is reflected into the lens. Nanette and Savannah were photographed in a park on the east coast of Oahu, Hawaii, where the light changes dramatically. The color temperature issues involved in creating this image will be discussed later in this book.

er angles to the camera in order to create a rim or hair light. The sharper angle of reflectance of these light sources will make them appear brighter in the image. Rim lights also tend to be smaller light sources and therefore appear to have more contrast than the generally larger main light.

The angle of incidence=angle of reflectance law can also help solve one of the trickiest problems in portrait photography: photographing someone with glasses. Removing the glass and photographing your subject with just the frames can look fake, while the reflection of the light in the glasses can be distracting. A subtle shift in the angle of the eyeglasses will move the angle of reflectance off of the chip plane.

ON-CAMERA FLASH IS SOMETIMES USED AS A LIGHT MODIFIER FOR OUTDOOR PHOTOGRAPHY.

On-camera flash is sometimes used as a light modifier/fill source for outdoor photography. This technique can be fairly easy but may result in "red-eye." Red-eye is caused by the light hitting the retina of the eye and bouncing back into the camera where it "burns" a red spot in the retina. The retina is highly reflective, so the problem occurs when the strobe is too close to the chip plane. The only way to eliminate red-eye is to make sure that the strobes are on a different angle than the film/chip plane—such as when the strobe is attached to a bracket or light stand.

Understanding how light bounces off of reflective surfaces is also critical in positioning fill cards. A fill card is a reflective surface placed opposite the main light and used to fill the shadows that are created by the main light. It is not enough to simply stick a piece of white, gold, or silver (or whatever else you wish to use!) card on the other side of your subject. The angle at which the card is placed will have a dramatic effect on your image. Position your fill card at the same angle as (but opposite) your main light for the best results.

ADDITIVE NATURE OF LIGHT AND ITS APPLICATIONS

We have discussed the fact that digital capture currently simply does not have the exposure latitude of negative films. The smooth transitions from highlight to shadow are much more difficult to control. There is a tighter limit on the range of lighting ratios available because your blacks will lose detail and your highlights will blow out faster. You can "subtract" light from a scene by using scrims or open shade, but as we will see later, these techniques might actually increase your difficulties. The odds are that you will be controlling the contrast of your scene by adding light to bring the image into balance. Portrait photographers often talk about the range from highlights to shadows in terms of lighting ratios. However, to fully understand how lighting ratios work, it becomes necessary to revisit the concepts behind lighting ratios and to reexamine one of the basics of photography: the f-stop. In actuality, f-stops are anything but basic. Understanding f-stops is critical to knowing how to preplan your lighting ratio. F-stops also help define one of the most difficult aspects of photography: the additive nature of light.

The theory behind the additive nature of light is nowhere near as complicated as its use. The concept is quite simple: your exposure increases as the number of lights illuminating part of your scene increases. The amount of light added to your exposure is predictable and easy to understand—if we were using whole numbers. The confusing part comes when translating the "simple" math to f-stops.

F-stops, or aperture settings, are constant from camera to camera and lens to lens because the numbers represent a ratio of the actual diameter of the lens opening to the focal length of the lens. Therefore, the actual size of an aperture of f5.6 will be different on a 50mm lens compared to a 100mm lens, but the relative size will be the same. F-stops are in direct relation to each other: any given f-stop is exactly twice as large or ½ as large as its adjacent stop. For example, the lens opening at f5.6 is exactly twice as large as that at f8 and exactly half as large as f4. Therefore, f5.6 lets in twice as much light as f8 and half as much light as f4. So, keeping the shutter speed constant, you would need half as much light to create the same exposure at f4 as you would need at f5.6. Conversely, you would need twice as much light to create the same exposure at f8 as you would need at f5.6.

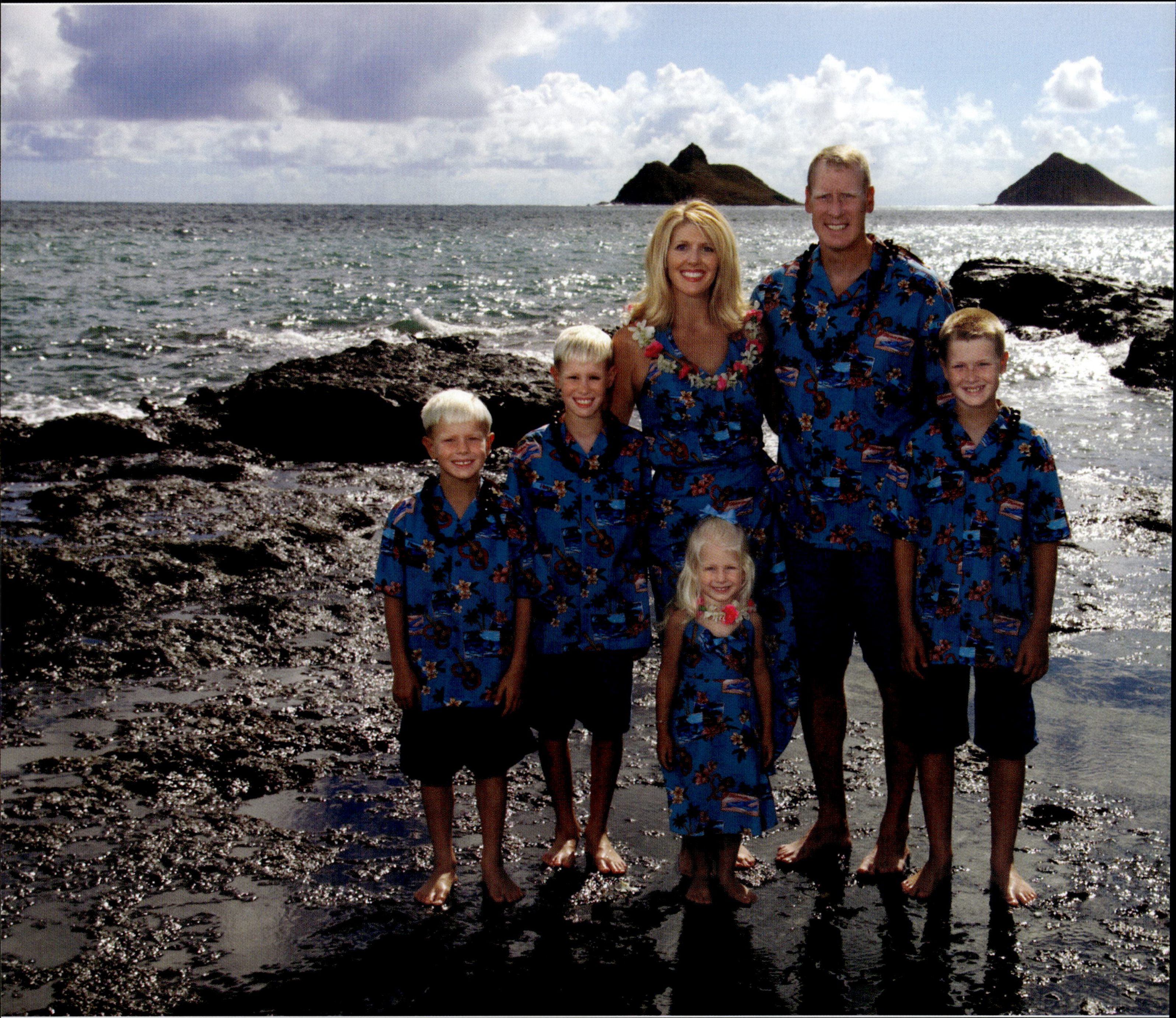

David Taylor used a fairly complex lighting scheme to balance a heavily backlit scene of a family with really blond hair! He used a combination of two strobes and the ambient light to balance the scene. One flash was housed on a bracket attached to the camera while a second portable flash was off-camera left. Each strobe was set 1 stop less than the background ambient exposure. Using hypothetical numbers, let's say that the background ambient reading at his chosen shutter speed was f8. Each strobe would then be set to read f5.6—each providing half as much light as f8 and equaling f8 when combined. David used a layer mask similar to the one described in the introduction to further darken the background. I also like the repetitive pattern of the posing of the family and the islands behind them.

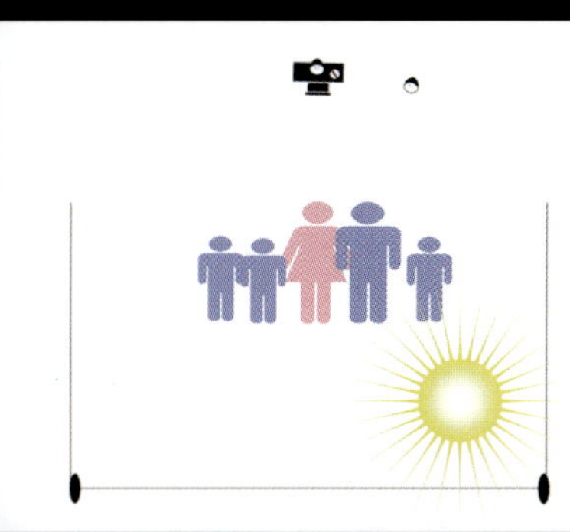

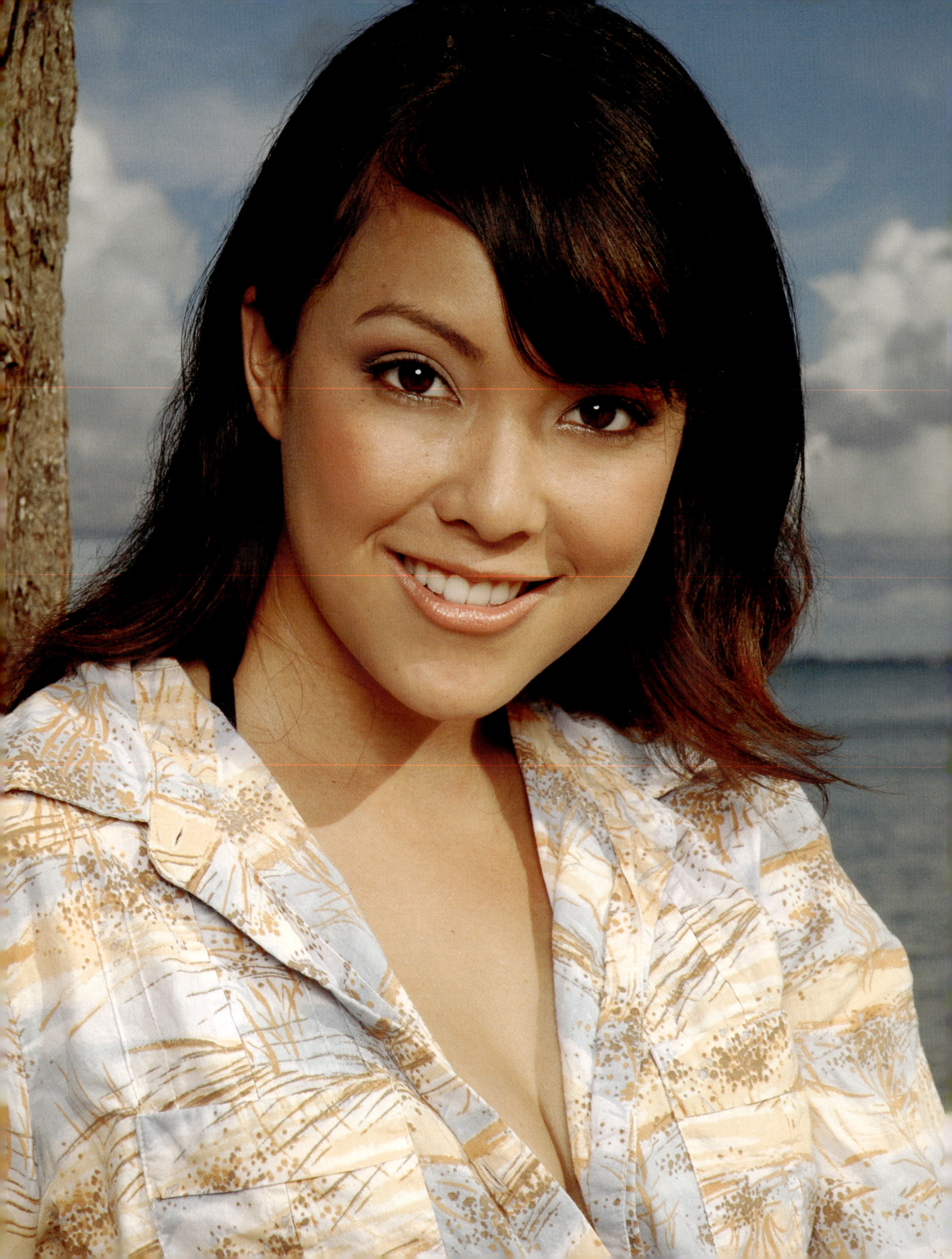

THINGS TO CONSIDER WHEN CHOOSING A LENS

There is some confusion about how depth of field is determined. The common—and correct—notions are that the size of your lens opening and the distance from the camera to your subject impact the amount of your image that is in focus. A smaller aperture and a greater distance from camera to subject will both increase depth of field. For the technophiles out there, both of these facts are related to the "circles of confusion" that are created by forcing light into a cylinder (the lens). A larger lens opening will result in a larger circle of confusion. An image is focused by bending and manipulating the beams of light into a pinpoint focal point. Your foreground will increase in sharpness as it approaches the focal point because the circles of confusion are getting smaller and smaller as they are forced into the pinpoint that makes up the key focal plane. Similarly, as the image progresses beyond the focal point, the circles of confusion expand, resulting in less sharpness in the background.

Larger circles of confusion are more difficult to force into a pinpoint, so you have larger "circles" in front of and behind your focal point—and a shallower depth of field. Similarly, at any given aperture, an increased distance between the camera and subject will increase the depth of field because there is more room to force the circles of confusion into the pinpoint. The process is more gradual, so the circles get smaller and smaller over a greater distance—with more of the image in focus.

An incorrect notion is that the focal length of your lens is inversely proportionate to the depth of field at a given aperture and set distance. It is true that an image photographed with a wide-angle lens will appear to have more in focus than the same shot taken from the same distance at the same f-stop with a telephoto lens. It is the increased field of view that creates this illusion. If the center portion of the image taken with the wide-angle lens was magnified to match that taken with the telephoto, then the depth of field surrounding the target would be the same.

Similarly, the perspective between the objects in the image does not change as the focal length changes. Changes in perspective occur when the camera is moved closer or farther from the subject. Many people who are shooting with a short lens will move in closer to create a larger representation of the object. It is the act of moving closer that shifts the perspective. In general, a portrait photographer will not need to worry about this because the choice of lens is usually predetermined by the nature of the work. A medium telephoto lens is the most common choice of lens for portraiture because it renders the most pleasing representation of your subject. Wide-angle lenses distort the image at the edges and elongate the foreground, especially when close to the subject—think noses!—and long telephoto lenses can compress the facial features too much. There will be certain applications for the extreme lenses, but they will be relatively rare. If you do need to use a wide-angle lens for portraits, try to keep your subjects as centered as possible and don't get too close—unless you are going for a particular effect.

Facing Page—This image of Kathryn demonstrates two of the factors currently under discussion: she was photographed with a 35–70mm zoom lens that was maxed out to 70mm. A 70mm focal length on a digital camera is equivalent to a 105mm lens on a 35mm camera and represents a nice midrange focal length with which to create portraits. The image was created by combining the ambient light under the tree with a strobe light. Understanding the implications of the additive nature of light allowed me to create the balance between the exposure on Kathryn's face and the background.

Light therefore needs to be considered as an ever changing variable based on the surroundings (e.g., available light versus a multi-setting strobe unit) and the photographer's choices (e.g., the choice of working aperture). We can begin to explore the additive nature of light and lighting ratios if we assign light the variable value of "X." X stands for a unit of light that represents a measured f-stop—any measured f-stop. The relationship between f-stops, or units of light, that was mentioned above is constant. So, the following is true for any unit of light, X:

1 stop less light equals ½X
2 stops less light equals ¼X
3 stops less light equals ⅛X
4 stops less light equals 1⁄16X

Conversely,

1 stop more light equals 2X
2 stops more light equals 4X
3 stops more light equals 8X
4 stops more light equals 16X

Let's use f5.6 as the exposure for the main light to look at some real-life examples.

LIGHTING RATIOS

This simple notion forms the basis for the additive nature of light and lighting ratios. For the sake of argument, let's start with a light source giving a value of f5.6. If we add a light that yields f4, then the additional light would add ½ stop to the exposure (because f4 is exactly ½ of f5.6) for an overall exposure of f5.6½. If the second light were positioned as a fill light, then this combination would yield a lighting ratio of 3:1. The chart shown to the right details the relationship between selected f-stops and the resulting ratios and final exposures.

The lighting ratios depicted are fairly common, but what do they mean? The majority of scenes photographed will have a highlight side and a shadow side. Lighting ratios are simply ways to describe the amount of light illuminating the highlight side in relation to the light illuminating the shadows. Lighting ratios refer to the amount of light—or number of units of light—that illuminate the subject on the highlight side versus the shadow side. A greater difference between the two sides indicates more contrast and a deeper shadow side. We can figure out the lighting ratios because light is additive in nature. The amount of light striking a subject is equal to the combined value of each light that illuminates the subject. If only one light is used (A), then the exposure is X. If two lights are used and each light is of equal value (A=B), then the exposure is X plus X or 2X because two equal units of light are illuminating the subject.

Most lighting situations that involve the use of more than one light to illuminate the subject call for lights of unequal power. In these cases, the more powerful light is known as the "main" or "key" light, and the less powerful lights are known as "fill" lights. Fill lights are

F-stop	2	2.8	4	5.6	8	11	16
Relative stop	-3	-2	-1	X	+1	+2	+3
Value	⅛X	¼X	½X	X	2X	4X	8X

Ratio	2:1	3:1	5:1	9:1
Difference between main light and fill	Equal	1 stop	2 stops	3 stops
Relationship between main and fill	Equal	2X	4X	8
Units of light on shadow side	1	1	1	1
Units of light on highlight side	2	3	5	9
Examples	main: f5.6 fill: f5.6	main: f5.6 fill: f4	main: f5.6 fill: f2.8	main: f5.6 fill: f2
Highlight exposure	f8	f5.6½	f5.6¼	f5.6⅛

The above chart shows how different f-stops relate to each other to create different lighting ratios. The chart shows a 9:1 ratio for demonstration purposes. However, a 9:1 ratio is simply not a feasible option given the current state of digital capture. The medium does not yet have the latitude needed to maintain detail at such extremes. The narrow latitude of digital capture lends itself to images that appear to have more contrast, so a 5:1 ratio would still be fairly dramatic. Classic portraiture hovers in the 3:1 ratio range.

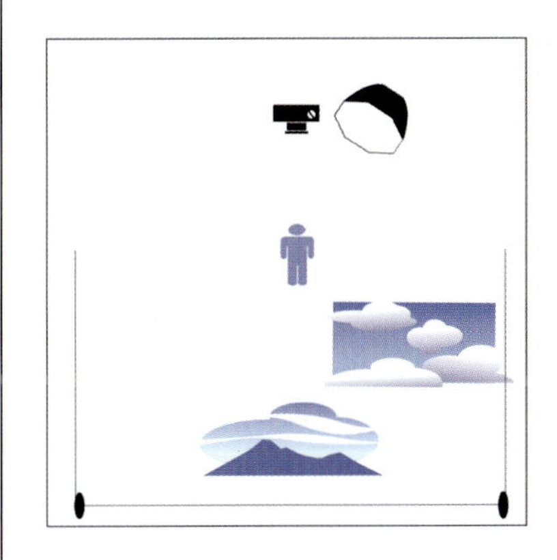

Here is an example of using a strobe in conjunction with the ambient light to create a pleasing lighting ratio. What was a sunny afternoon quickly turned cloudy. A strobe was fit into a halo-style softbox. The shutter speed was dragged to 1/60 second to allow the ambient aperture to approach that of the strobe, allowing detail to show in the background. The overall exposure was f8 at 1/60 second. The image appears to have a 2:1 to 3:1 ratio. The look on the little boy's face is priceless!

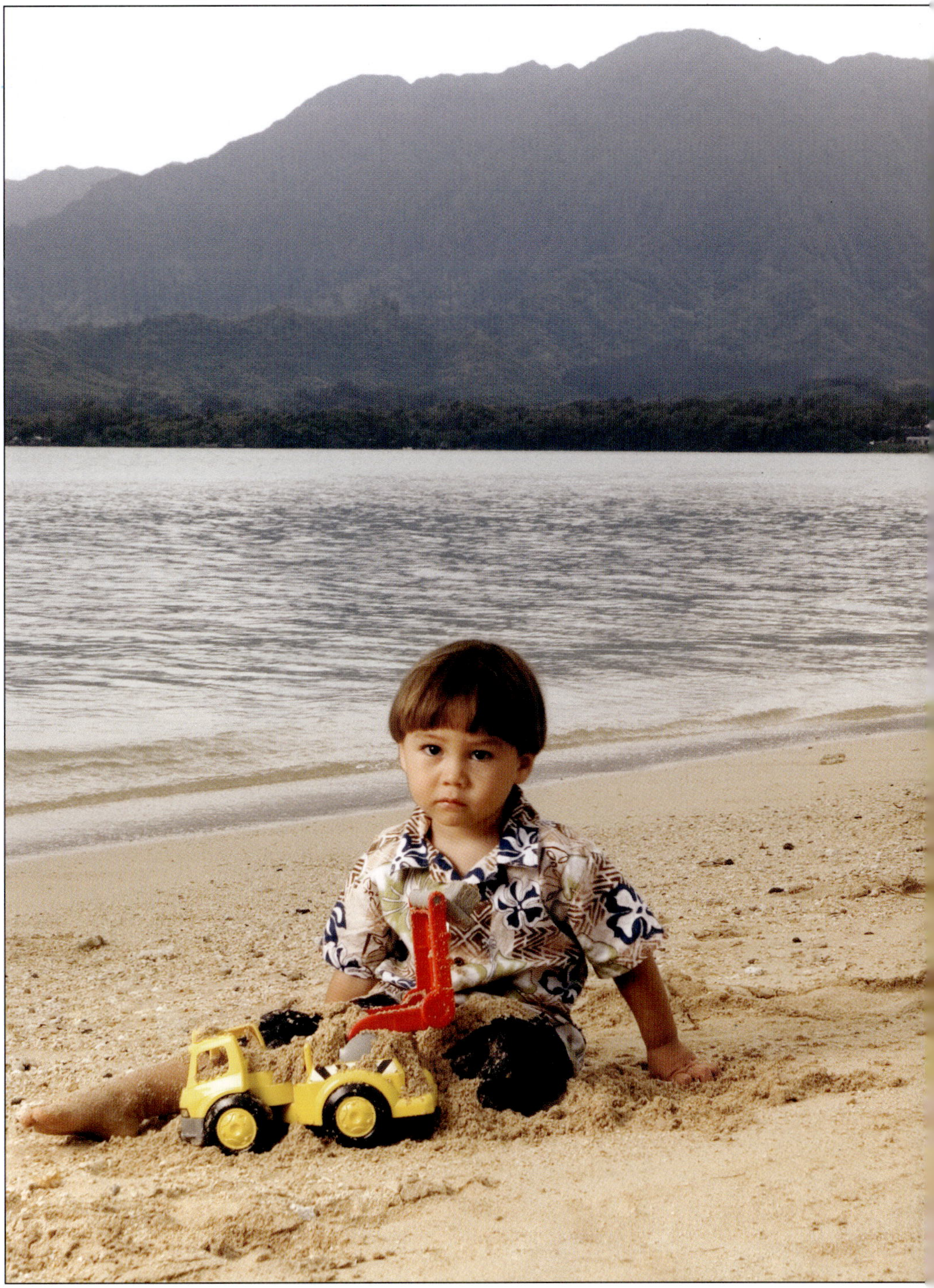

used to provide light on the shadow side of the subject. The final exposure is determined once again by adding the values of light that illuminate the highlight side of the subject. Consider these examples:

Your main light has a value of X. Your fill light is set to provide 1 stop less light than your main light. From the chart below, we know that the first fill light has ½ the power of the main light. Your final exposure on the highlight side is X plus ½X, or 1½X. Remember that X represents a given f-stop, so by adding this fill light, you have added ½ stop to your exposure on the highlight side of the subject. In the example above, the main light was set at f5.6 and the fill was set at f4 for a 3:1 ratio and a final highlight exposure of f5.6½. We could change the values to f8 and f5.6 respectively. The final exposure would now be f8½, but the ratio would still be 3:1.

As the chart on the facing page indicates, using a fill light that is 2 stops less than your main light would add ¼ stop of light to your highlight exposure.

Calculating lighting ratios is relatively easy if you are in a studio and are using "power" fills. A power fill light is simply the use of an additional strobe to provide extra light rather than using cards or reflectors to catch light from the main light to bounce it into the

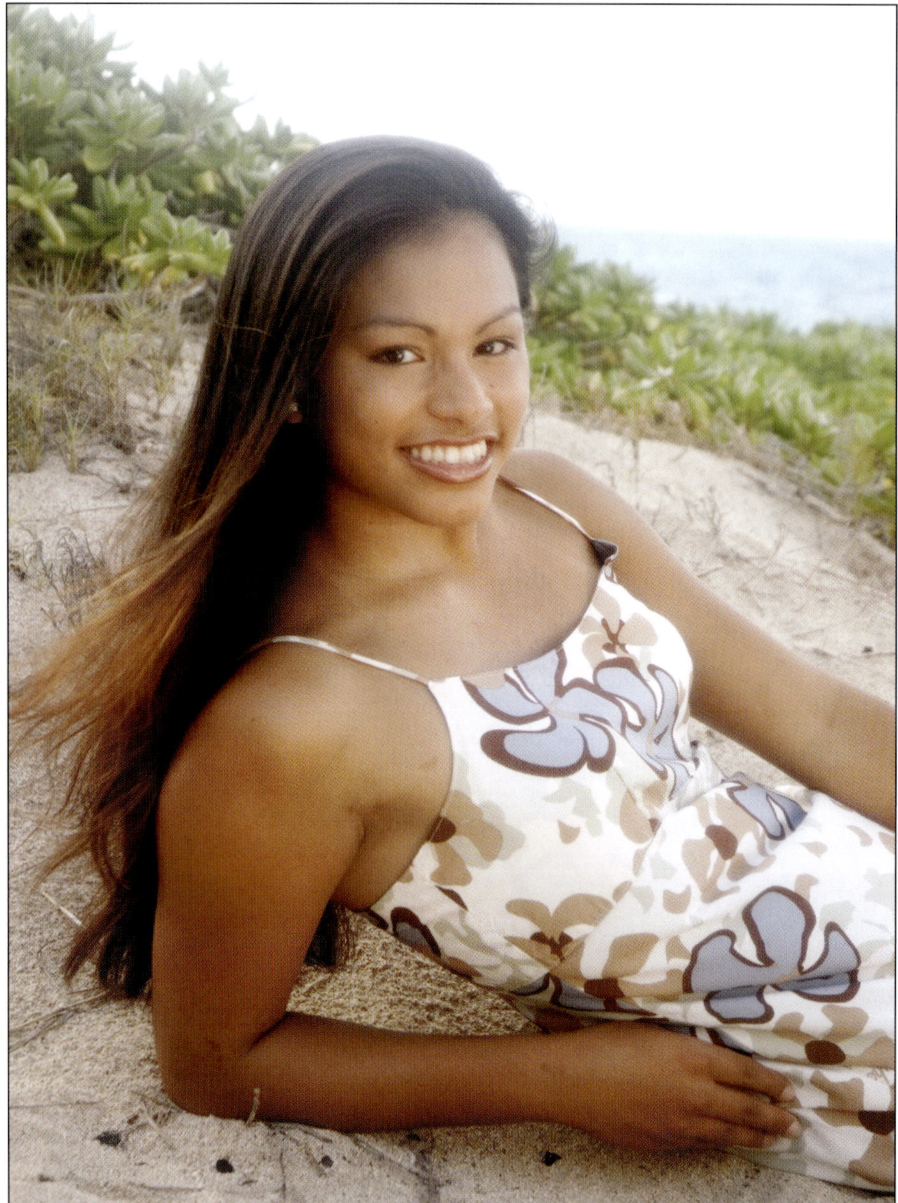

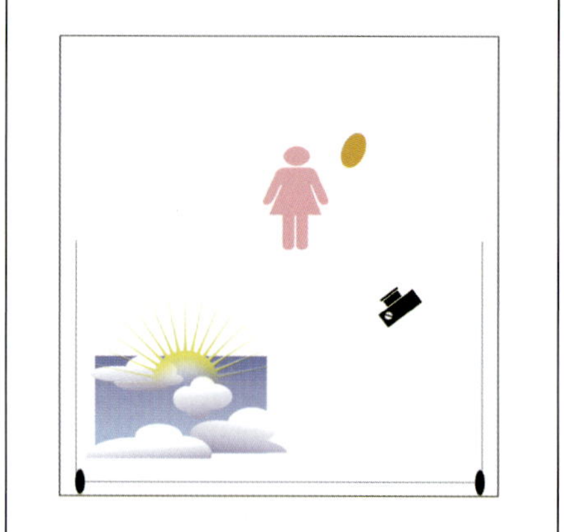

Karielle was photographed on a beach on the east coast of Oahu. The sun was constantly moving in and out of a cloud cover. We shot quickly each time the sun was on the fringe of a cloud. The sun was beginning to set behind and to Karielle's right. A silver/gold reflector was used to bounce some light back onto her to add some contrast and create sparkling catchlights in her eyes.

shadows. Calculating the values and impact of power fills was just detailed. By definition, a fill light adds light to the image without affecting the direction or impact of the main light. An accurately placed power fill light adds the same amount of light to the shadow side as it does to the highlight side. As noted above, lighting ratios describe the number of units of light that illuminate the shadow and highlight sides of your subject. Using power fills—or strobes—outdoors works in the same way, except when the ambient light changes due to cloud covers!

Using strobes outdoors can certainly be an effective way of bringing the scene into balance for digital capture. However, there will be many times when a strobe is not the answer. Sometimes a simple reflective surface placed opposite the main light will do the trick. Another advantage to using a fill card for portraiture has to do with the catchlights. Portrait artists tend to prefer a single—or at least one dominant—catchlight in their subjects' eyes. A strobe outdoors will create a second strong catchlight while the catchlight from a reflector tends to be softer, especially if the fill card is white.

CHAPTER 3

OUTDOOR LIGHTING

MAGIC HOUR

Outdoor lighting can be frustrating to control. As we have seen, sunlight is often an unusable source of light because it produces too much contrast through most of the day. However, there are times during the day when the natural light is soft and beautiful. The sun is low on the horizon so it is directional, creating opportunities for a nice "modeling" effect ("modeling" refers to using light and shadow to create a three-dimensional feel to a two-dimensional medium). The rays of sunlight travel longer distances as the sun peaks over the horizon. The light rays are broken up more by

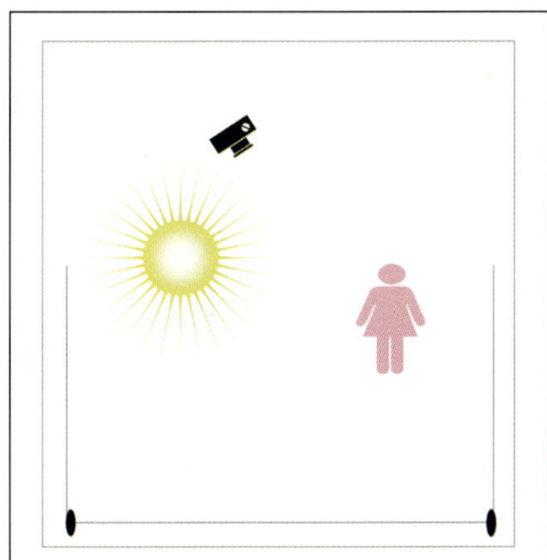

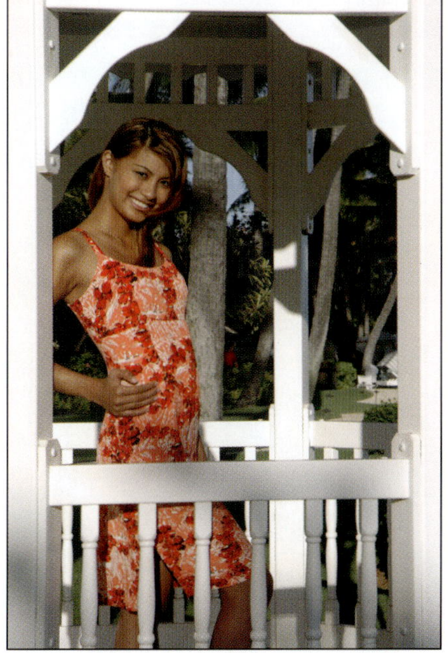

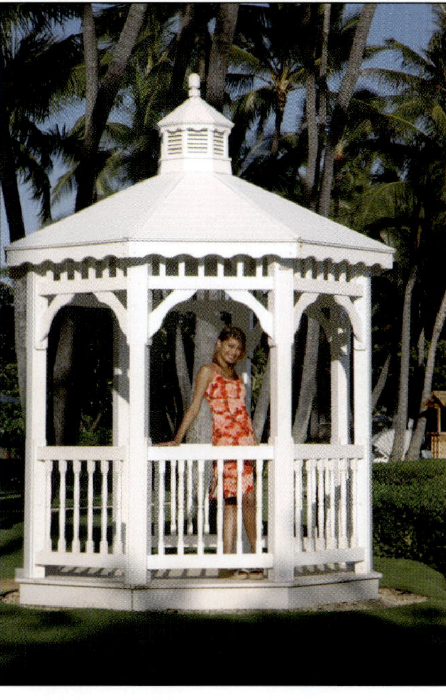

Above and Center—Ruthchelle Melchor was photographed in this seaside gazebo just as the sun hit that magic point. The light was softer in the late afternoon but still had a sense of direction. Ruth was positioned so her face was lit by the setting sun, rather than in the shade of the gazebo. A meter reading was taken with an incident meter with the dome of the meter placed at her cheek and pointed to the camera. It can be difficult to maintain the whites of your image even when the light illuminating your highlights is the same as that lighting your subject; therefore, your metering has to be extremely accurate. The white posts of the gazebo are almost blown out in this image—but not quite! **Right—**The beauty of magic light is its ability to light the entire scene with the same beautiful light. Moving from the relatively personal image of Ruth (above center) to more of an environmental portrait was as easy as changing the focal length of my lens.

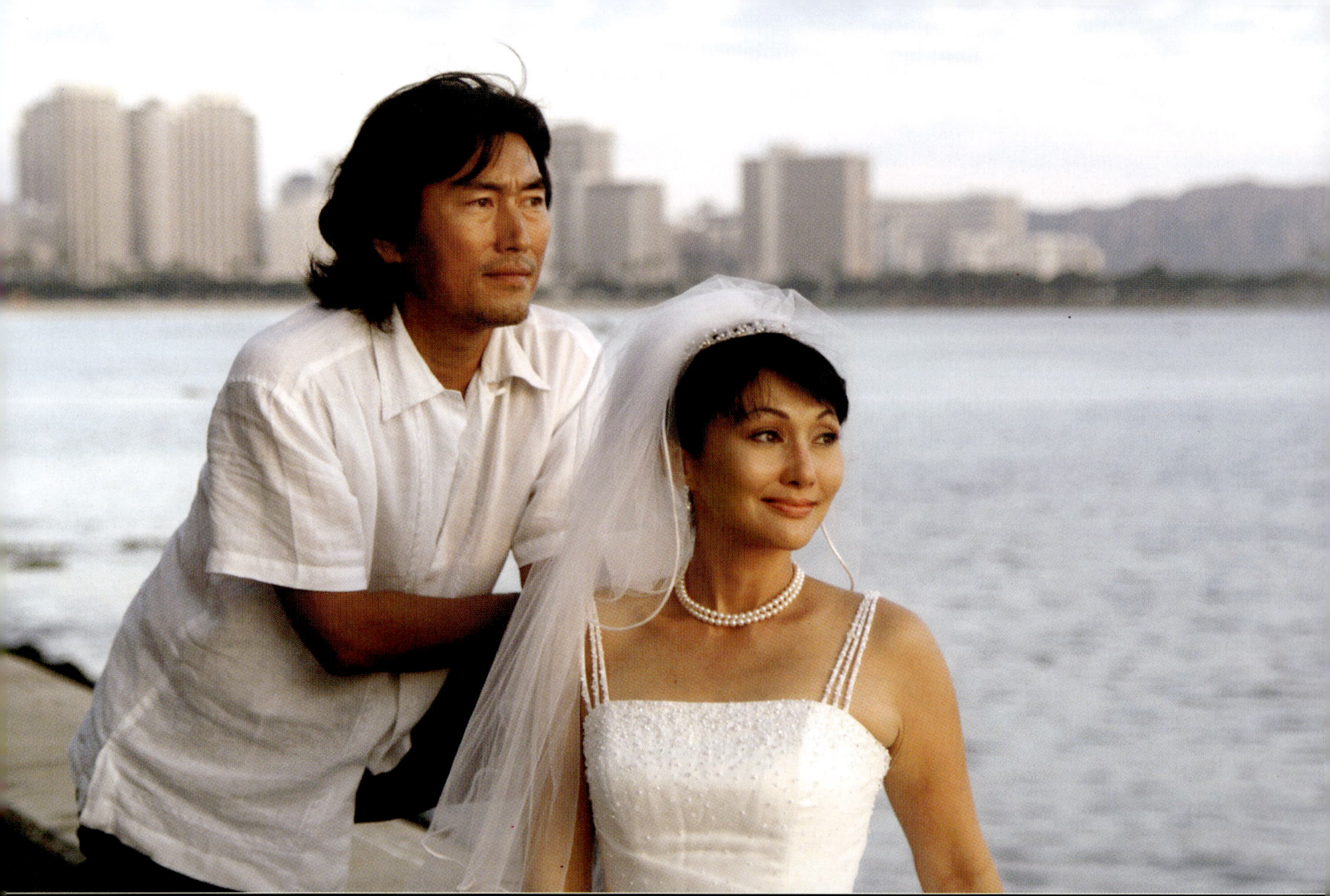

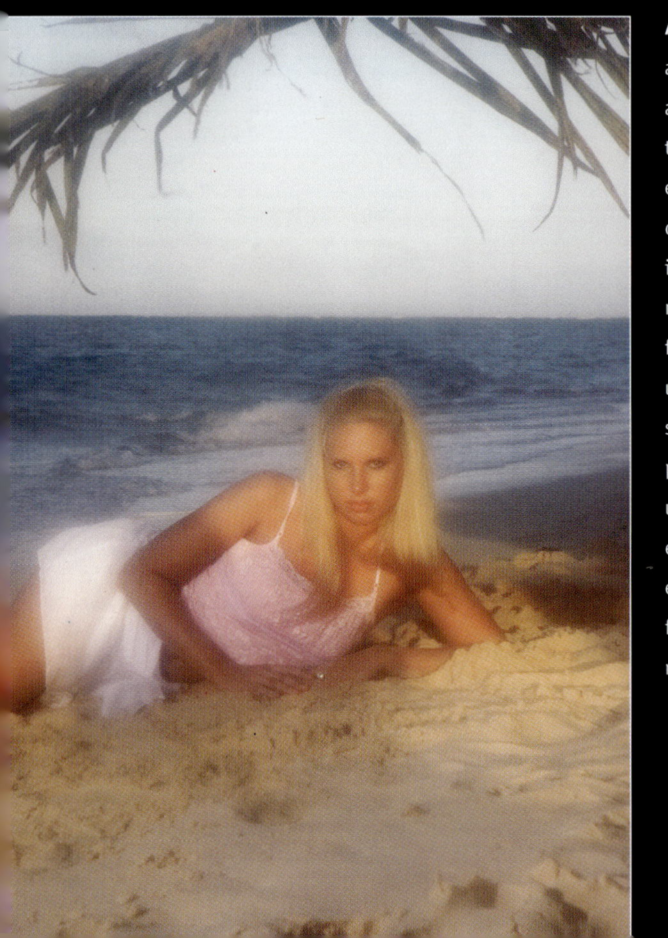

Above—David Taylor used a modification of magic light to create this elegant yet casual wedding portrait. The sun is setting to the right of the photographer and would create a split lighting effect if he posed the couple looking toward the camera. Simply turning the couple's faces toward the light solved the problem and reestablished the effect that magic hour is known for—soft, directional light that is warm in nature. The couple was properly placed for this type of image: they are off center, with room in the image to follow their gaze. Waikiki in the background is well out of focus, so it does not become a distraction; rather, it sets the location. The sense is one of anticipation for the future! **Left—**Shadows from the surrounding area (and photographer!) can be used to frame the photograph too. Amy Raquel was photographed just before the sun slid behind the mountains. The sun cast long shadows from everything in its light's path, so we positioned Amy in the one openly sunny spot. Portrait photographers often use soft focus filters to achieve a nice misty feeling in their images. There are also several ways to achieve the desired look in Photoshop. This time, however, nature provided her own soft focus filter as the surf and wind combined to slowly coat my skylight filter with saltwater. It probably wasn't great for the camera, but with Amy's help it resulted in a pretty image!

atmospheric interference, so the quality of light at sunrise and sunset is softer than at other times during the day. Furthermore, it is the shorter blue and green waves that are affected most by the fragmentation of light, resulting in the predominantly amber hue of early morning or late-afternoon sunlight. The naturally beautiful light is known as "magic hour"—aptly named because this is about as much time as you have to shoot under these ideal conditions!

Generally speaking, there is no easier time to create outdoor portraits than when the sun is rising or setting behind you. The light illuminating your subject is usually the same as what is illuminating the background, so the range of exposures is easier to control. Flare is not an issue in these situations because the light behind your subject is often not greater than the foreground. The lowered contrast of the light is also more forgiving when shooting white garments.

You need to shoot fast in these instances because the magic light fades fast. The exposure will drop dramatically as the light fades, so meter frequently. The sun sets in the west, so the benefits of evening magic hour are most noticeable when shooting into the east. The reverse is true for early-morning shoots.

The images on the facing page are examples of beautiful magic hour portraits. No fill was used to create these images.

However, magic hour light can still be tricky. The sun needs to be low enough in the sky for your subject to be able to comfortably look into the light. You'll know if you start using unmodified sunlight too early. The next four images clearly show the difference that approximately one-half hour made in the comfort of the models. The first set features an environmental portrait of a young athlete. Ku'uipo was photographed at a basketball park high in the hills. The sun was at a position that provided strong directional light, but it was soft enough to allow her to look in the direction of the setting sun. Sunlight at this level allows for some flexibility in how it will be used. Ku'uipo's mom and dad stood just to her right holding a large gold reflector. The sun was used alternatively as a main light with

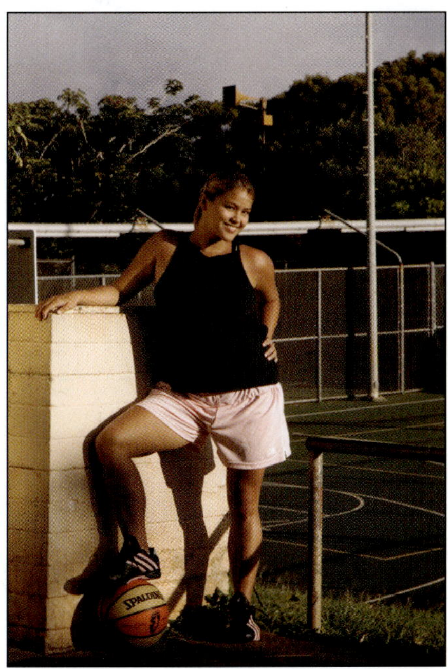

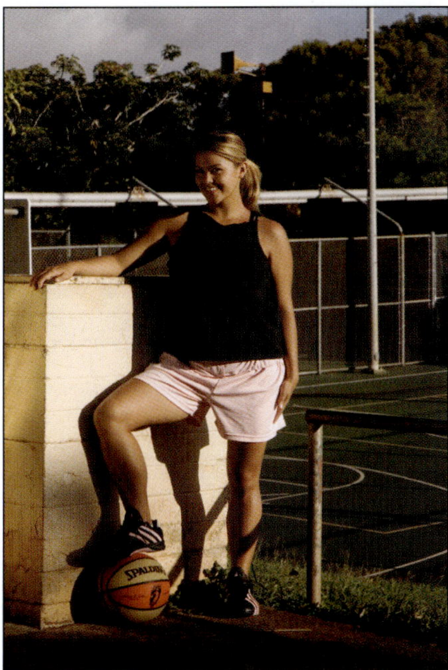

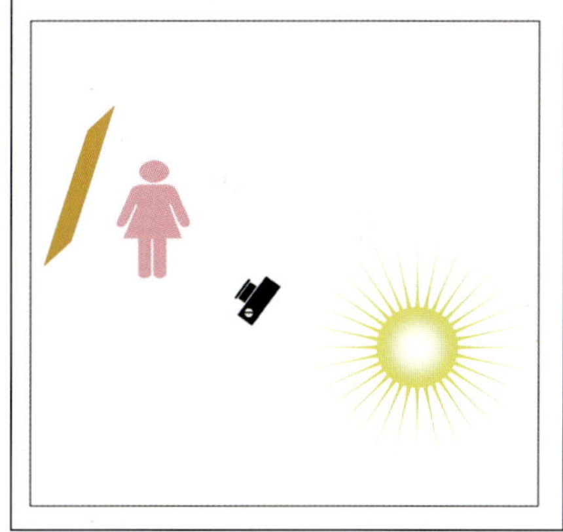

Ku'uipo was photographed in a park to depict her interest in basketball. One of the challenges of environmental portraits is working with the scene that you are given to tell a story and create a visually pleasing image. There were many strong lines crossing and intersecting within the image. Ku'uipo was positioned in a spot that would show part of her world to the audience while keeping the focus of the image on her. Note that many of the lines lead directly to her. Sharp diagonals and crisscrossing lines can be tough to work with and, in general, you want to keep strong lines from passing behind your subject's head. Sometimes it is a tradeoff. I could have shot from a higher position to drop the fence line lower, but that would have made Ku'uipo look shorter than she is. Alternatively, I could have shot from a low perspective, but that would not show an integral part of the story: the basketball court. Ultimately, I chose to show the court, keeping as natural a perspective of Ku'uipo as I could—and live with the fence behind her head. The main light was changed from the sun to the reflector simply by having Ku'uipo turn her head.

the gold fabric acting as a fill source and then as a large edge/rim light when the gold fabric provided the main illumination.

Sometimes you will get to a scene and think that the sun is low enough because the shadows on the ground are long and there is a beautiful balance between your subject's skin and the backdrop. However, the sun may still be too harsh for your subject. This photo of Debbie Brown is almost magical: the light illuminating her was the same as that lighting Diamondhead behind her, the whites of her outfit were not blown out, and there was a nice direction to the light, which formed

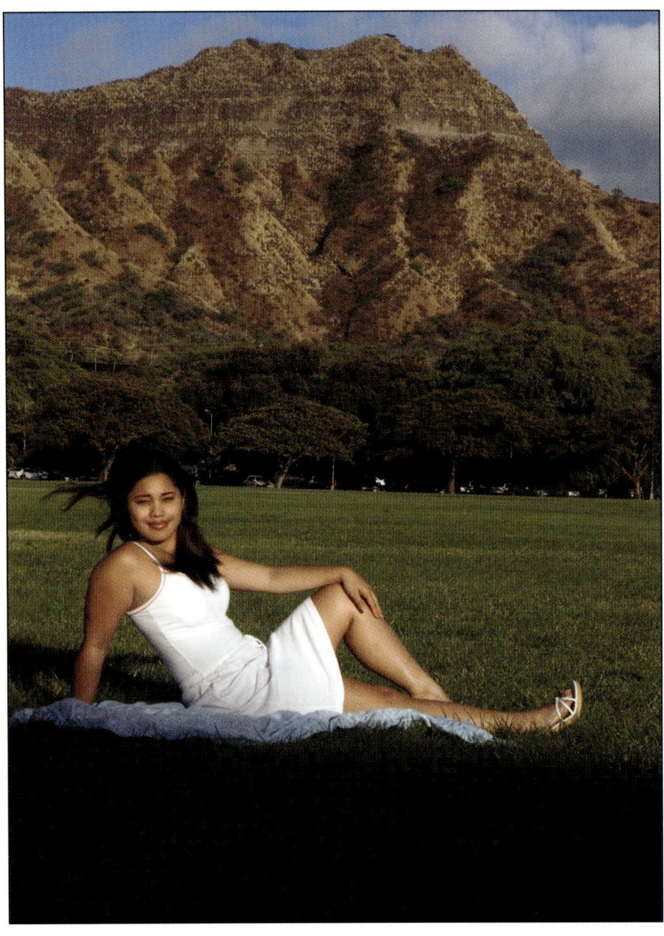

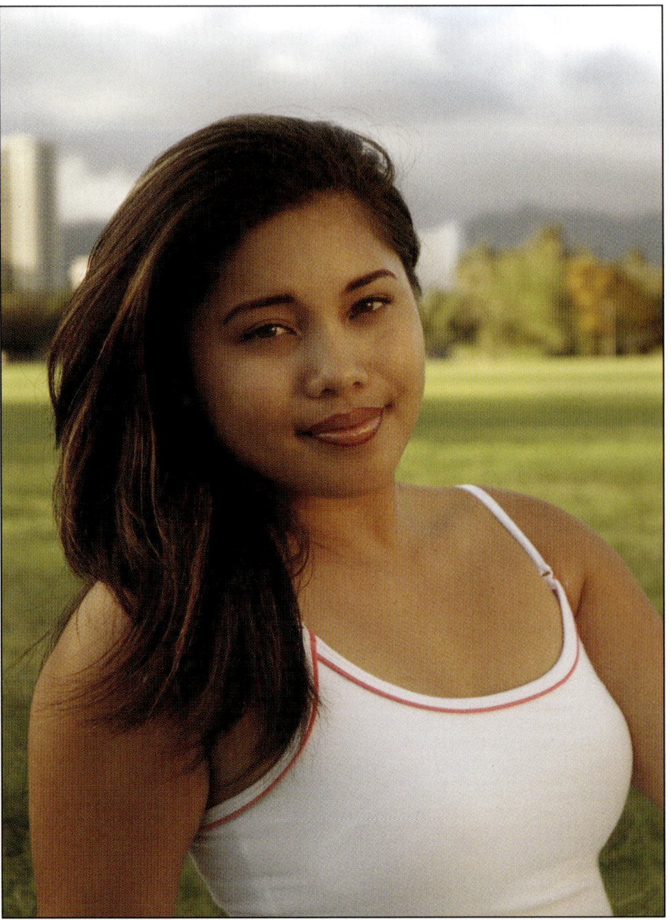

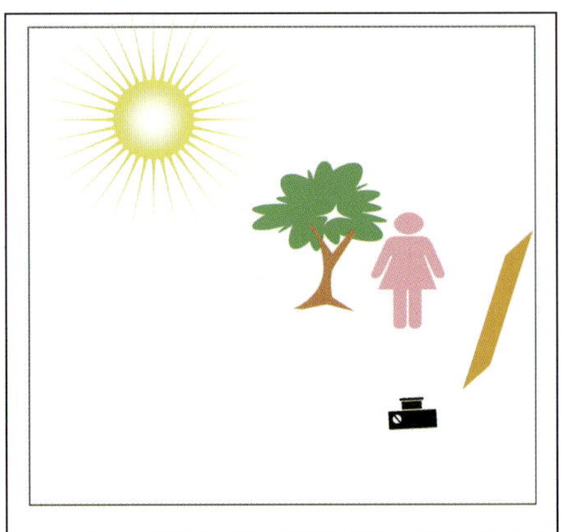

Left—Kapiolani Park in Honolulu, Hawaii, is a stunning park with the ocean, Diamondhead, and Waikiki as potential backdrops. The sun was still a bit too harsh for Debbie Brown, who tried her best to keep her eyes open—and just managed to do so. Here is a tip to use when you find yourself in a similar position: have your subjects close and rest their eyes, and have them open them on a certain count: "Okay, close your eyes and open them on 'two.' Ready? 'One, two.'" Snap the photo when their eyes are open. **Right—**One solution to the problem above would have been to use one of the scrim/reflector or strobe techniques described later in this chapter. In this case we simply turned Debbie around and photographed her with Waikiki as the backdrop. She was positioned on the fringe of the shade cast by a large tree. Using open shade with lighter areas behind your subject is a very risky technique that is also detailed later. Positioning Debbie as close to the sun/shade fringe as possible assured us that there would be some wraparound effect from the sunlight and that the inverse square law wouldn't eat as much light as would happen if we had her sit farther into the shade. A large gold reflector was positioned close to her to bounce some sun back into the shade. These tricks were all used to provide some direction to the light illuminating Debbie's face and try to keep the bright background from becoming too overexposed.

If the scene behind your subject is still too bright, then you can move the model farther in toward the tree and use the trunk as a backdrop. The trunk is lit by the same light as your subject, and you will not lose detail in the highlights—assuming that you have a dark tree trunk! The use of a silver/gold reflector adds direction and contrast to the image.

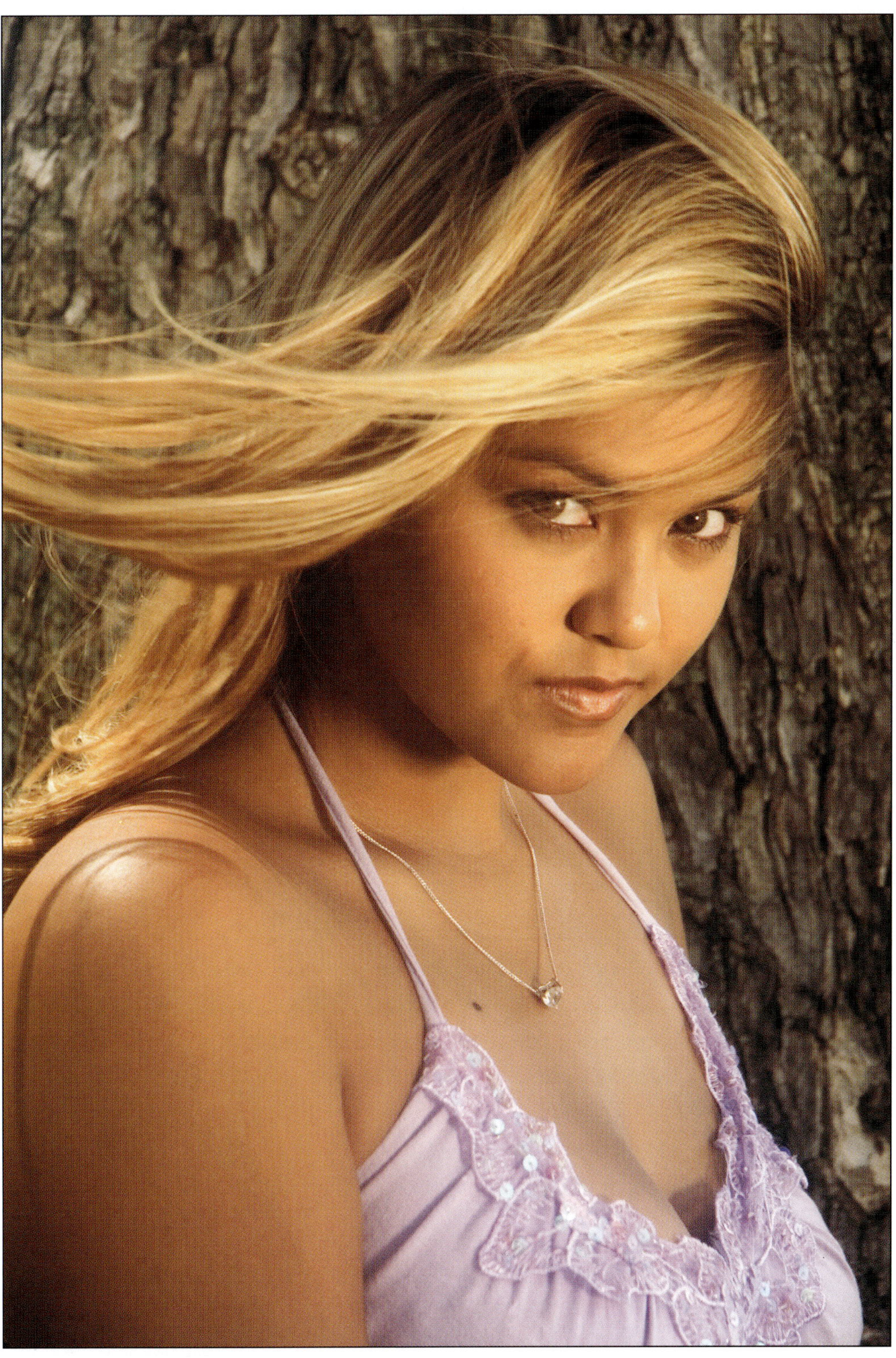

beautiful contours on her face. The problem is that she was fighting to keep her eyes open. This image is passable—her eyes are open barely enough to keep the image out of the recycle bin.

There are also situations where the area behind your subject is a great deal brighter than what is falling on them—even with the sun in the magic position. This situation is not uncommon along some of the shores of Hawaii. Clouds form quickly over the mountain ranges and block the setting sun. However, the clouds tend to be fairly small and localized, so the area behind the subject is lit with bright sunshine. The light blocked by

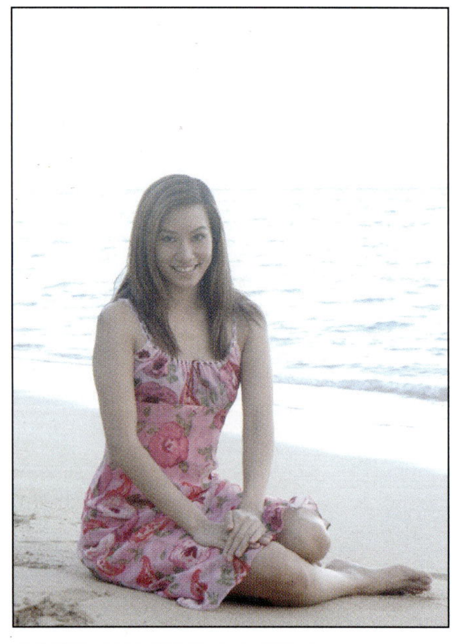

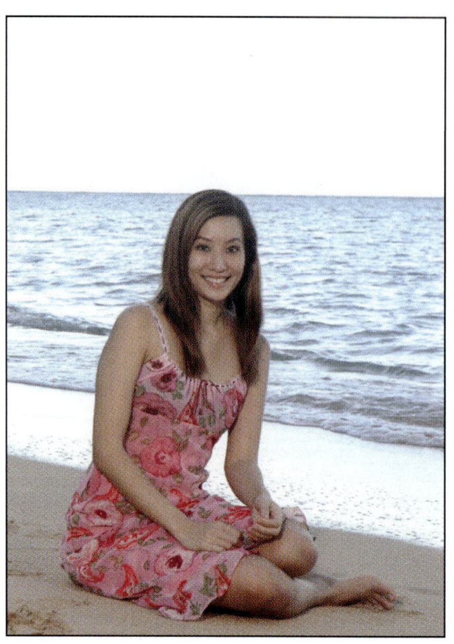

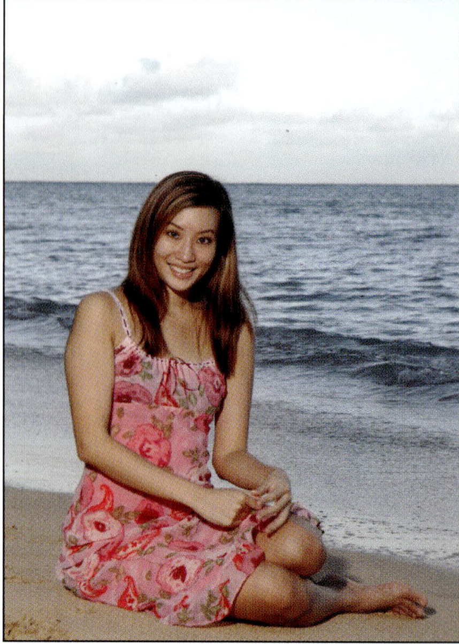

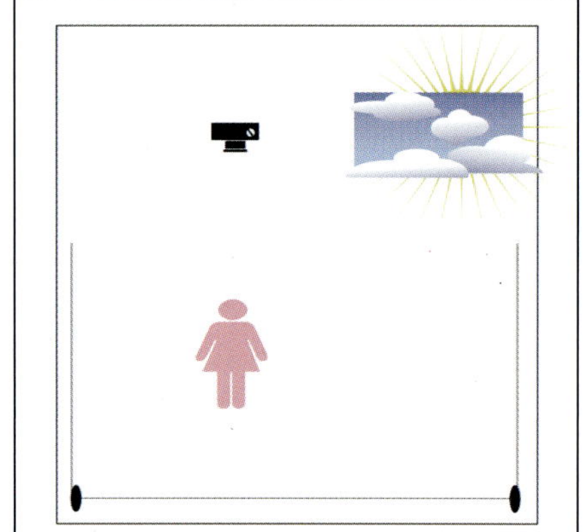

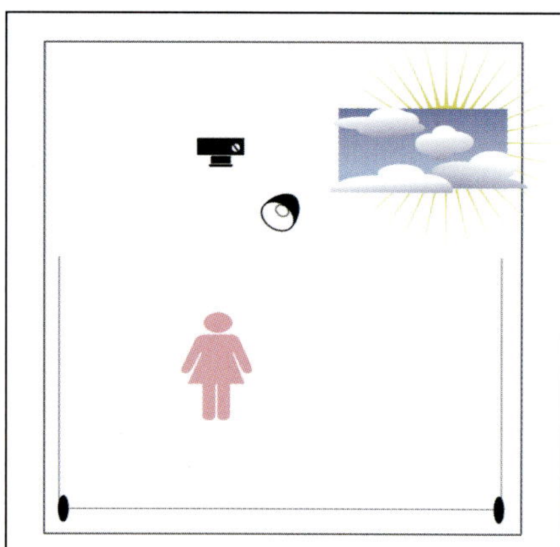

Left (Top and Bottom)—The sun was in the magic position for these images of Brooke Tanaka. However, it was tucked behind some clouds, which would normally result in a usable—if flat—image. In this case the clouds were localized and cast a shadow on the foreground only; the skies were bright and blue behind her. Therefore, the light behind Brooke was at least 2 stops brighter than the foreground, creating a difficult lighting situation. Any attempt to get a proper exposure on Brooke badly overexposed the background and yielded a flat, ugly main light effect. **Center (Top and Bottom)—**The image was improved by introducing a strobe head with a 30-degree gridspot to overpower the flat light and to bring the foreground level up to match the backdrop. The shutter speed was then adjusted to control the look of the backdrop. The strobe became the main light, so a faster shutter speed did not have much impact on the exposure of Brooke, but it did greatly affect the ambient light behind her. **Right—**I changed the shutter speed and checked the preview window on my camera until I got the general look I wanted. I then re-metered the scene to make sure that the exposure reading by Brooke's cheek was accurate. **Facing Page—**The final exposure in this series was 1/250 second at f8. The ocean is a rich blue, the sky has some pretty shades of blue, and Brooke looks great! By the time we created this image, the ambient light dropped a little to increase the dramatic effect.

the clouds is a great deal less intense than the light on the backdrop. Metering for your subject will greatly overexpose the backdrop and can create a lot of flare. One way to fix the situation is to bring in a strobe. For the above images, the strobe was about 3 stops hotter than the foreground ambient light and became the main light. The "ambient" light was the fill. The background ambient light was controlled by adjusting the shutter speed. Increasing the shutter speed made the strobe more of a main light, nullifying the flat light. I kept checking the preview screen on my digital camera to check the backdrop until I got what I wanted. I then re-metered the scene, made the appropriate changes to the aperture settings, and went into "shoot" mode!

The exposure for the lousy photograph of Brooke was f5.6⅓ at 1/30 second. The final image was shot at f8 at 1/250 second—there is almost 4 stops difference between the two. I cannot honestly say that I "knew" to change the exposure by 4 stops, but the captions for the above images show how it was done.

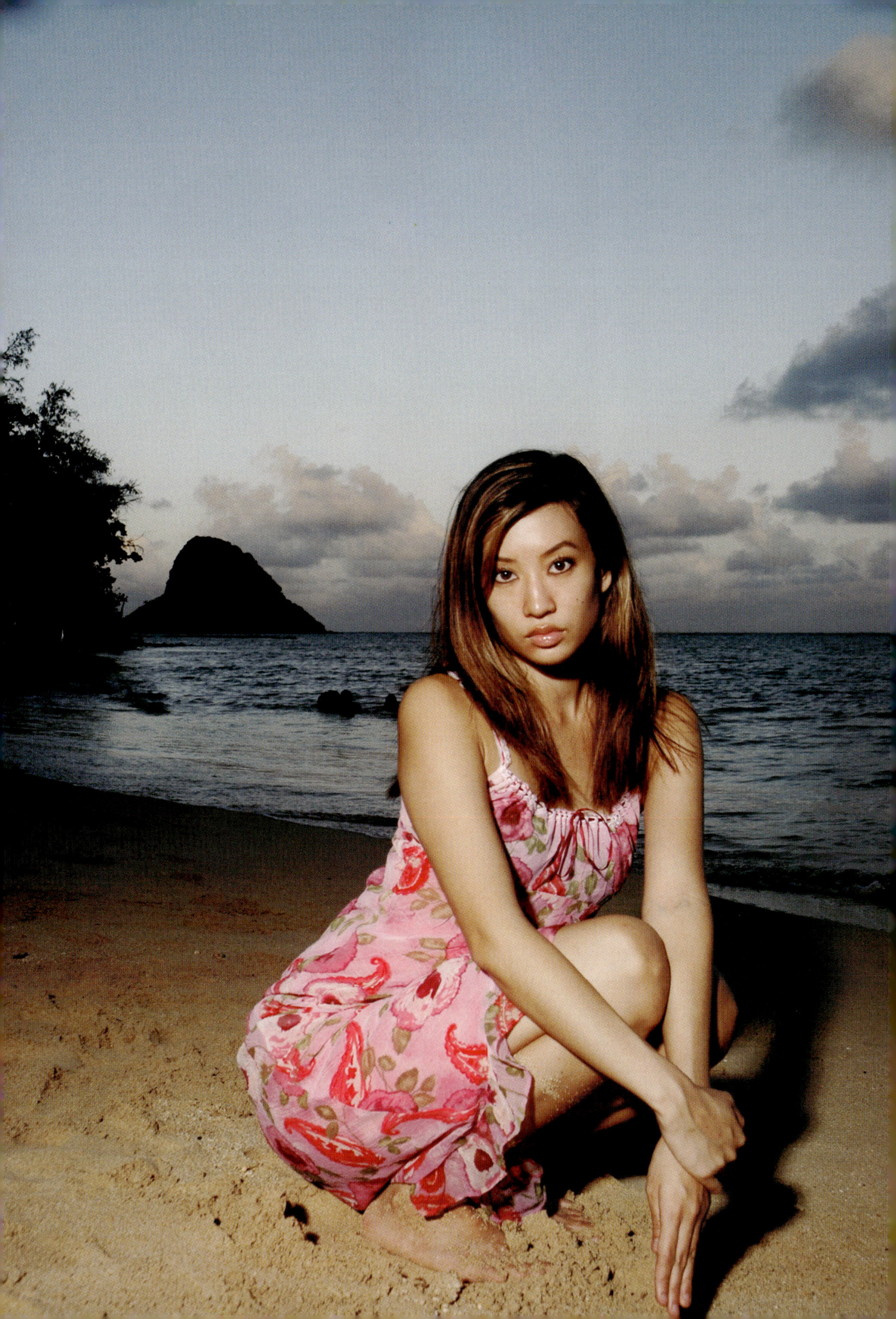

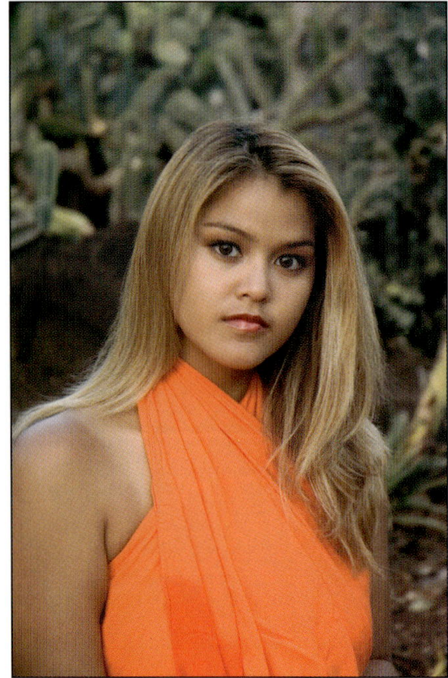

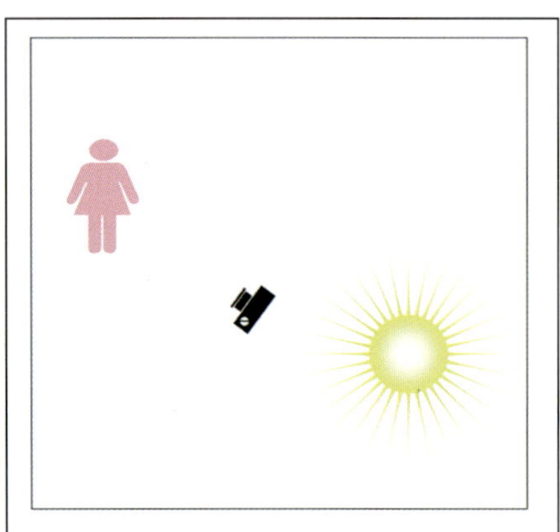

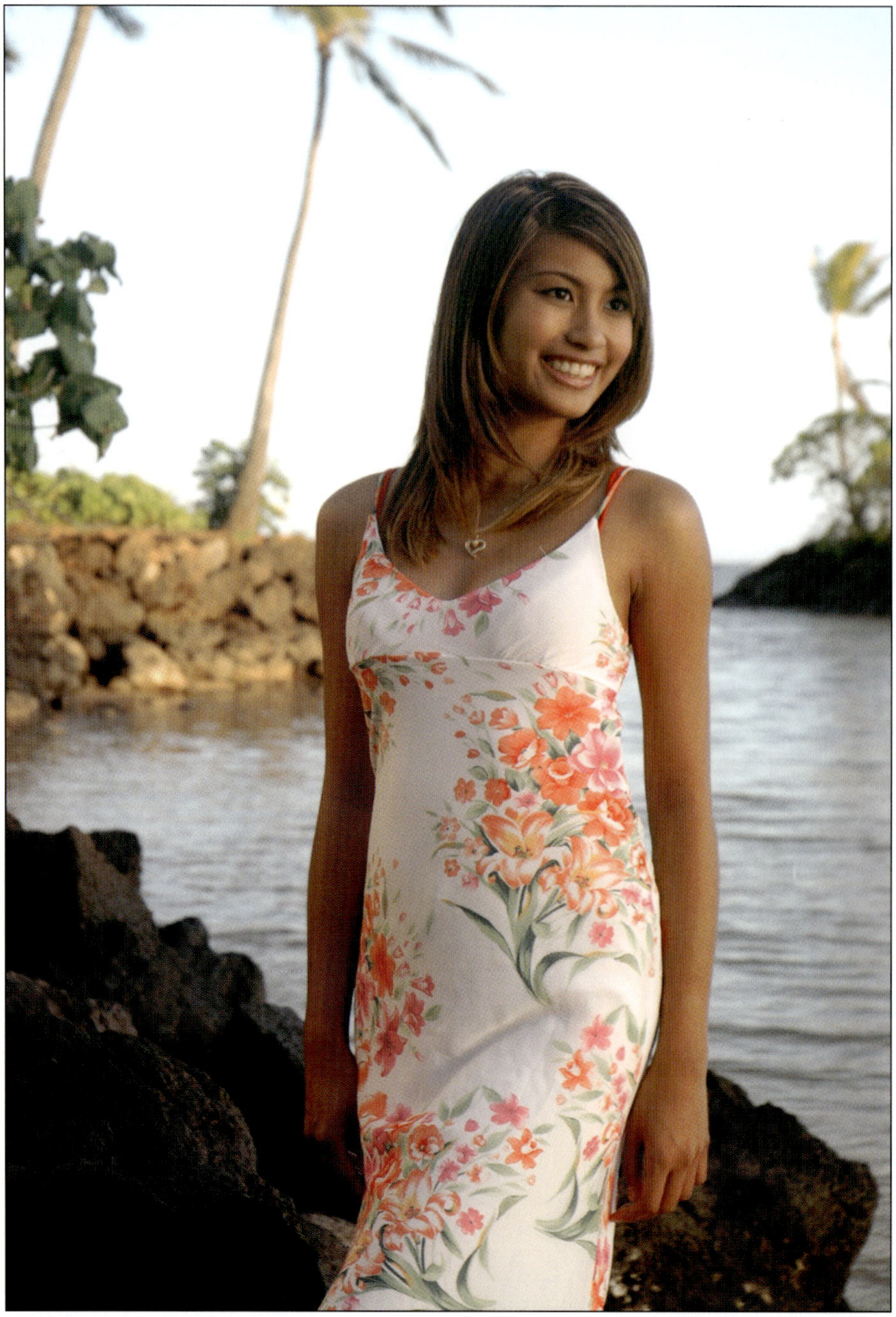

Left (Top and Bottom)—This stoic portrait of Ku'uipo was one of the last few shots of the day. The sun was essentially gone, and the last rays added a very soft quality of light that accentuated the mood of the photograph. You must meter continually because the light drops off incredibly fast at this time of day. I think we dropped about 2 stops in five minutes. It is advisable to use a tripod for these shots because you'll be shooting very slow and wide open. This shot was one of a couple that I was able to capture without motion blur because I was handholding the camera. **Right—**The image of Ruthchelle Melchor was also captured as the last rays of sunlight disappeared. In this case I had Ruth turn her face into the setting sun to grab whatever modeling effect remained in the fading sunlight.

TWILIGHT

Magic hour is beautiful but short-lived. Many portrait artists continue to create beautiful images before or beyond the magic light. The first or last rays of sunlight can be used to produce spectacular images. The light values during twilight change rapidly, so you need to be sure to meter your scene on a frequent basis. If you are shooting your portrait session early in the morning, then the light values will increase rapidly. The "forgiveness latitude" for digital capture is extremely limited on the overexposure end of the spectrum, so you need to keep checking the exposure to maintain the highlights in your image. Conversely, the light will drop off dramatically as you shoot beyond magic hour in the evening. You have a little more room for error at the underexposure end of the spectrum, but not much. The changing quantity of light may also necessitate a change in the image that you have previsualized. Modifying the aperture will alter the depth of field of your image, and changing the shutter speed will eventually affect how motion is recorded in your portrait.

CREATING IMAGES ALL DAY LONG

Portrait photographers cannot be expected to make a living by creating images during the brief window of time that twilight and magic hour provide. On the other hand, direct sunlight is practically useless as an unmodified light source during the rest of the day.

The keys to creating beautiful outdoor digital portraits all day lie in applying the laws of physics detailed earlier to modify the existing light to design the image that you desire. You will often need to increase the size of your light source relative to your subject in order to create a softer quality of light. Other times you will have to add light to a scene to create a sparkle to the image, bring the scene into an acceptable contrast range, and even salvage an unusable situation.

Portraiture, almost by definition and with few exceptions, involves using soft, even lighting to create images with subtle and smooth ratios. The laws of physics dictate that the quality of light will get harsher as the light source is moved farther from the subject; hence the difficulties with direct sunlight. Yes, it is a huge light source, but as was noted above, its extreme distance from the Earth turns it into a pinpoint light source.

However, we can manipulate sunlight to fit our needs. Essentially, the light emanating from the sun can become the basis for what we choose as our light source. We can bounce or diffuse the direct sunlight to create the light that we need. The reflector or the diffuser becomes the light source! Diffusers will generally spread the light and create a larger, softer light source. Reflectors bounce the existing light, and therefore, the impact that the reflector has on the quality of the light will depend on the size and material of the reflector. A small silver card will reflect harsh light onto your subject, but a large white board will create a softer bounce.

CLOUDS/OPEN SHADE

There are times when nature provides her own diffuser. A cloud cover can create soft and beautiful light that is easy to work with. Don Herzig created this beautiful portrait (below) on a farm in Tennessee just before it poured. There must have been a momentary break in the clouds because the gorgeous hair light adds the contrast needed to keep the image from becoming too flat. The image was created with the camera on automatic mode, which worked in this case because the

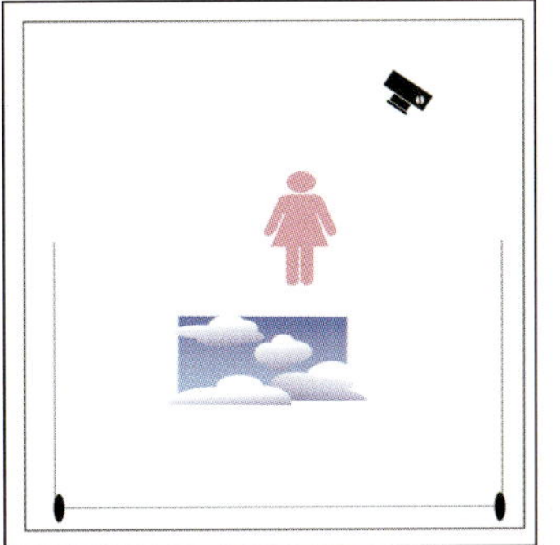

Don Herzig used what nature gave him to create an alluring portrait. Overcast skies presented soft light that illuminated the background and foreground evenly. There was enough sunlight breaking through the clouds to add a beautiful hairlight that keeps this image from becoming too flat.

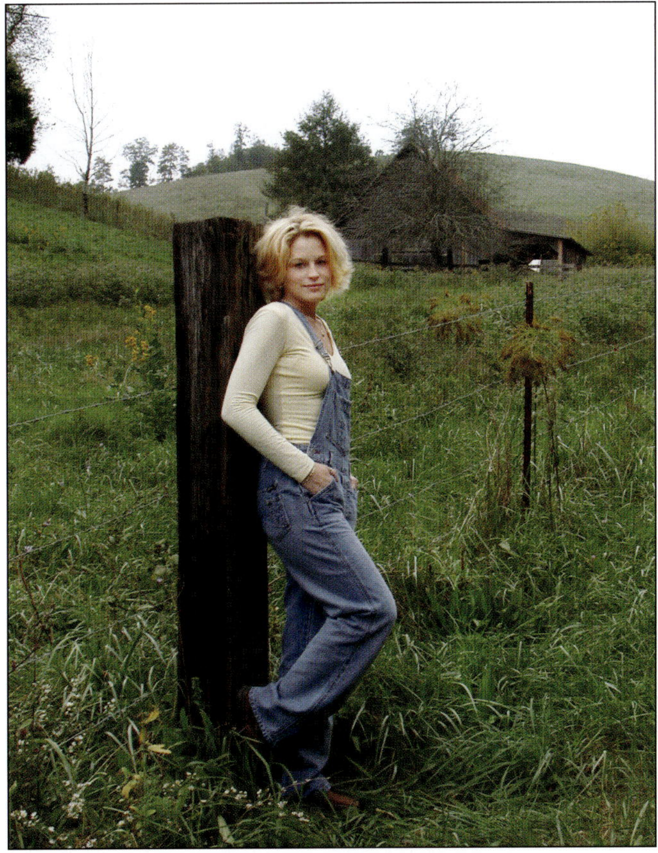

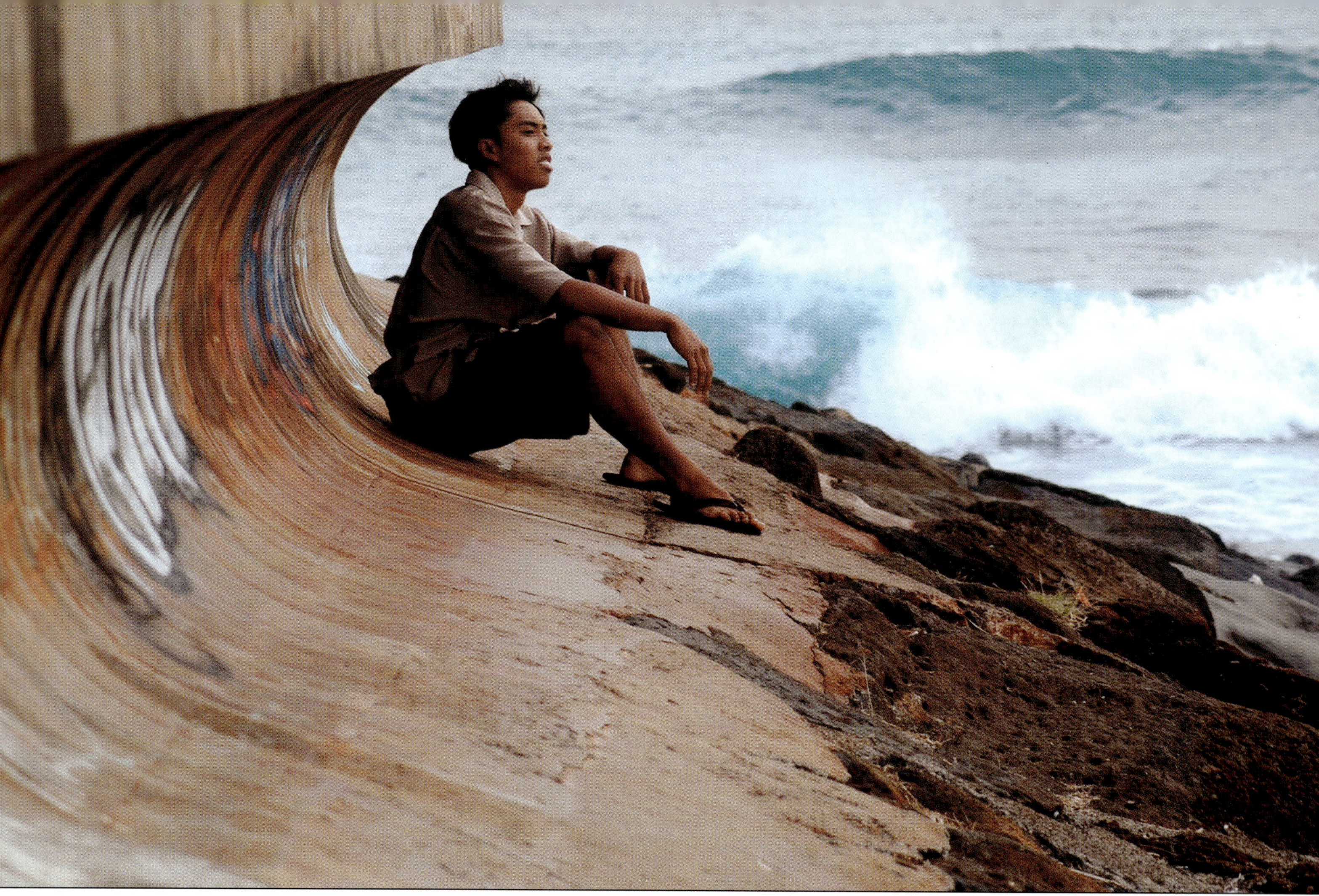

Stan Cox II used the location of this portrait to serve two purposes. First, as mentioned below, he used the curve of the tube to create direction in a situation where the light was flat. Secondly, the location helped tell a story about Stan's subject. The young man is clearly comfortable within his surrounding—the surf seems almost an extension of himself. The image was created using only available natural light.

light was even across the entire image. Don very effectively used the location to tell a story about this young lady, and the choice of wardrobe along with her positioning is perfect. Don tackled the tricky aspect of posing hands nicely by having the model tuck her hands into her pockets—once again creating a very natural feel to the portrait.

It is difficult to rely on overcast or cloudy days to give you enough contrast to create a successful image. Those days often produce flat and boring light. You'll have to find a way to create some sense of direction out of flat light.

In the image above, Stan Cox II did just that by positioning his subject under the arc of a cement tube. The lighting was very flat and the mist from the ocean lowered the contrast of the image even more. The tube seems to act as a negative fill and create directionality in the light. Stan completed the image by using a curves adjustment layer to add about 3 points of red (by using the drop-down menu in the curves dialog box and choosing the red channel) and tweaked the contrast using the master RGB channel.

So, overcast skies can certainly increase the size of your light source, but it can come at a cost. You'll be better off shooting on a sunny day and finding ways to increase the size of your light source by using the environment and/or artificial means. The easiest way to increase the size of your light is to find open shade. The light illuminating your subject is diffused by the trees, overhang, or whatever is creating the shade. The surrounding areas can also provide some fill by reflecting light into the shady areas. The light becomes indirect and diffused—and therefore larger and softer than the direct light—but maintains some direction.

It can be difficult to determine the direction of the light in open shade, but it is necessary to study the light in order to meter the scene properly. Your base exposure is the highlight side of your subject's face. Everything else has to fall within the narrow range of plus or minus 2 to $2\frac{1}{2}$ stops. Once the direction of light and your metering point is established, you decide how to create the lighting ratio that you decide on. You may want to move your subject closer to the edge of the shade, allowing more of the unfiltered light to illuminate the highlights. Conversely, the inverse square law dictates that the highlights will fade as you move your subject deeper into the shade.

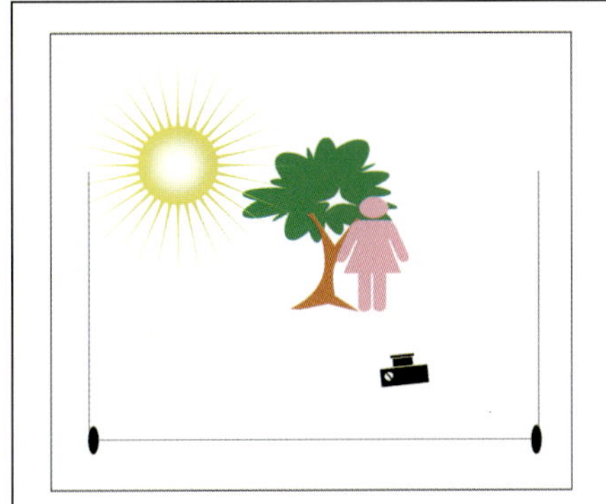

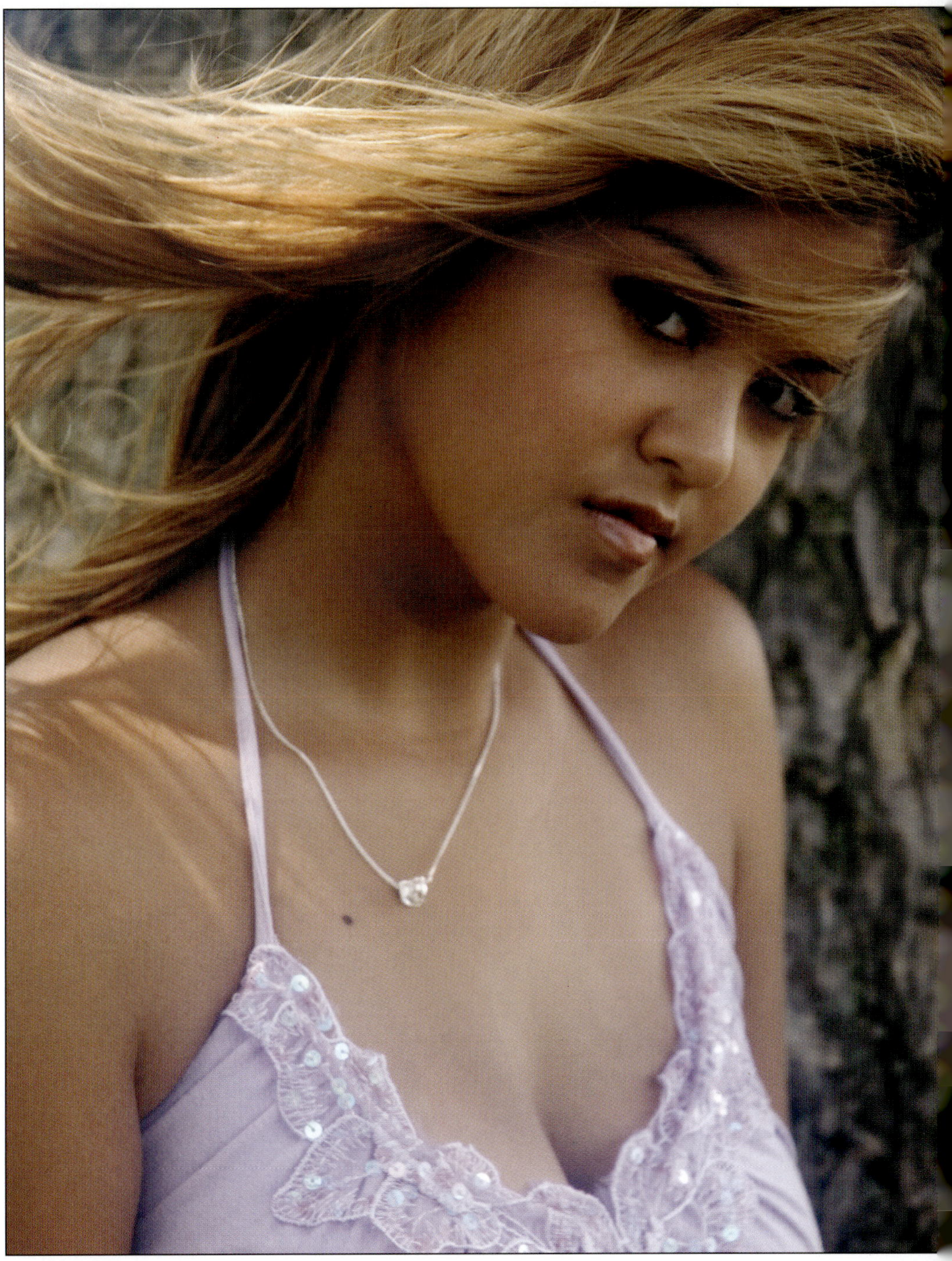

Open shade can be an effective place to create a pleasing portrait in otherwise unflattering conditions. It is important to look beyond your subject to see if the background is lit by the same light as your subject or if it is lit by direct sunlight. If the backdrop is lit by the same open shade, then you will not have a problem keeping the scene within the exposure range of digital capture. Ku'uipo was photographed against a large tree trunk to ensure that the field behind the tree would not be visible. The light behind the tree was at least 3 stops brighter than the open shade and would have recorded as extremely overexposed. Light filtering through the branches was used to highlights Ku'uipo's hair and provides some contrast to the image. An image on page 59 shows the same scene with the use of a silver/gold reflector.

The ratio of light moving from the highlight side to the shadow side of your subject is not the only lighting extreme to watch for when creating a portrait in the shade. Your exposure will be accurate for the light falling upon your subject in the shade. However, that light will be as much as 2 or more stops less than the light surrounding the shade. Any part of the scene that lies outside of the shade will be grossly overexposed and well beyond the range of digital capture.

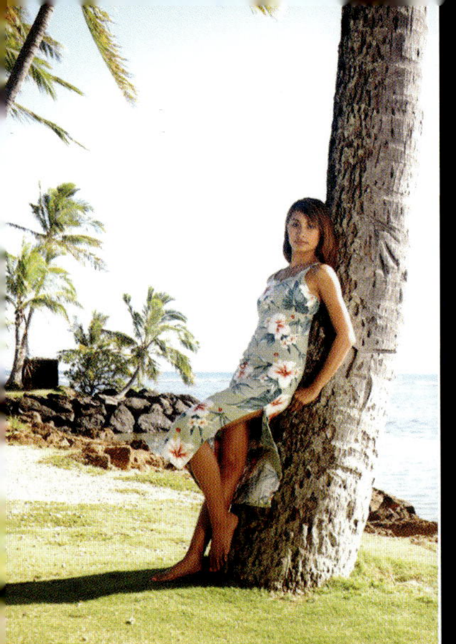

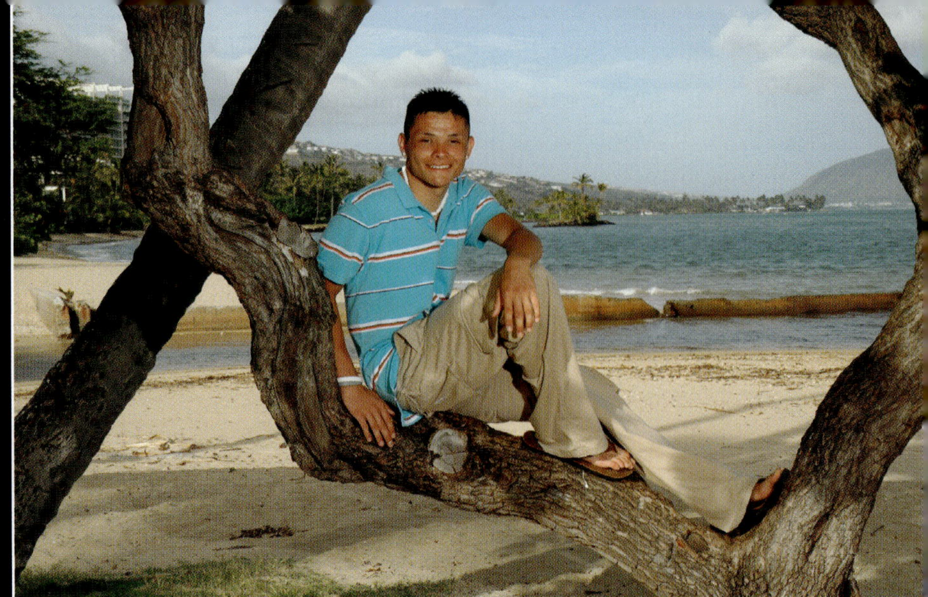

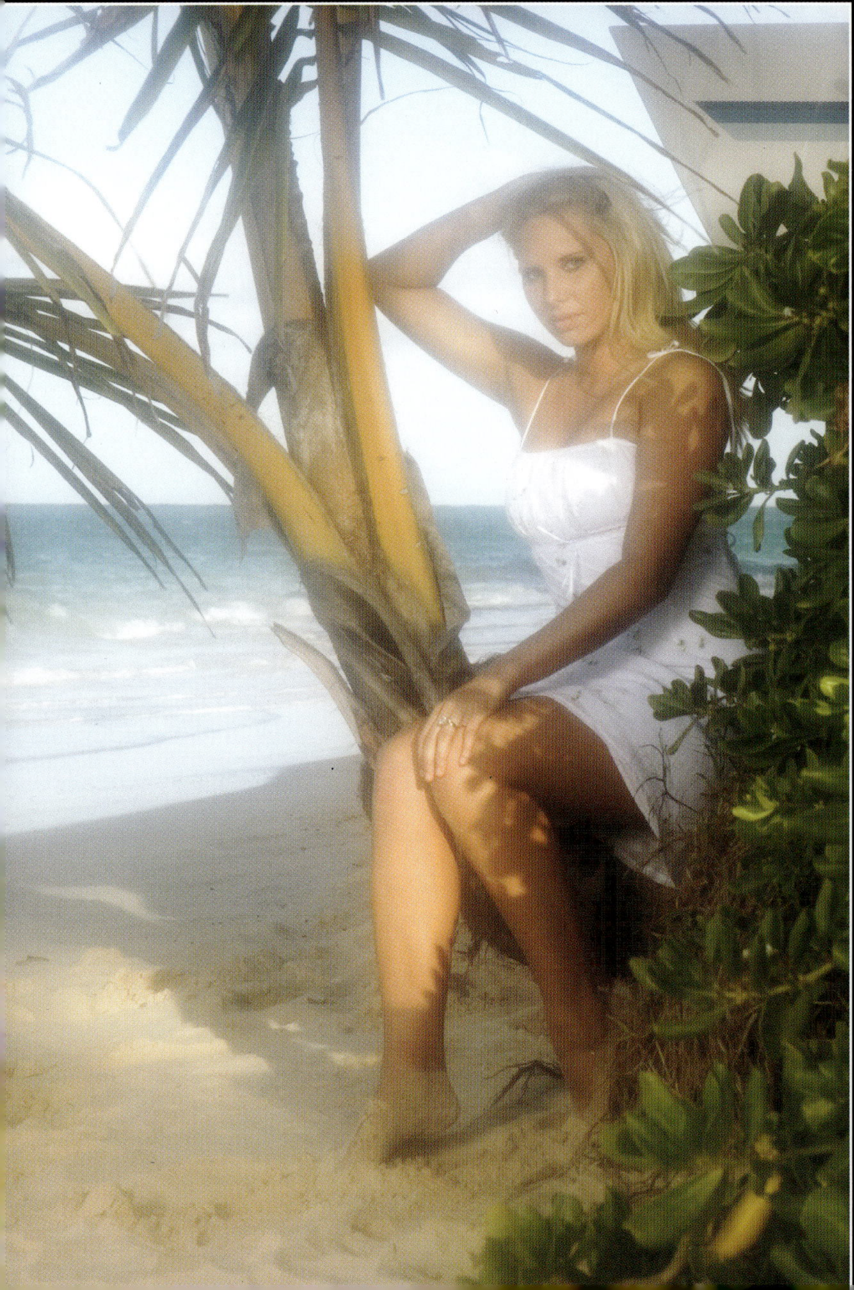

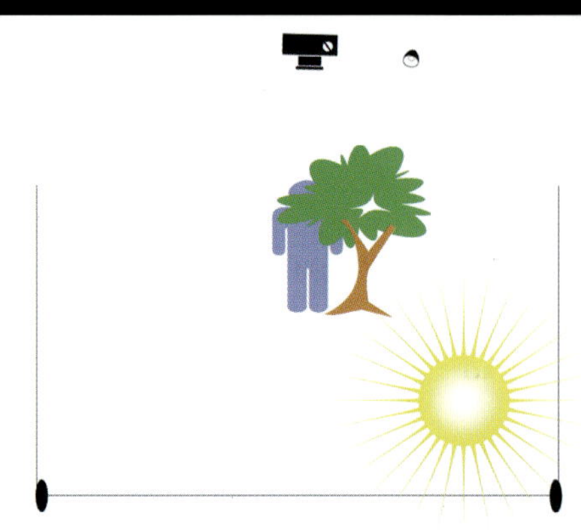

Top Left—Ruthchelle Melchor was photographed a a beautiful beach park. Unfortunately, you can' tell because the background was between 2 and 3 stops brighter than the light on Ruth! **Top Righ and Above**—One effective way to modify the situ ation is to introduce a strobe to the scene. The setup for this image created by Stan Cox II was similar to the one above. His subject was in the shade of a tree. Rather than simply expose for the light under the tree (which would blow out the background), Stan took an exposure reading of the background and set his portable flash unit to expose his subject at the same exposure. The use o strobes outdoors is detailed later in this chapter. **Left**—The same technique is demonstrated here but we used a halo-style softbox to create a softe lighting effect for this portrait of Amy Valero. The ambient light under the tree was f5.6$^{4}/_{10}$, and the combined exposure with the strobe was f8$^{4}/_{10}$ (sho at f9). The background is still somewhat overex posed, but the strobe turns the backdrop into pret ty pastels rather than a patch of white.

SCRIMS

There are many situations when you will want to modify the existing light but will either not have access to open shade or the shaded areas will not work for the image you have in mind. Fortunately, there is a way for you to bring the shade with you. Scrims, or translucent fabric stretched over a frame, can be used to provide beautifully soft light in almost any situation. Sunlight hits the scrim and turns it into a light source as large as the piece of fabric used. The light that passes through the fabric is what illuminates your subject. The light is much softer and diffused, but the direction of light needed to create a three-dimensional feel to your image is maintained. The main difference between using a scrim versus open shade—aside from the portability of the scrim—is the effect that these two techniques will have on the color temperature of the light. Open shade raises the color temperature (resulting in a bluish shift) while white fabric will lower the color temperature of the light (resulting in an amber cast). I personally like a warmer tone in my images, so I like using scrims. Create a custom white balance to neutralize the color shift, use the photo filters adjustment layer in Photoshop, or shoot the image in RAW and change the color temperature in the conversion if the amber hue is too great.

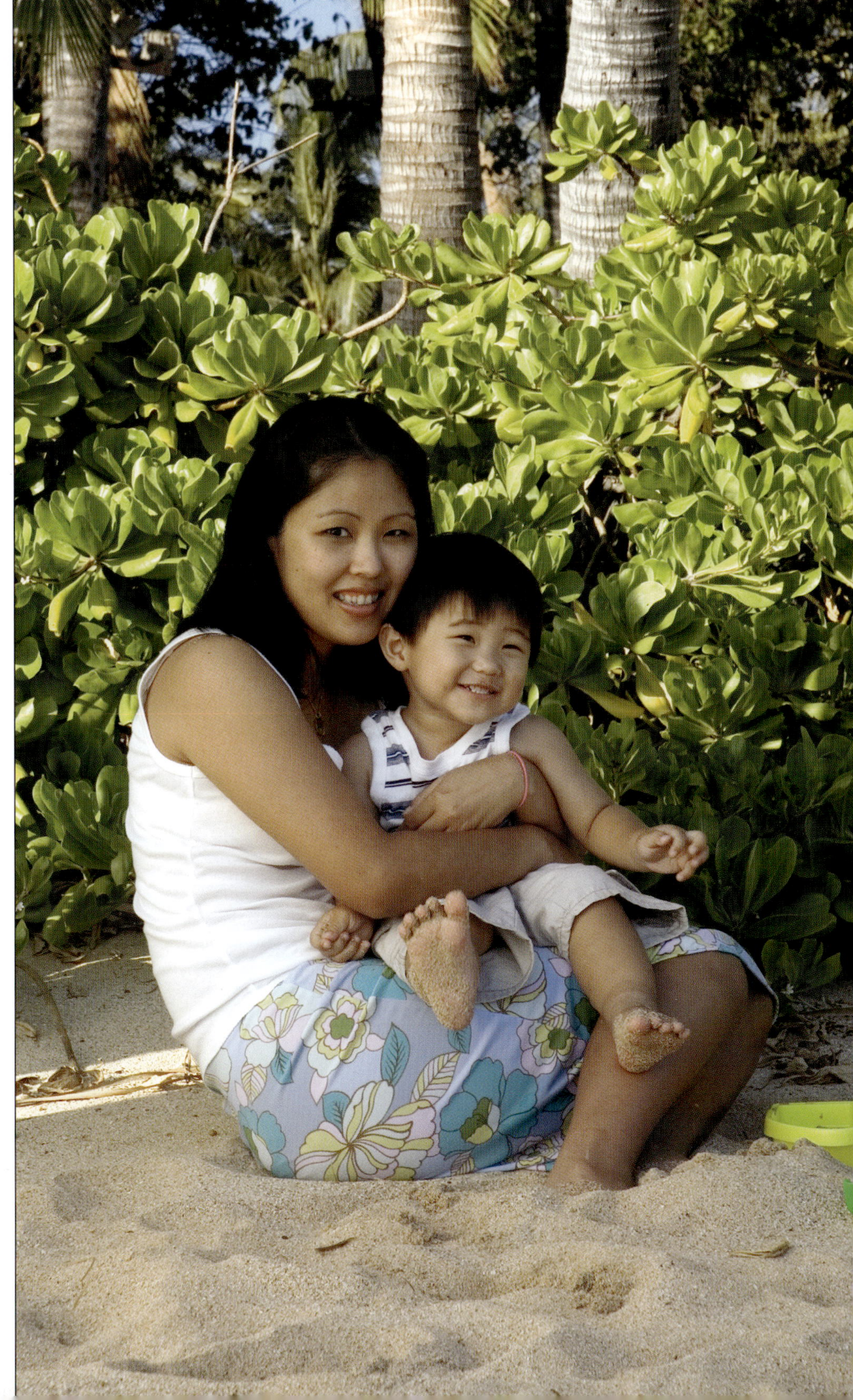

Jenny and her son were photographed on a brightly lit beach on Oahu, Hawaii. The direct sun would have created harsh shadows, and the green plants behind them would have been very dark. Green plants often record darker than one might think, so adding a scrim to the scene served two purposes here: it softened the light from the sun and allowed me to open the lens up to allow more detail to show in the greenery. The blue sky in the background still maintained enough detail, and the only "telltale" sign of the scrim is the overexposed patch of sand that is still lit by direct sunlight. The use of the scrim also made it much easier to maintain the whites in Jenny's shirt.

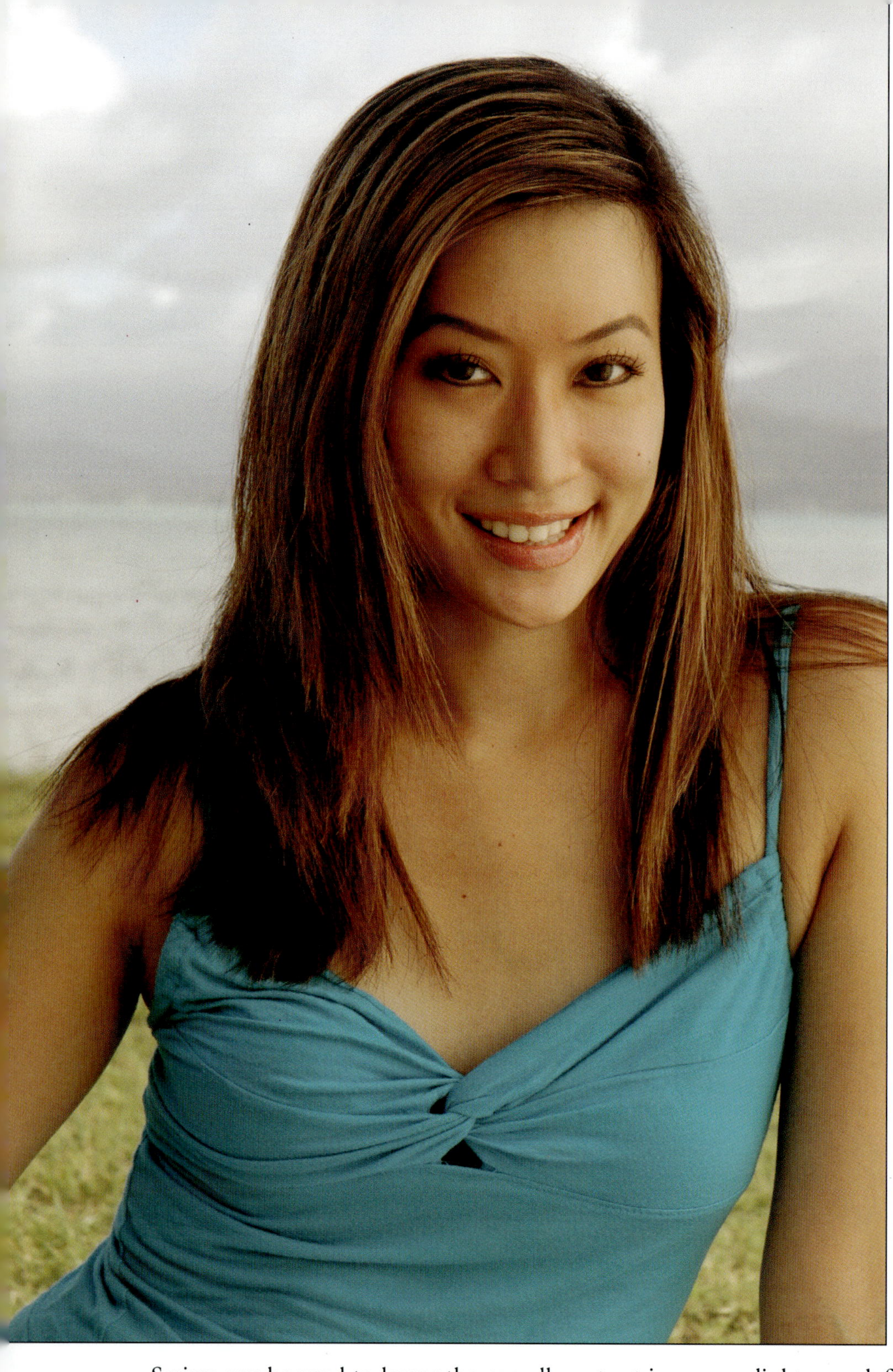

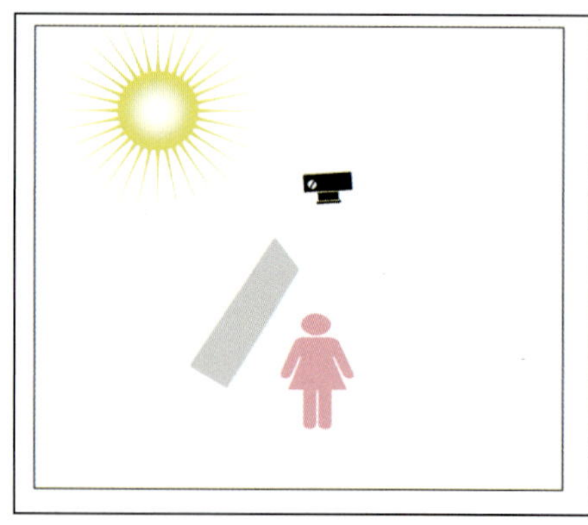

Brooke Tanaka was photographed on a northeast beach on the island of Oahu in Hawaii. The autumn sun was setting at camera right, creating a severe side lighting situation. The harsh light was modified by placing a 77x77-inch Photoflex Litepanel scrim on Brooke's left. The back edge of the scrim was positioned parallel to the subject's back, so the majority of the scrim was in front of her. In essence, this was like feathering a softbox in the studio; the majority of the light source skimmed across Brooke, allowing the soft light to wrap around her, adding its own fill to the shadow side. The backdrop was lighter than normal because the light illuminating Brooke is at least 1 stop less than the light hitting the ocean. However, the fabric is thin enough that it doesn't "eat" too much light, and the backdrop, while bright, is still within the range of digital capture. The light falling on Brooke is soft and beautiful, and there is a faint catchlight.

Scrims can be used to lower the overall contrast in a scene as well. They will lower the exposure values of the main light, which when positioned properly can be used to bring a scene into the exposure range of digital capture. An example would be when your subject is in direct sunlight against a dark backdrop (such as bushes or trees). The odds are that the shadows in the dark backdrop would go black without detail if the sunlight were left unmodified. However, the scrim will cut the exposure of the main light by 1 to 2 stops. Opening your lens or selecting a slower shutter speed will also affect the exposure of the background, allowing more detail to show in the shadows.

However, scrims can create the same problems with your backdrop as open shade when the background is lit with full sunlight. A bright backdrop will be greatly

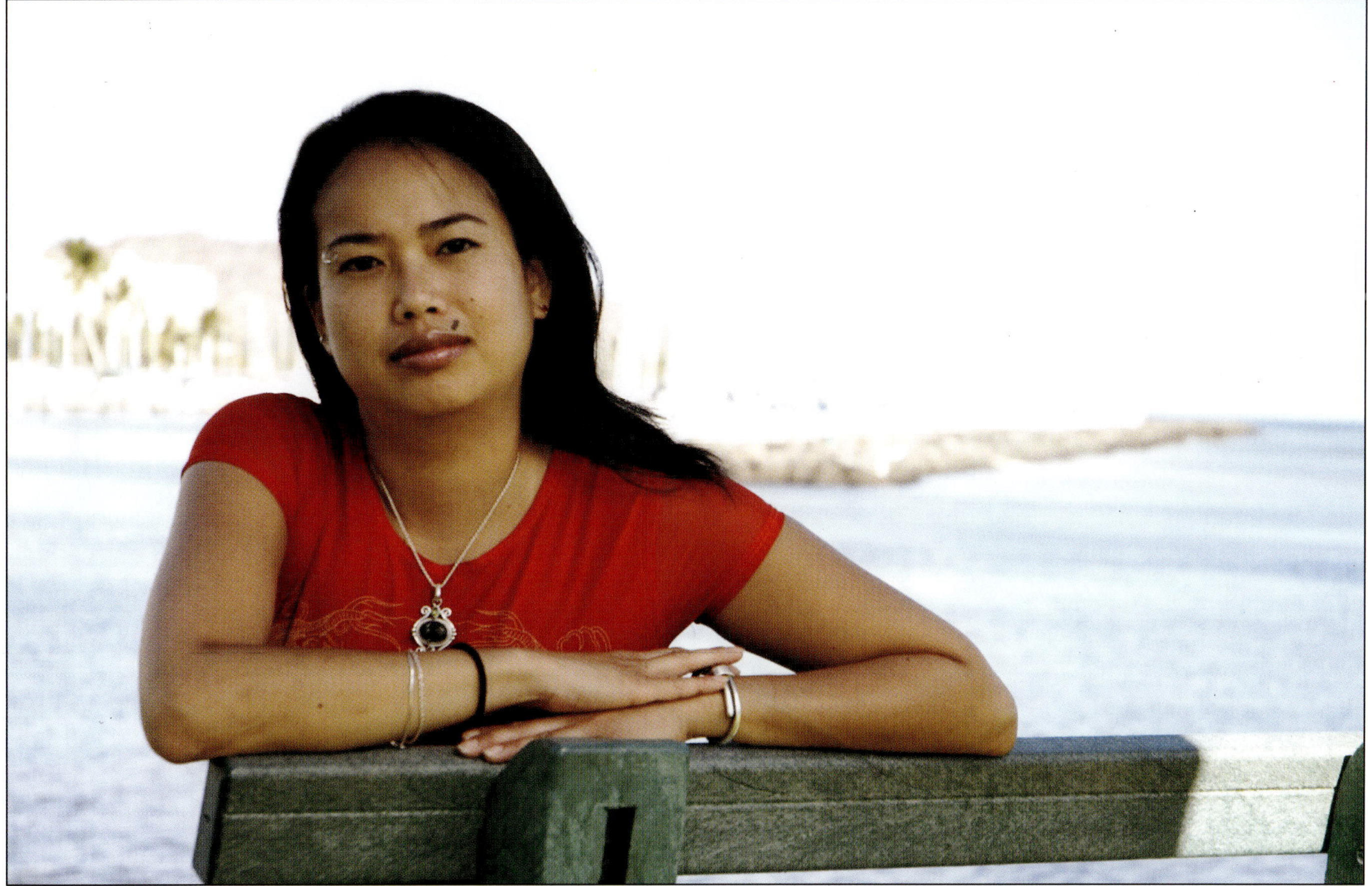

Cheryl was photographed in the afternoon when the sun was setting but was still high enough to create difficult shadows from a tree that was in front of the bench. One solution was to use a scrim over Cheryl to cut the light and even out the shadows. This technique eased the harshness and created a nice soft lighting scheme for her, but the backdrop was now about 3 stops overexposed and lacked detail—there is no way to tell that Cheryl was seated in front of a beautiful marina in Honolulu. We'll bring Diamondhead back later in this book (see page 87)!

overexposed compared to the exposure set for the skin tones. The light, while beautiful, can also be a little on the flat side. Your image can also lack a catchlight, depending on where you place your scrim.

Scrims come in different thicknesses, so the amount of light that is "eaten" by the scrim—and therefore the effect it will have on the backdrop—will vary according to the fabric used.

REFLECTORS

Adding light to the scene will address the issues of better balancing the background light to the foreground and will also ensure that your portraits have sharp and clear catchlights. Two ways to add light to an outdoor scene are to use reflectors and/or strobes. Reflectors are extremely versatile and can be used in isolation or in conjunction with scrims.

To say that reflectors "add" light to a scene is not technically correct. Reflectors take the available light from one area and bounce it into a different area, increasing the light values in the "bounced" section of the scene. This important distinction means that reflectors are very easy to use and meter. Strobes, on the other hand, actually add light to the scene and require an understanding of a complex mathematical interplay of exposures.

Reflectors can be used as a fill source or as a main source of light when your subject is in shade. Your choice of reflector will be determined by the needs created by the scene. A white reflector will provide less light than a silver or gold card, but the reflected light won't be as harsh, and it will be easier for your subjects to keep their eyes open without squinting. An added benefit of white reflectors is the effect they have on the

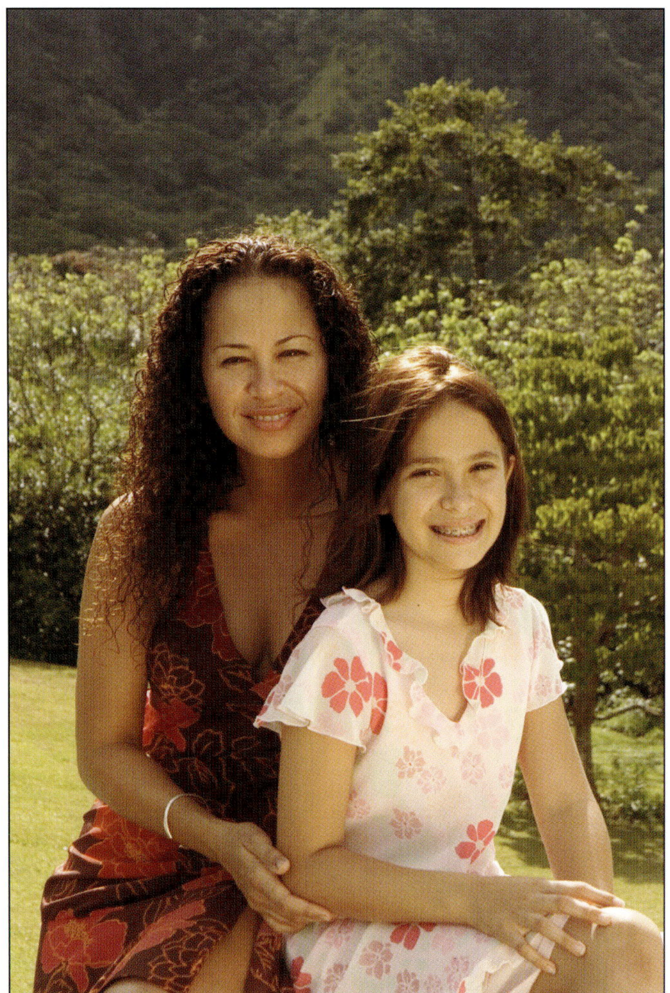

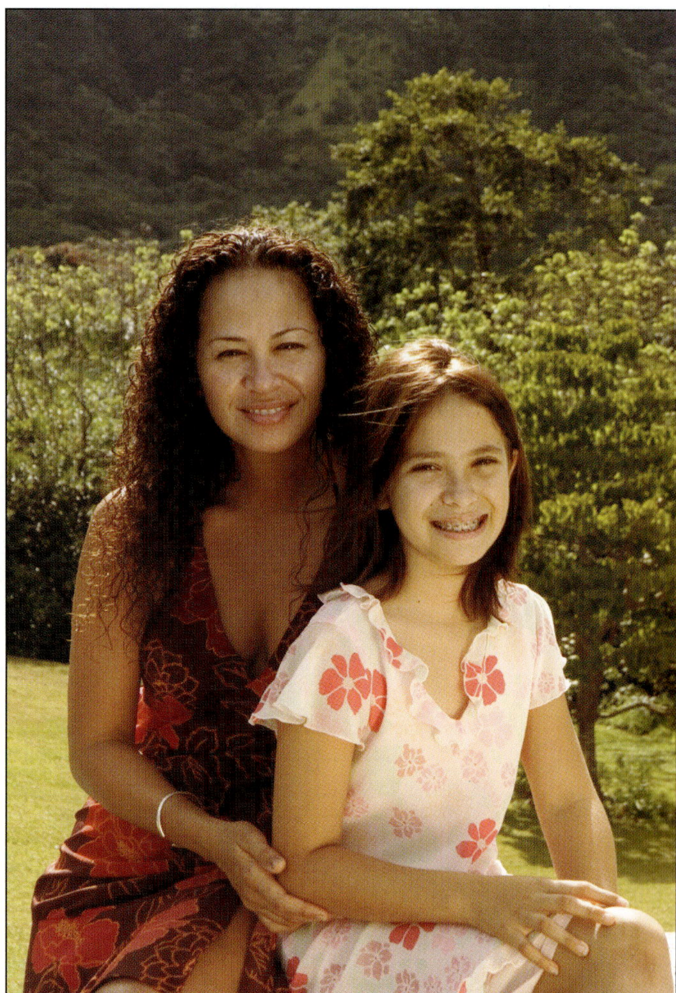

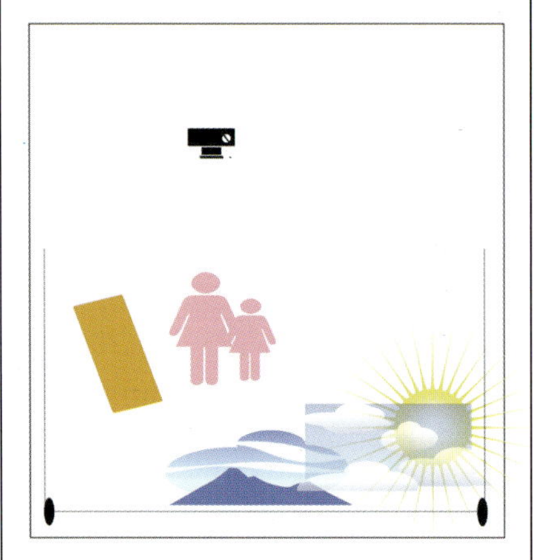

Nanette and Savannah were photographed in a beautiful park on Oahu, Hawaii. The park, while stunning, is difficult to shoot in because of the almost constant cloud cover over the mountains. There are also areas of almost constant sunshine, and the conditions change back and forth continually. Two lighting techniques were used to combat the dramatically changing lighting conditions. A large gold reflector was put in place to bounce the sunlight into our family's faces when the sun was out, and a strobe was set up to use when the sun was hidden behind the clouds. The ambient light read about f5.6$^{2}/_{10}$ at $^{1}/_{250}$ second. The exposure with the gold reflector was f8$^{1}/_{3}$ (f9). The exposure with the strobe was also f9, so it was easy to switch back and forth—we simply removed the hot-shoe PC cord adapter when the sun came out and replaced it when the sun went behind the clouds. We tried a barebulb strobe technique, which in this case proved to be too harsh for my tastes. This technique, and its problems for this session, was described earlier in chapter 2. Here is the final image after the application of the above Photoshop enhancements.

color temperature of the light. Your image will have a slight blue cast because of the color temperature of open shade if you do not set a custom white balance to capture your image. Light bounced off of a white surface will lower the color temperature of the light and will at least partially counteract the blue hue.

The sun was high and behind Nanette and Savannah (above), creating a nice backlit scene. The light on their faces, however, was not flattering. A Photoflex 77x77-inch gold LitePanel was placed low to camera right and was angled up to catch the light from the sun and bounce it back into their faces.

PHOTOSHOP TIP: SELECTIVELY CHANGING THE COLOR TEMPERATURE

1. Open the image to be manipulated.
2. Open the layers palette.
3. Click on the adjustment layers icon at the bottom of the layers palette.
4. Choose Photo Filters.
5. Pick a #80 or #82 series (cooling) filter. These filters raise the color temperature of the image. I wanted a subtle effect, so I chose the #82 filter.
6. Move the slider (intensity) until you get the desired look and click OK. I chose a density of 15 for the image of Nanette and Savannah.
7. Select the brush tool.
8. Set the foreground color to black.
9. Paint in the underlying layer where you do not want the effect to be seen—you have even more control here because you can also set the opacity of the brush. I left the brush opacity at close to 100% because I wanted to raise the color temperature only in Nanette and Savannah's faces. The filter has essentially been erased in all areas except for the faces.
10. Your final bit of control lies in the fact that you made all these changes on an adjustment layer, so you can also set the opacity of the adjustment layer to your liking—or delete it and start over again!

The sun provided a beautiful hair light and also illuminated the background, keeping the scene in balance. The light reflected from the gold reflector created a warm glow to Nanette and Savannah's faces. The reflector changed the color of the light by adding the gold hue and also by lowering the color temperature of the sunlight. The sun was beginning to set, so the color temperature was beginning to shift to a lower temperature anyway.

The addition of the gold reflector may create an effect that is too warm for some tastes. If this happens, you can use the technique described above to modify the color temperature of select portions of the image in Photoshop.

Reflectors can save the day when you arrive at a scene where the light is not quite at the magic position. We have seen a couple of examples in this book where the sun was still too high and created shadows that were too dark and/or created a situation where the subject had to squint. Adding a reflector can help with the shadows but can make it even harder on your subject. If you need to bounce more light into your subject's face, then have them close their eyes until you are ready to shoot. Shoot fast when they have their eyes open, and let them rest frequently.

Reflectors can be used effectively to provide a fill source of light. Reflectors will bounce light into the shadow side of your subjects' faces and can help create a more pleasing lighting ratio.

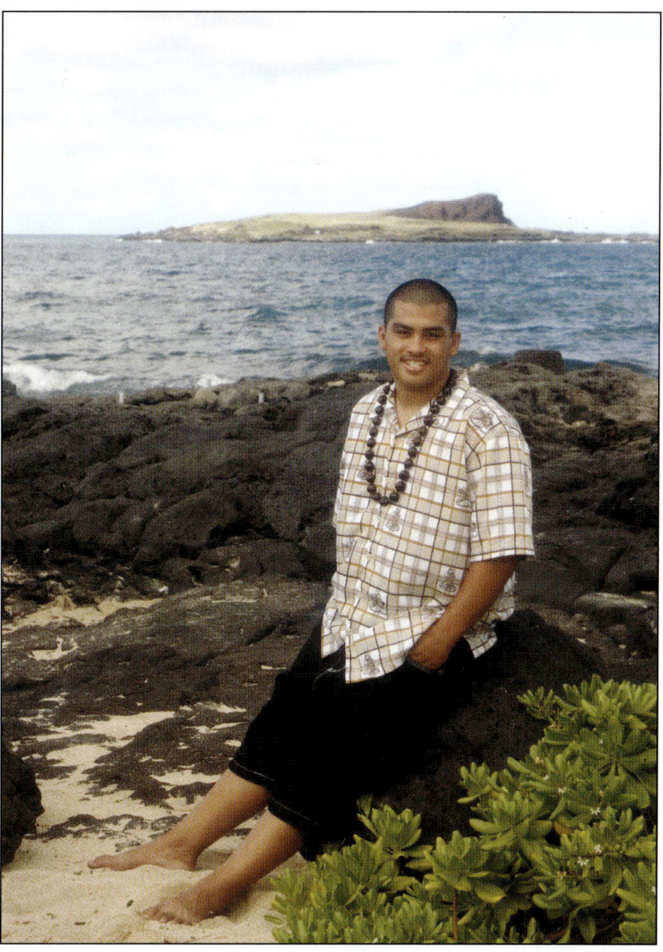

We had to let Kelroy get used to the double dose of fairly high sunlight and a silver/gold reflector before we were able to capture this pre-magic hour portrait.

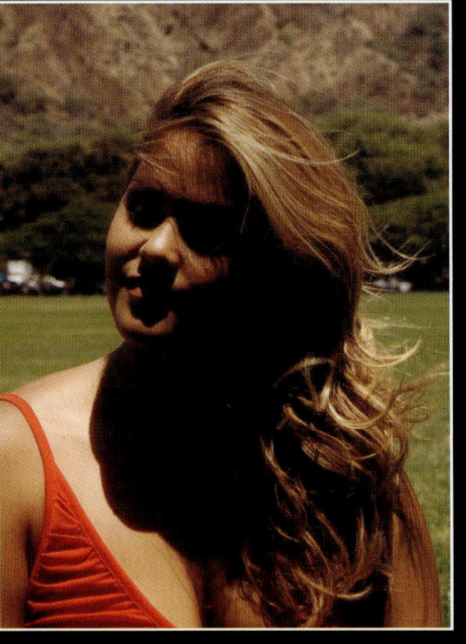

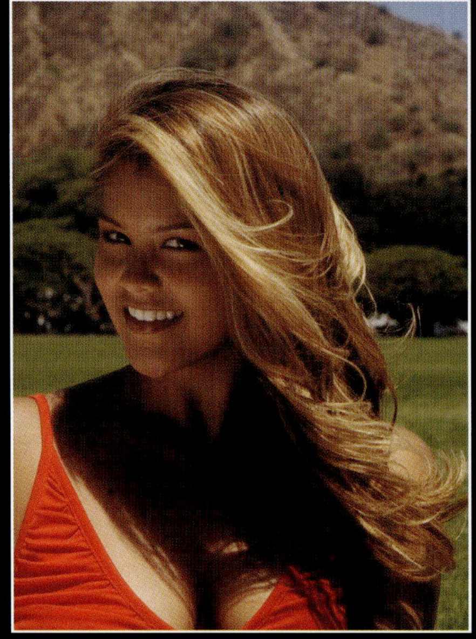

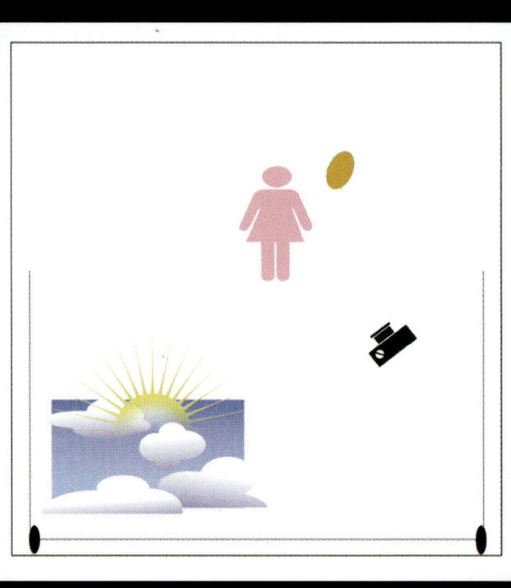

Left—This series of photographs shows the effect of using different-colored reflectors to modify high, direct sunlight. Silver and gold reflectors will bounce more light into the shadows, but they can be more difficult on your subject. We start this sequence with an image taken in Kapiolani Park on Oahu, Hawaii. It was about 1:30 in the afternoon, and the light was harsh and unflattering. The background is beautifully exposed, but the light on Ku'uipo is awful. Note: The images in this series were purposely cropped to show the effect of the light modifiers on Ku'uipo's face as well as the background. **Right—**A white 42-inch reflector was positioned low to catch the light and bounce it back into Ku'uipo's face. Ku'uipo had an easier time looking in the direction of the reflector, but she had to be positioned carefully for the white to adequately fill the shadows.

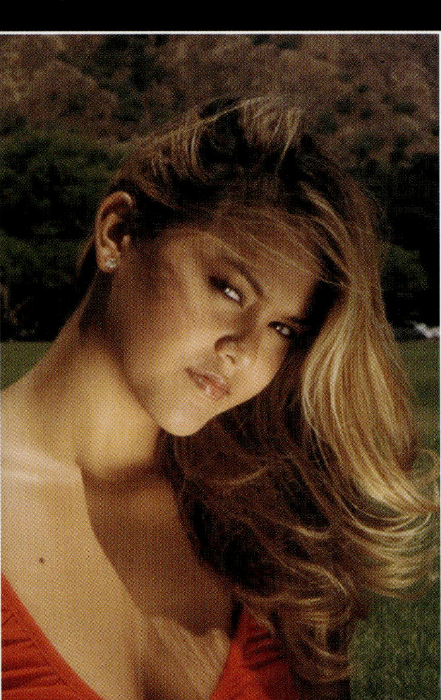

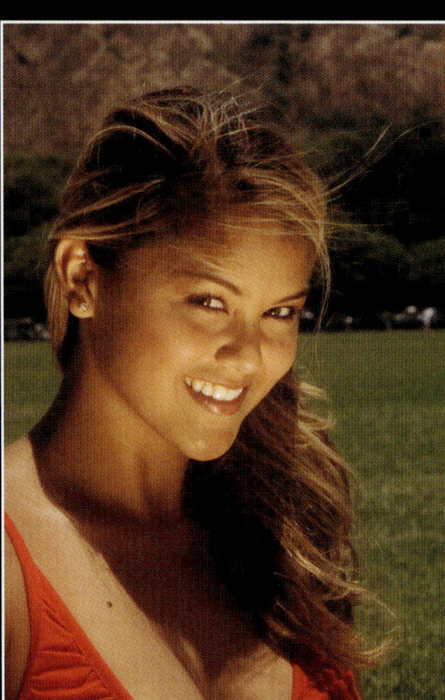

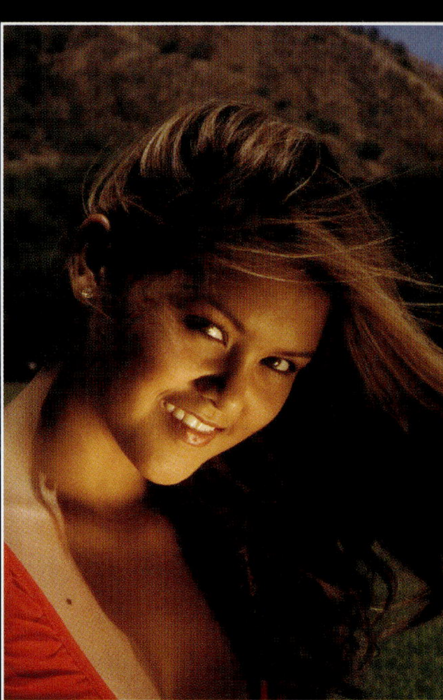

These three images show the effects of using a silver, silver/gold, and gold reflector. Each color did a better job of filling in the harsh shadows created by the sun, but with the change in reflectivity, it became increasingly difficult for Ku'uipo to keep her eyes open. These reflectors can be extremely bright. I asked Ku'uipo to keep her eyes closed until I was ready to shoot. I tried to get two or three shots each time she opened her eyes, but I was lucky to get one shot each time. Ku'uipo is a beautiful young lady who is also a very good sport! Notice how the backdrop seems to be richer in each successive image. Each reflector bounced more light into Ku'uipo's face, changing the exposure, which in turn underexposed the backdrop a little more each time.

SCRIMS WITH REFLECTORS

There will be many times when you will need to use a reflector or strobe with a scrim. There are several ways to use reflectors in conjunction with scrims.

As noted above, silver and gold reflectors will bounce more light into a darker area of your scene but may actually be too bright or produce too much contrast on the subject. If this occurs, a piece of thin translucent fabric can be placed over the reflector to "cut" the light somewhat. The light will pass through the fabric twice (it will pass through the fabric on the way to the reflector and again as it bounces back), so use a fabric half as thick as you think you need. Remember that silver reflectors raise the color temperature of the light, and white and gold will lower the color temperature.

Reflectors, placed on the opposite side of your subject, can take the direct sunlight and bounce the light back into the "shade" created by the scrim and replace the "pop" (and catchlights) lost by using the scrim.

Mirrors can be used as very bright reflectors. Combining open shade, a scrim, and a reflector can create beautifully soft portraits with a kick. Position your subject under a group of trees. Set up the scrim on the fringe where the shade separates from the sunshine, and set up the reflector or mirror in the direct sun,

We return to the series of images of Brooke Tanaka for this demonstration. Earlier we saw an image of Brooke in direct sunlight and then with a scrim to cut the contrast of the sunlight. To create this image, we added a 77x77-inch gold reflector on the opposite side of Brooke. The white scrim and the gold reflector combined to create a beautifully warm image that simulates a sunset portrait. The use of the reflector raised the amount of light under the scrim by at least $^1/_2$ stop, creating a better balance between the backdrop and the exposure of the light illuminating Brooke. In the previous image, the direction of the light was determined by the scrim, and the shadow side was the right side of Brooke's face. Now the reflected light became the dominant light source, and the diffused light that passed through the scrim became the fill source.

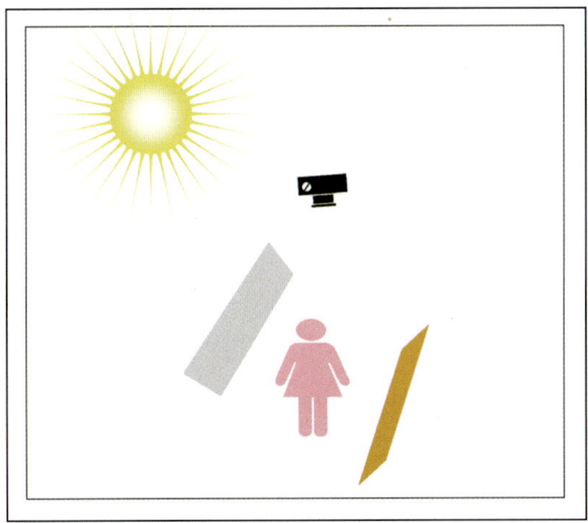

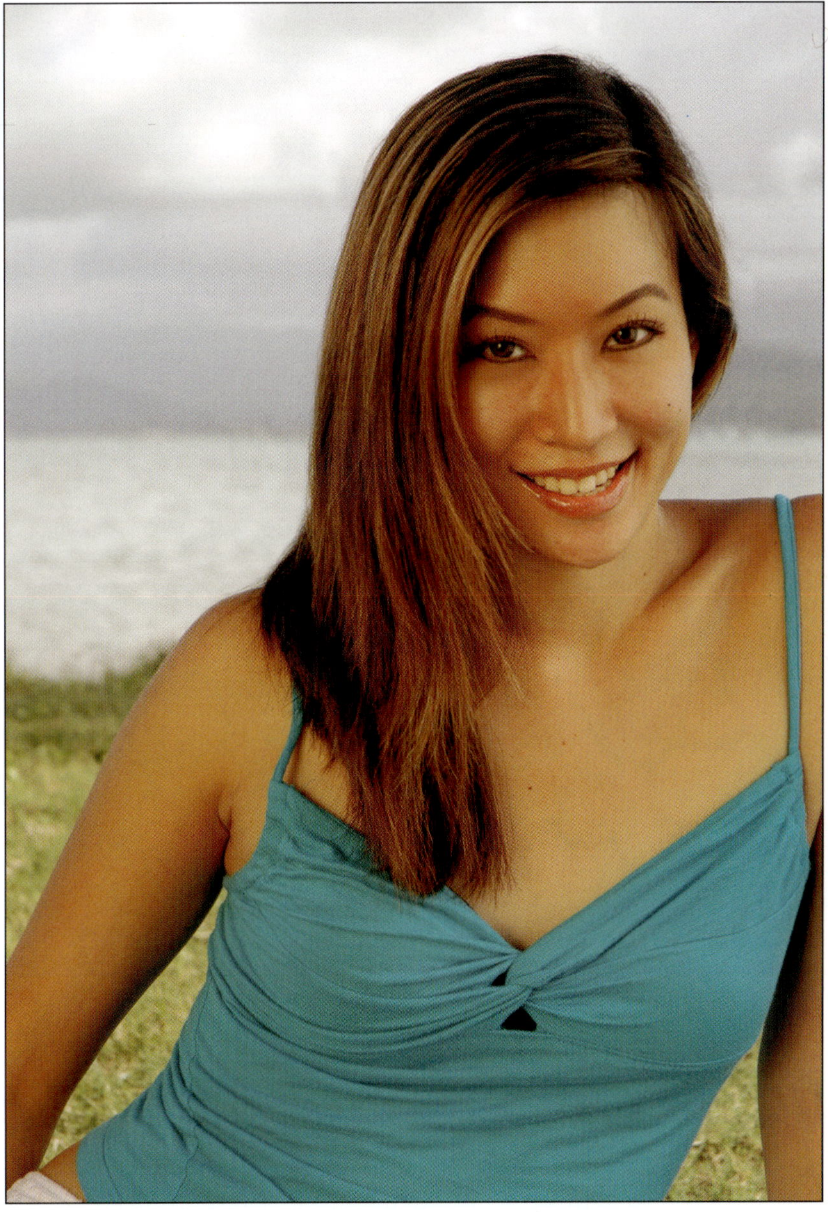

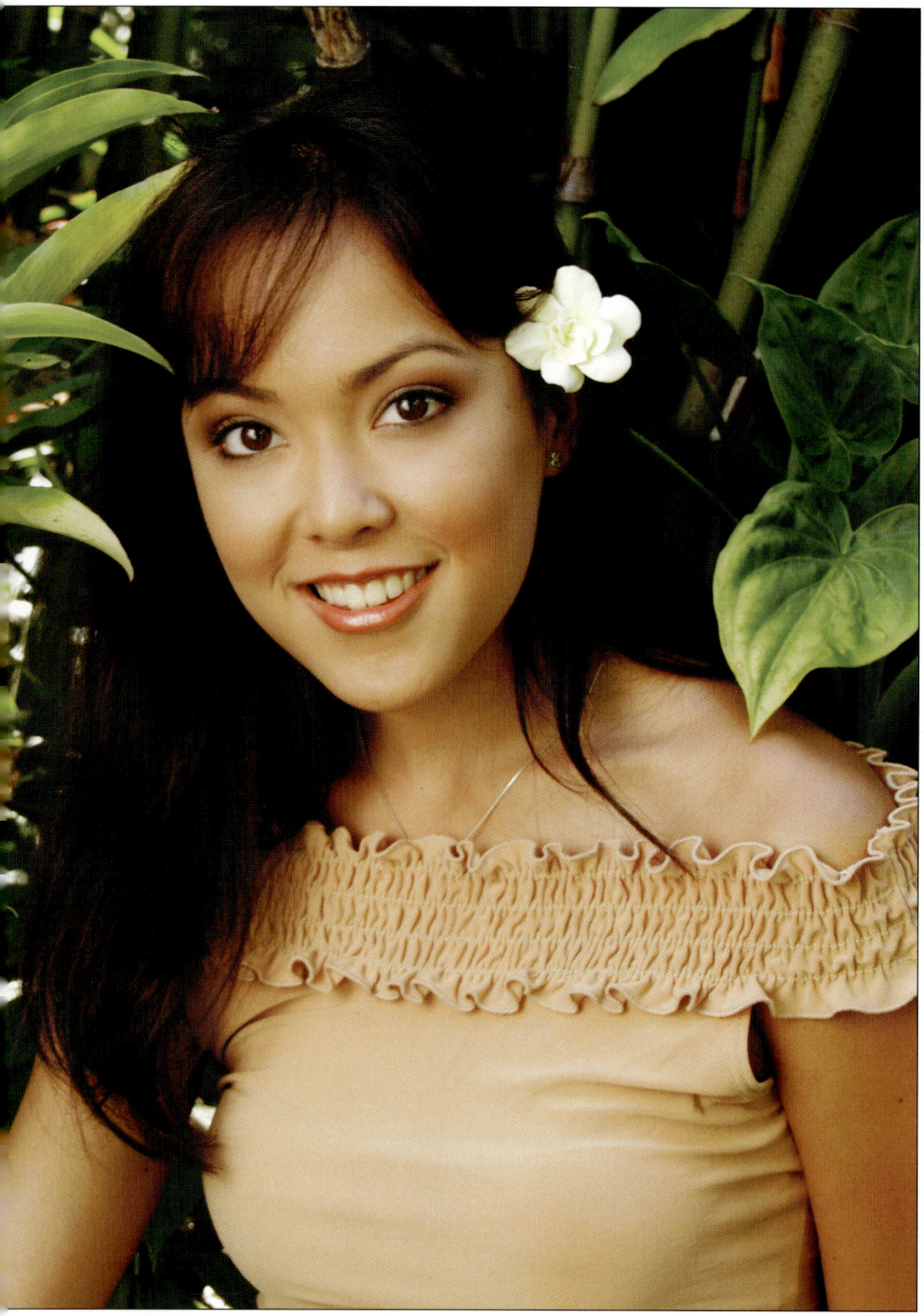

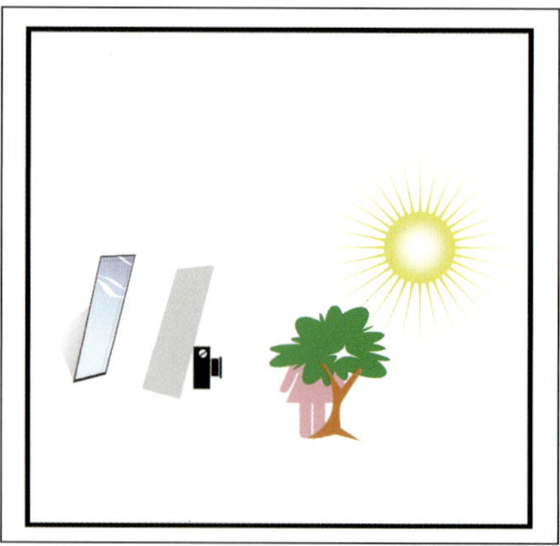

The main light for this portrait of Kathryn was the light diffused by a 77x77-inch Photoflex LitePanel. The source of the light was direct sunlight bounced off of a Plexiglas mirror.

angled to bounce the light through the scrim. Rather than having a harsh light under the trees, the light is spread and softened by the scrim. The light will be soft and beautiful, and there will be catchlights in your subjects' eyes.

The light on Kathryn (above and facing page) is soft and beautiful, but there is little detail in her hair and the leaves are dark behind her. There are ways to bring back some of the lost detail. In the Photoshop tip on the facing page, you can see how blending modes and layer masks can be used to complete the task.

It is not uncommon for portrait photographers to add a hair light to a studio portrait. Hair and rim lights add a spark of contrast and visual interest to the image.

PHOTOSHOP TIP: RESTORING SOME LOST BACKGROUND DETAIL

1. Make a duplicate layer by hitting ctrl/cmd + J.
2. Find the blending mode drop-down menu in the top-left corner of the layers palette.
3. Choose Screen from the list. The screen blending mode will lighten all pixels that have a value less (darker) than 128 (midtone).
4. The result is pretty bad, but we will fix that! Go to the layers drop-down menu and select Add Layer Mask>Hide All. You will be back where you started.
5. We are going to paint the screened layer back in, but only where we want it and at different strengths depending upon what we want to lighten.
6. Select the brush tool from the tool palette and set the foreground color to white. White will reveal the masked layer, and black will hide the masked layer. Note: If, while painting, you create a stroke of the actual color—white or black—then go to the layers palette and click on the mask icon in the active layer box to get back to working on the layer mask.
7. Notice that the toolbar at the top of your Photoshop window has an opacity slider. You can control how much of the masked layer you want to show through. I painted in Kathryn's hair and some of the dark holes behind her at 100%, the leaves and stems at 50%, and I even lightened the mask of her face at 25%.
8. The image looks much better, but I wanted more detail in Kathryn's hair. I made a duplicate of the screened layer. The parts of the image that were still masked were unaffected, while the rest of the image was lightened some more.
9. However, I only wanted to lighten Kathryn's hair, so with the brush tool still selected, I set the foreground color to black. I set the opacity slider to 100% and painted a mask back over everything except her hair. The whole process took less than five minutes!

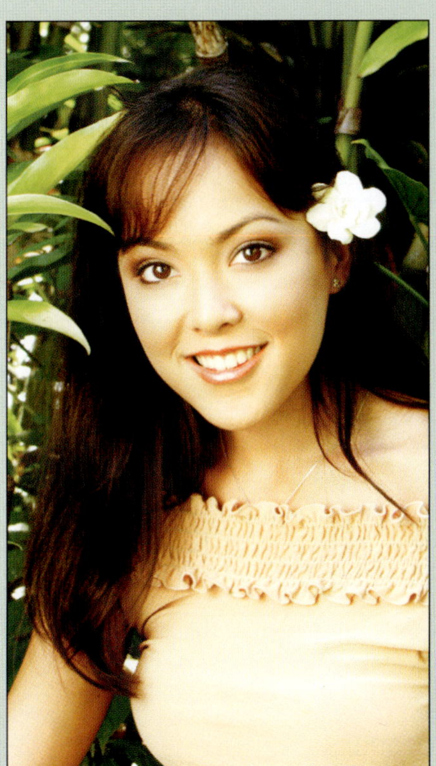
Step 3

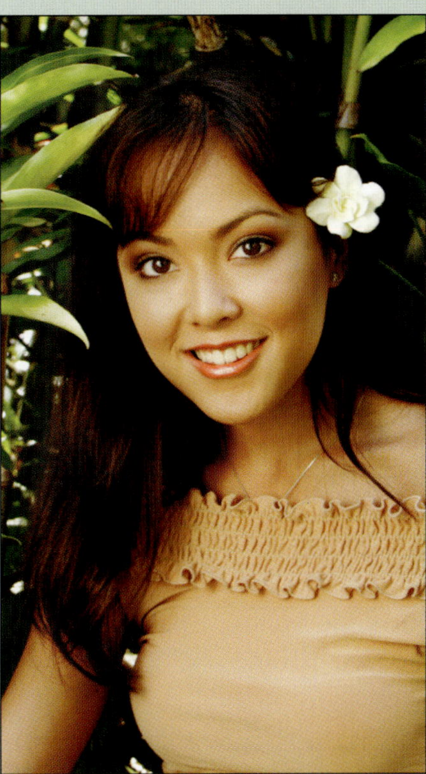
Step 7

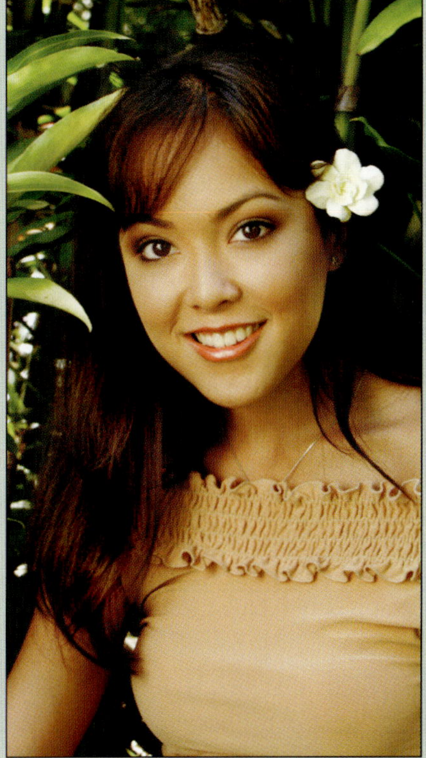
Step 9

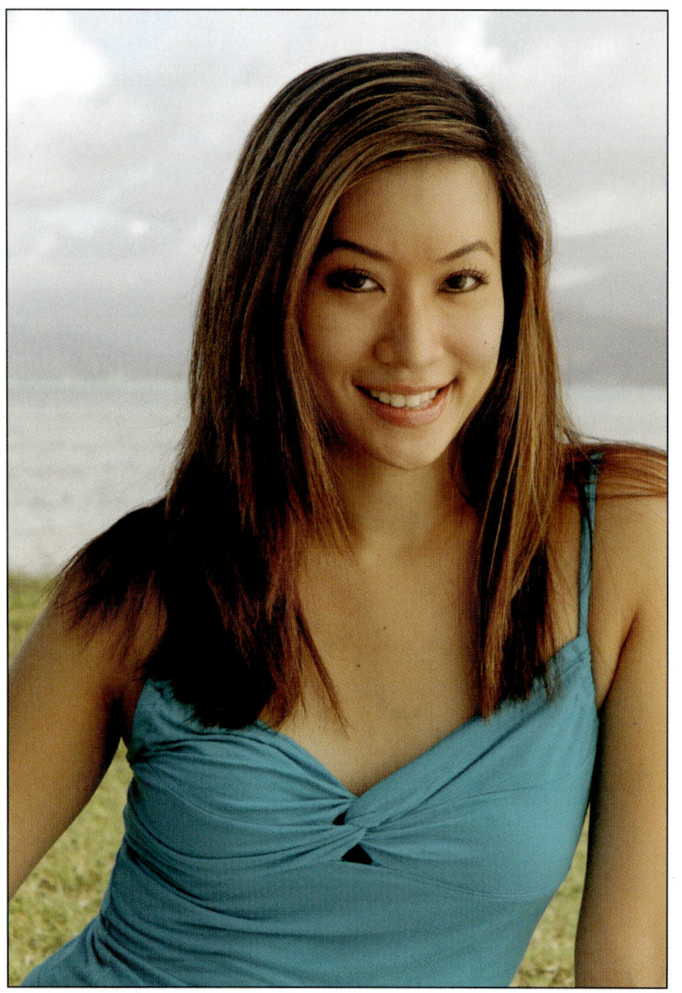

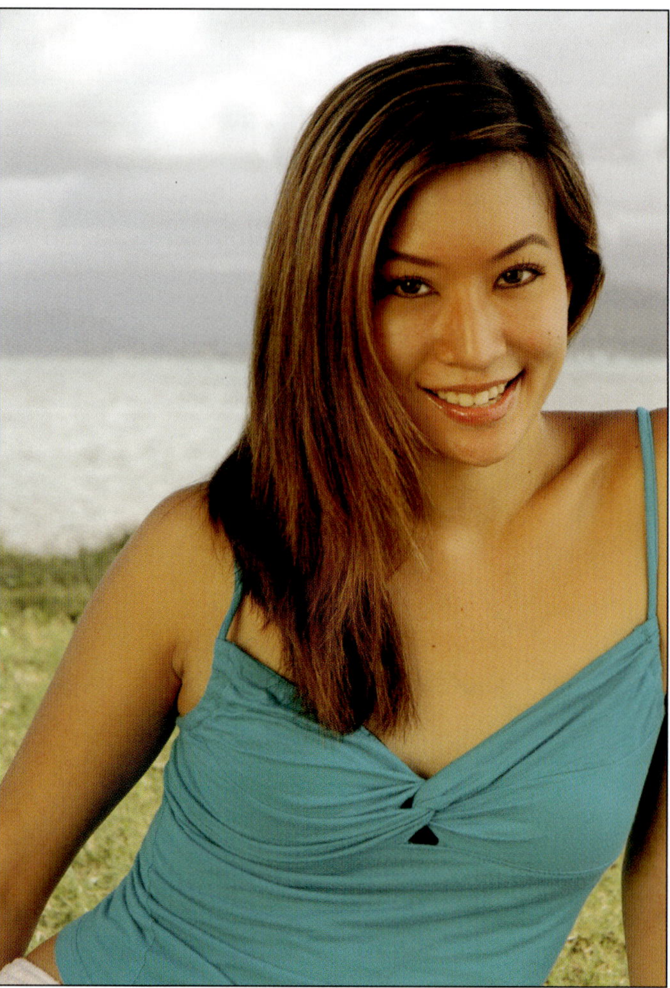

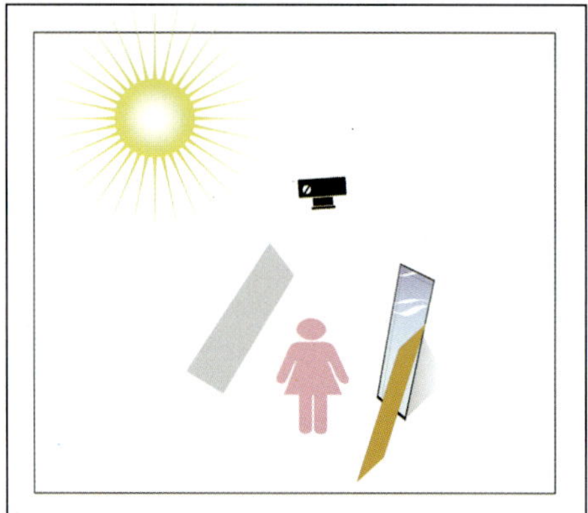

Left—The first image of Brooke Tanaka was created using just a scrim (see page 68). **Right—**In the second image, a reflector was added (see page 73). **Diagram and Facing Page—**We conclude the sequence by adding a hair light—a narrow mirror behind and to her right. The highlight this created adds a bit of realism to the scene: it's a bright sunny day on the beach (even though there are clouds behind her!). You can also position your subject(s) at the edge of your scrim, which will allow direct sun to light the hair while the diffused light illuminates the face and foreground.

The added lights also help to create a three-dimensional feel to the image and draw the viewer into the photograph. Hair and rim lights also add a realistic feel to location portraits—we have just modified the natural light to fit our needs and have a nice, soft light on a bright sunny day. Highlights help to create the illusion that the portrait was created with the same light that illuminates the surrounding area.

Smaller reflectors or mirrors can also be used to create this same illusion. To see their effect, let's conclude our look (above and facing page) at the series of images of Brooke Tanaka we began on page 34.

USING STROBES OUTDOORS

Strobe lights are often used to modify or accent the ambient light for an outdoor portrait. Using strobes

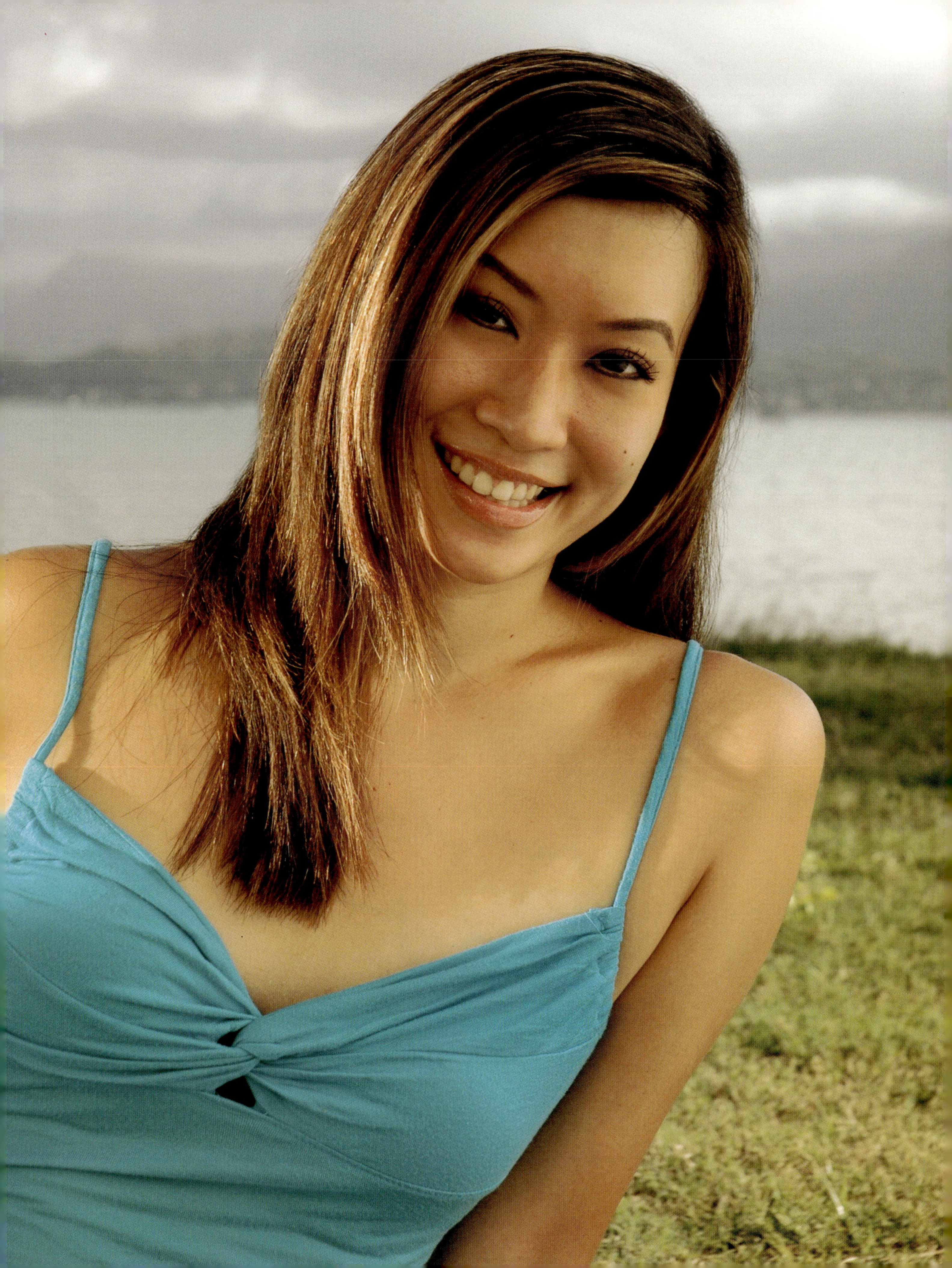

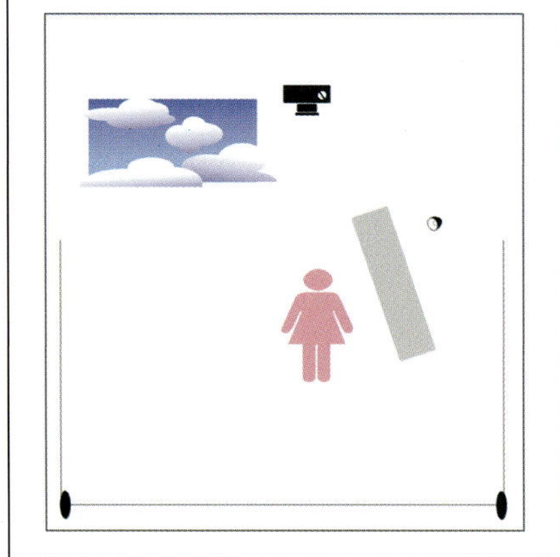

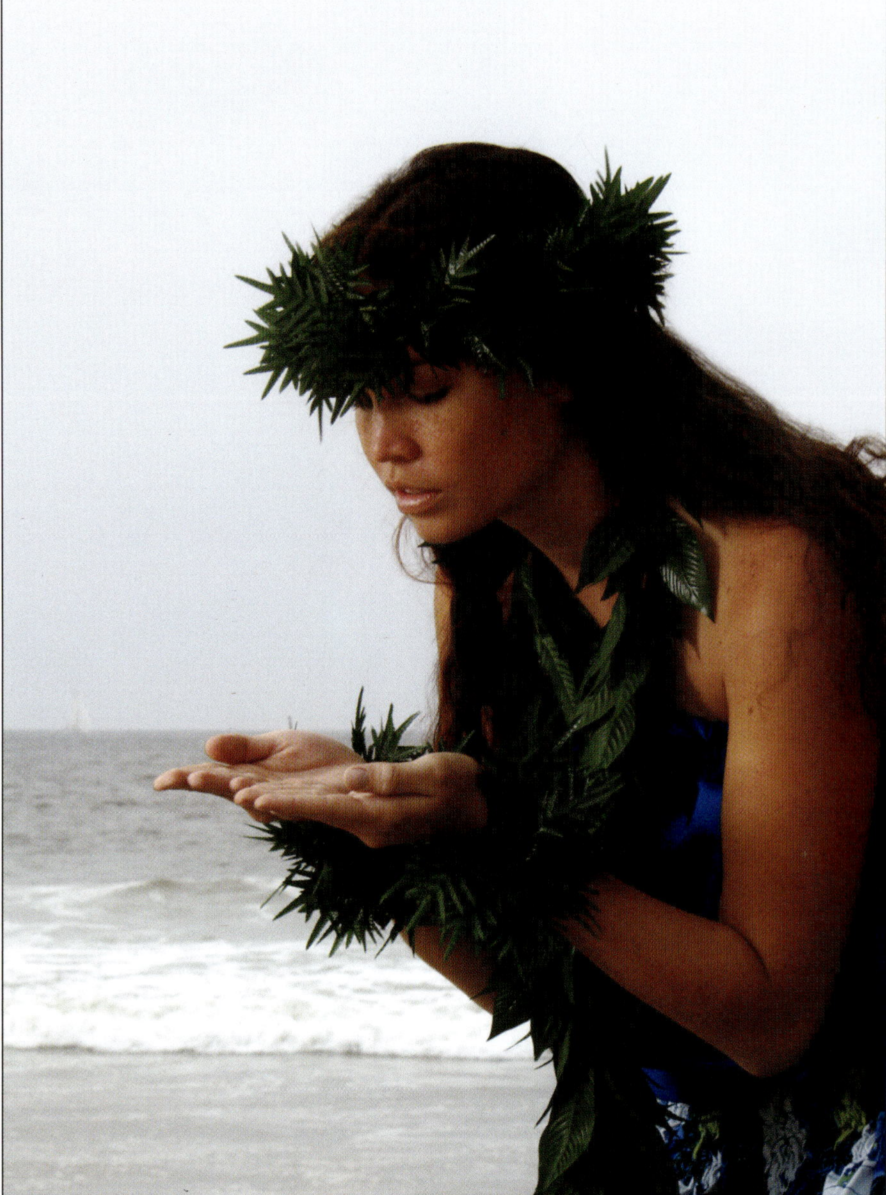

Strobes can be used to salvage a session on a day when Mother Nature isn't cooperating. Sometimes a cloudy day produces images that are easy to create and have enough contrast to work (as in Don Herzig's image on page 63. However, more often the results are flat and boring. The introduction of a flash can provide the contrast needed for a successful portrait. The image of Sanna Dioso was created on a cold, foggy, and cloudy day at a beach in Los Angeles, California. The ambient light read about f4 at $^1/_{60}$ second. A portable Sunpack strobe was taped to a light stand, and the flash was fired through a homemade scrim positioned about 45 degrees to camera right. The overall exposure read f8 at $^1/_{60}$, so the strobe output was about $1^2/_3$ stops greater than the ambient light.

outdoors is a great deal more complicated than lighting an indoor set. Photographers rarely need to concern themselves with the shutter speed in an indoor studio. The ambient light is usually much less intense than the light provided by the strobes, so as long as the shutter speed is set at the appropriate sync speed or lower, the only concern is the aperture. The only time that the ambient light would affect your exposure during an indoor shoot is when the shutter speed is extremely slow. The principles behind the additive nature of light and lighting ratios were introduced earlier in this book. Studio photographers have a relatively easier time applying these laws because they have full control over each light in the studio—and the fact that the shutter speed is usually not a factor in the determination of how the image will look.

The situation is vastly different when you bring your strobes outdoors. Now the changing ambient light plays a critical role in the equation, and your shutter speed is a vital component in how your image is rendered. The interplay of your shutter speed and aperture determines the look of an ambient light–strobe portrait, but generally speaking, the aperture is determined by the strobe setting while the shutter speed controls the effect of the ambient light. A bright backdrop can be toned down by choosing a fast shutter

PHOTOSHOP TIP: A SIMPLE TONING TECHNIQUE

Toned images have long been a popular product for portrait photographers. Any photographer who remembers the stench of some of the toners will appreciate the following technique. There are many ways to tone your images in Photoshop. I stumbled upon this incredibly simple approach as I was trying to remember how to use some of the more complicated methods, like the channel mixer adjustment layer technique described by Martin Evening (*Adobe Photoshop 6.0 for Photographers,* Focal Press, 2001). I started playing around with other possibilities because the book that details the channel method was 3000 miles away in my office. I knew that I wanted to work with layers and the layer blending options to create the effect, but the methods I was using were still way too convoluted. I was looking for a sepia tone to add an old-time Hawaii feel to the image of Sanna Dioso wearing a traditional hula outfit. I started by selecting a dark-brown color swatch as my foreground color. Then I created a new document that was the same size as the image of Sanna. I selected the paint bucket tool and "dumped" dark brown into my new document. I dragged the brown image on top of the image of Sanna (holding down the shift key to center the new layer). I changed the blending mode to color and was done.

The idea of having to create a new document to match the size of each image I wanted to tone seemed ridiculous, so I kept playing. I went back to the original document and made a duplicate layer by pressing ctrl/cmd + J. I then dumped the foreground color onto the top layer by using the paint bucket tool and changed the blending mode to color. This also worked, but I found an even easier way to do it. Here's how:

1. Open the image you wish to tone.
2. Select the toning color from the color swatches or color picker dialog box and set your choice as your foreground color.
3. Go to the layers drop-down menu and select New Fill Layer>Solid Color.
4. Choose Color as the blending mode in the dialog box.
5. Click OK.
6. Lowering the opacity of the fill layer will allow the colors in the original layer to show through. Go to the layers palette and lower the opacity of the fill layer until you get the exact mixture of tones that you desire.
7. If you want to change the color of the tone, then simply double click on the fill layer icon in the layers palette and choose a new color with the color picker. It really is that easy!

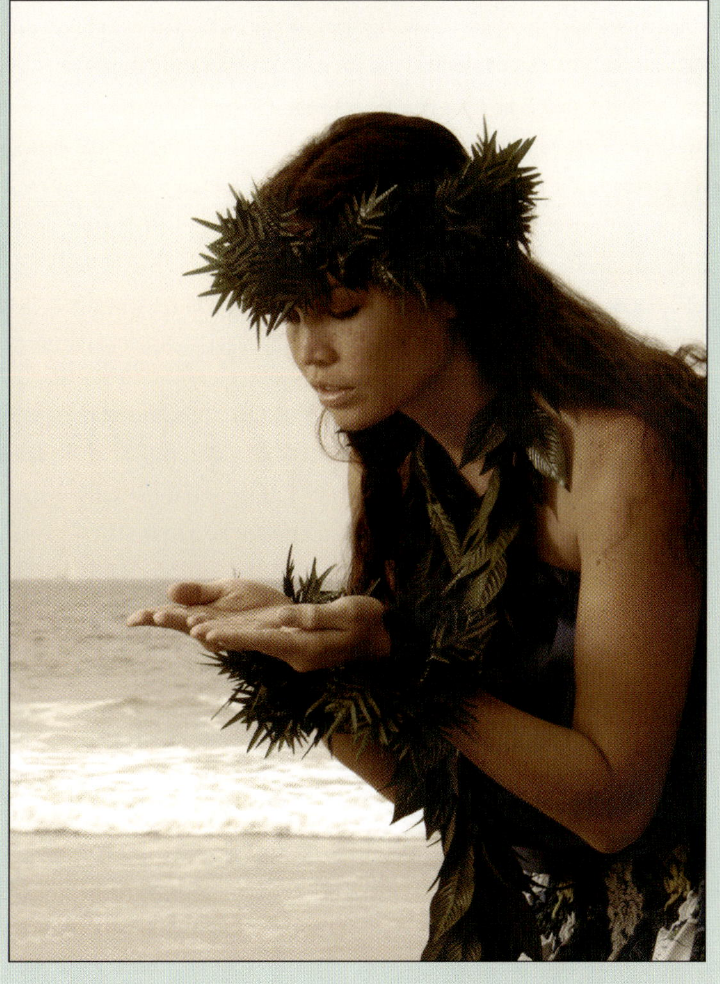

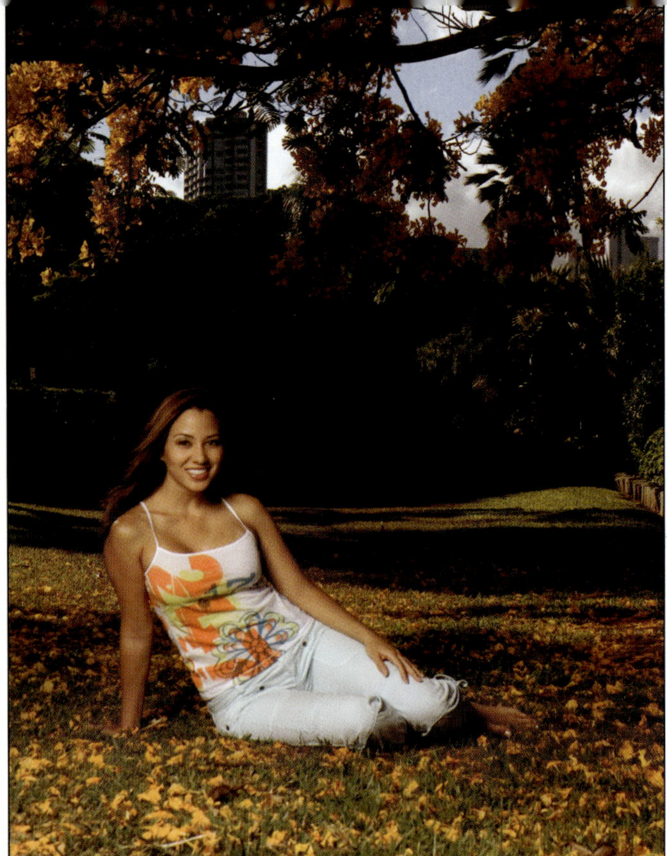

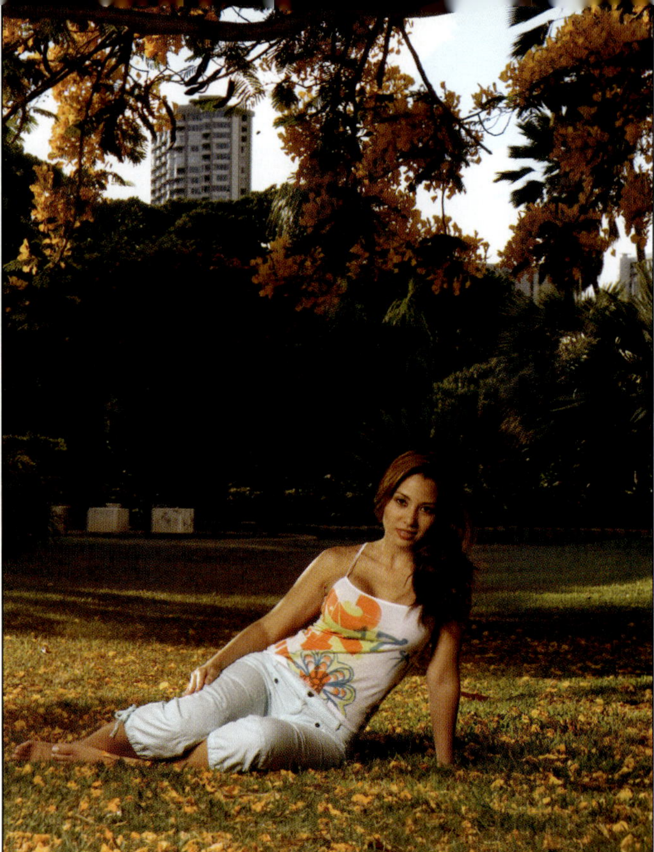

Above Left—We positioned Monica Ivey under a tree in a beautiful park in Waikiki. She was placed in the shade so the ambient light at her face was less than in the open sunshine behind her, and we had pretty patterns of light and shadows throughout the image. At $^{1}/_{500}$ second the strobe was close to the ambient light behind Monica. The aperture was f9. **Facing Page—**We slowed the shutter speed down to $^{1}/_{250}$ second. The shutter was dragged 1 stop, adding 1 stop more light to the backdrop. However, the strobe was not affected by the change in shutter speed. Monica was in the shade of the tree, so the shade still added a relatively small amount of light to the exposure at her face. In fact, slowing the shutter speed by a full stop only added $^{1}/_{3}$ stop to the combined exposure. However, the backdrop became lighter because the backdrop exposure was based on the ambient alone. The light from the strobe did not affect the backdrop, which was now $^{2}/_{3}$ stop lighter (remember we had to close the aperture $^{1}/_{3}$ stop). **Above Right—**Dropping the shutter speed down one more stop to $^{1}/_{125}$ second had no impact on the exposure at Monica's face but added an additional stop to the backdrop. Notice the highlights on Monica's right hand. The direct sunlight—even at this late time of day—is too bright for the highlights to be maintained at this exposure. The middle exposure (facing page) probably works the best of the three.

speed, while slower speeds will add detail to a darker environment. The addition of a strobe controls and balances the exposure on your subject. The strobes will not have much impact on the backdrop because the light from the flash will diminish rapidly as it passes your subject—unless your client is nestled tightly amongst a setting such as a group of trees or flowers.

Strobes can be either fill lights, co–main lights, or the main source of the light for your outdoor portrait. It is crucial to remember that, however you use the strobes, the overall exposure on your subject will be based on the light from the strobe and the ambient light at the particular shutter speed chosen. Changing your shutter speed will affect the backdrop but will also affect the impact of your strobe.

Assuming that the distance between your flash and your subject stays the same, the constant in the exposure equation will be the output of your strobe. The amount of light that the strobe adds to the overall exposure determines its impact (fill, co-main, or main). You will need a light meter that can read the ambient and the strobe light to arrive at the final exposure. You'll also need a meter that will show at least two of the three readings (ambient, strobe, and overall) for you to determine the lighting ratios and decide what impact each light source will have.

The examples above and on the facing page show some of the complexities involved with combining strobes with ambient light. We'll start by looking at what happens when you keep the power setting on

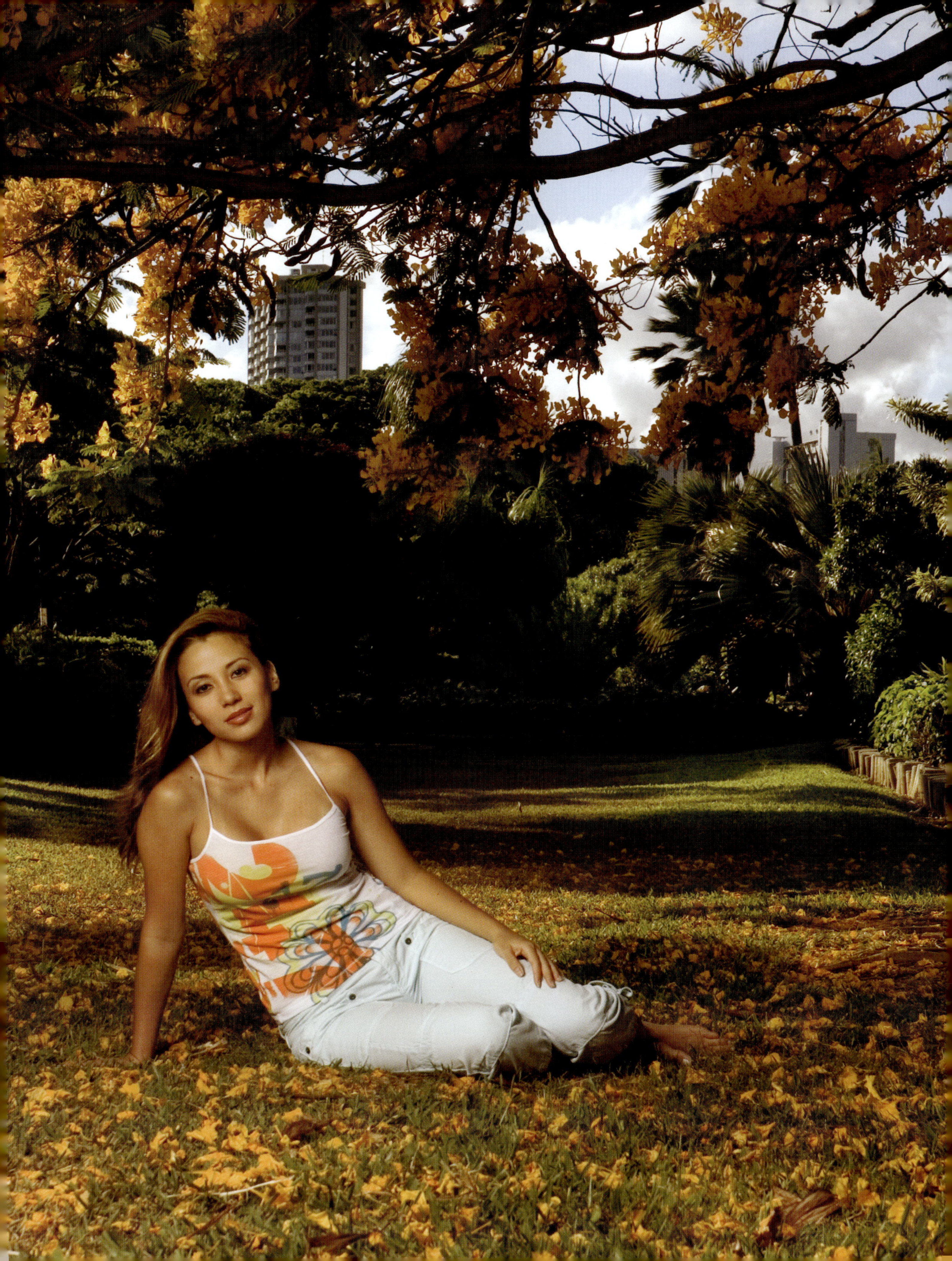

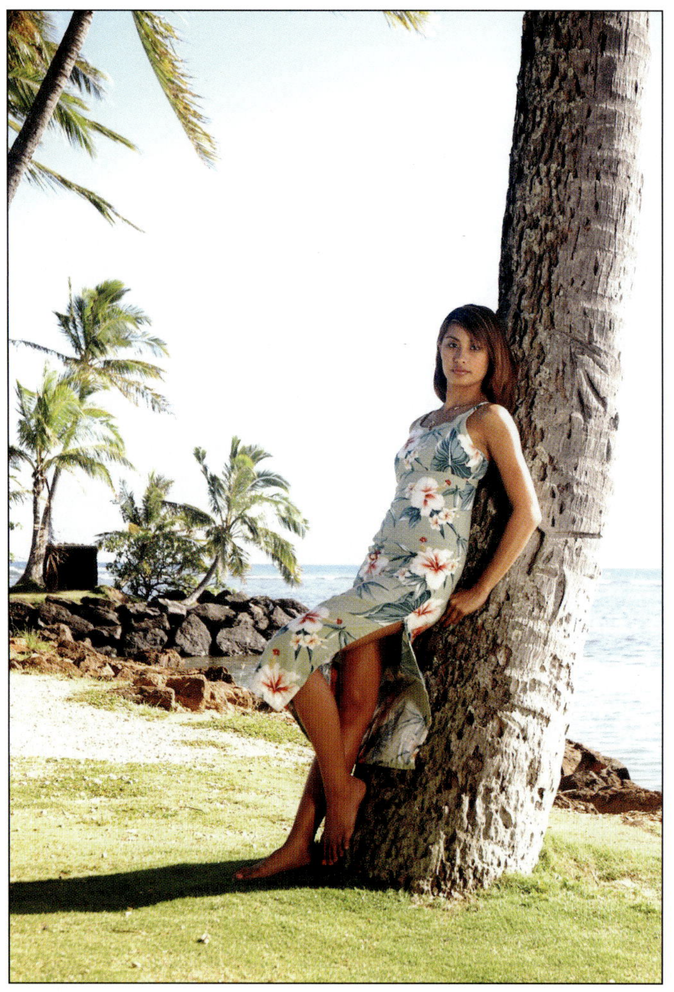

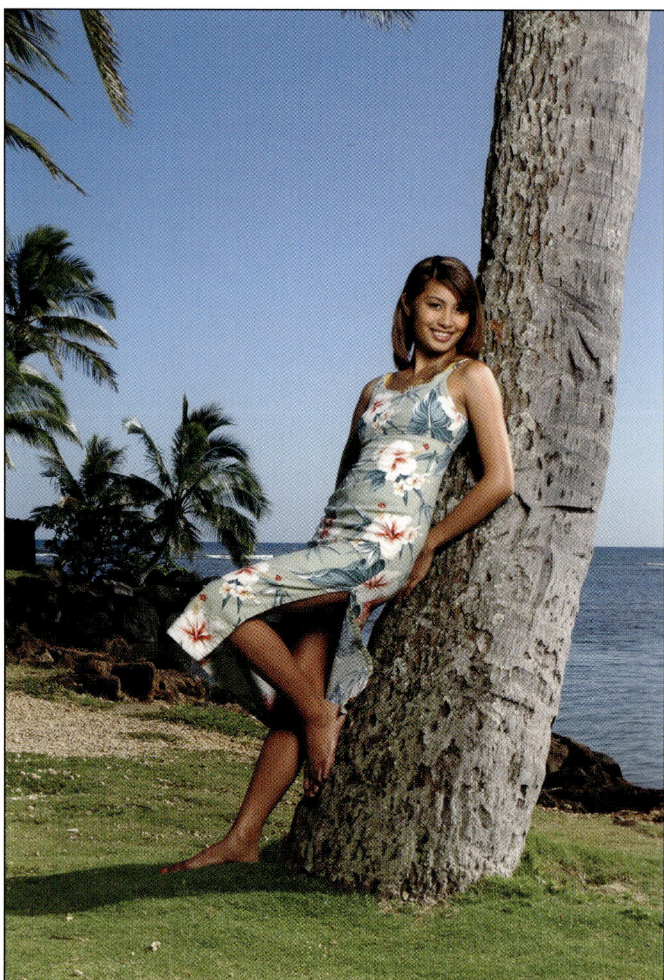

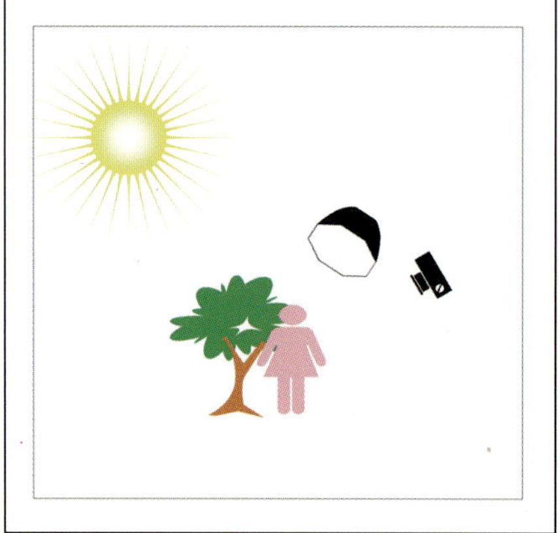

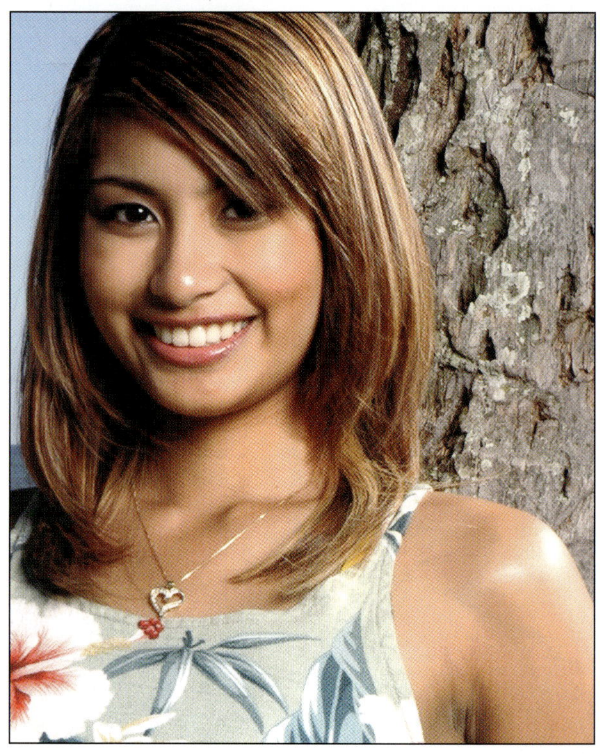

Top Left—We saw this image of Ruthchelle Melchor earlier when the potential difficulties of placing your subjects in the shade were discussed. Now we will examine one way to fix that problem and show what happens when you alter the power of the strobe without changing the shutter speed. **Top Right and Diagram—**In this image the combined light from the strobe and ambient shade was f11$^{7}/_{10}$, matching the light behind Ruth. The image is in balance with the backdrop, which is exposed beautifully along with Ruth's skin tones. **Right—**Unfortunately, the strobe and ambient light weren't balanced for the highlights created by the direct sunlight: a close-up version of the same setup shows that the highlights on Ruth's skin are a little hotter than you may like, even though the distant shot looked good. The sun acted as an edge light or a non-front light and needed to be metered with the dome pointed right at the sun.

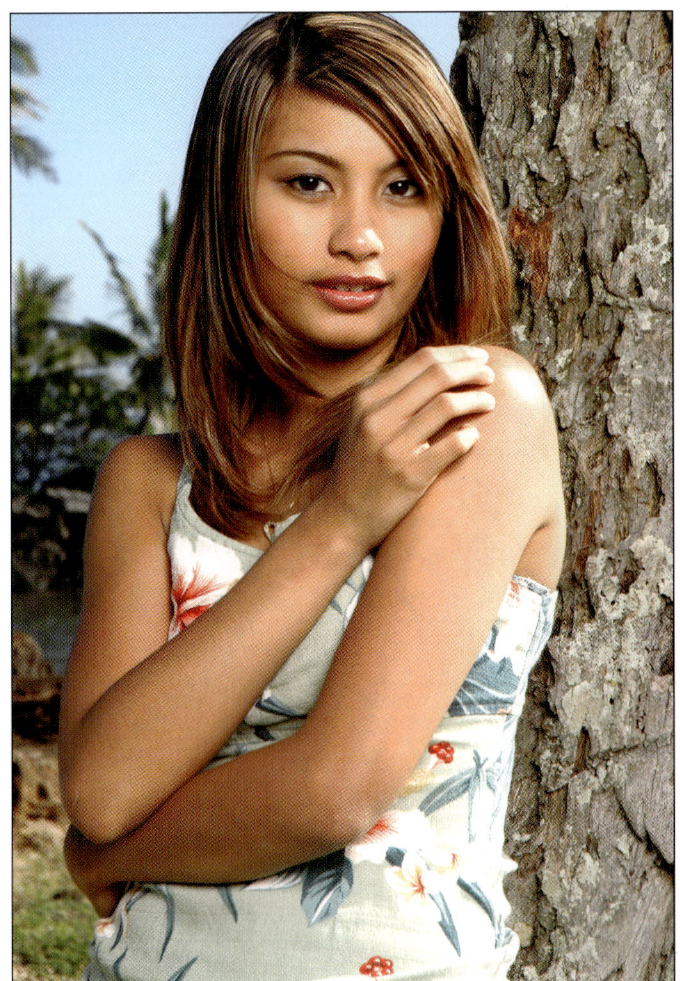

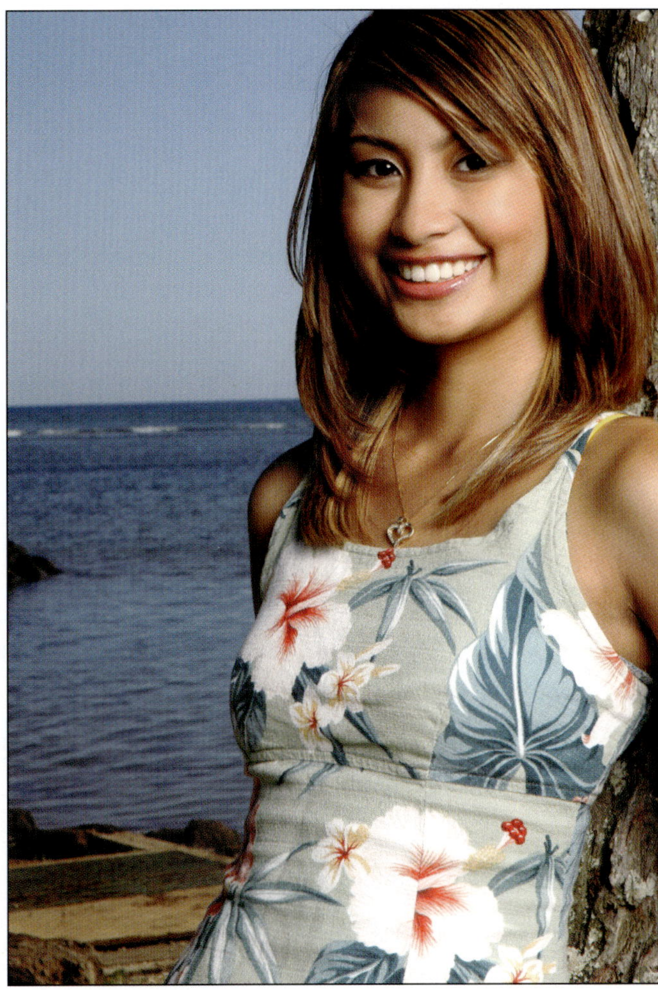

Left—For this shot, we dropped the power of the strobe by 1 stop. The combined light for the main exposure was f$8^{8}/_{10}$, which was a stop less than the backdrop. However, the strobe is still the main light in this image because it still 2 stops more light than the light in the open shade, but the backdrop is 1 stop lighter. However, you can see that the lighter backdrop comes at a high cost: now the direct sunlight creating the rim light is way too hot as we have lost detail in Ruth's skin tones around her hands, shoulders, and nose. We've been talking throughout this entire volume about how narrow the exposure range is for digital capture—here you see it clearly: 1 stop makes a pretty picture almost useless! **Right—**Next we bumped up the strobe to read a combined exposure of f$16^{2}/_{10}$, which is a $^{1}/_{2}$ stop more light than the backdrop. Ruth is still nicely exposed, and the backdrop is a little more saturated than in earlier photographs. The hot spot on Ruth's shoulder is not blown out either. So, you can make some major changes to your photographs by varying the power of your strobe, i.e., altering the f-stop.

your strobe and its distance from your subject constant but change the shutter speed.

It was noted earlier in this book that open shade could be a very effective way of creating a beautiful portrait when sunlight is too harsh. The shady areas provide beautifully soft light that still has some direction to it. Open shade can be a very effective way to soften the effects of high overhead sunlight—if your background is not lit by the open sunlight. You'll have a great deal of difficulty capturing a soft portrait if your subject is lit with open shade and your background is in sunlight. The proper exposure in the shade can be at least 2 to 3 stops less than the backdrop. Your carefully chosen location with the stunning background will look almost like a white seamless backdrop because you have opened your aperture to expose for your subject and grossly overexposed the backdrop. A reflector will not be of much use here because it is unlikely that you would bounce 3 stops of light back into the shade to illuminate your subjects.

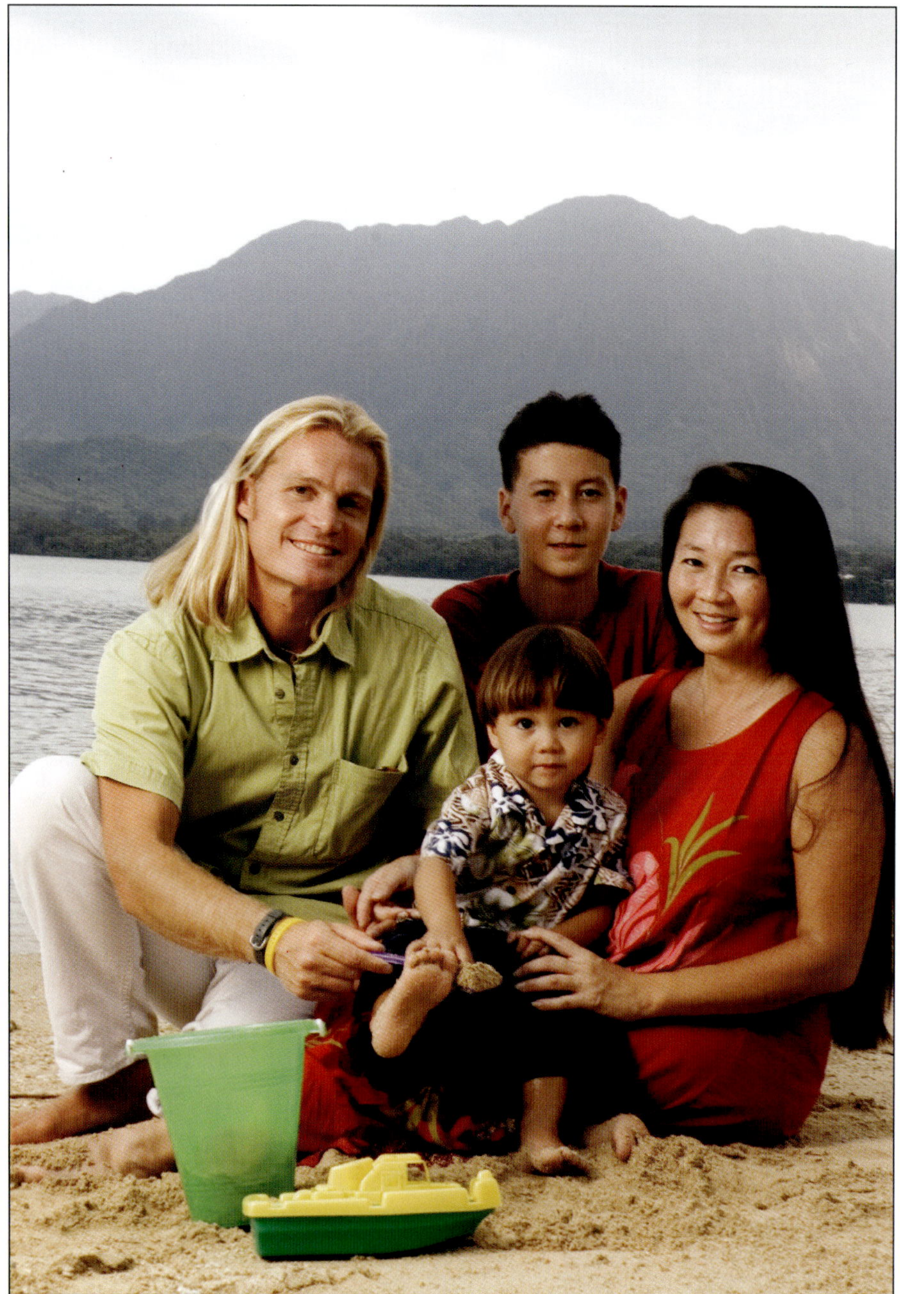

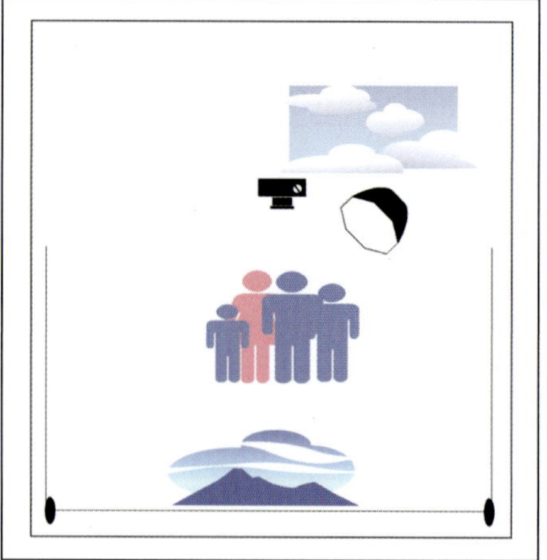

This portrait was taken on a day when the sun came in and out of the clouds. The images created before this one were brightly backlit, so the shutter speed was set at $^1/_{250}$ second. Thick clouds rolled in, and the ambient reading became about f2.8 at $^1/_{250}$. I wanted a working aperture of about f8, so I slowed the shutter speed down 2 stops to $^1/_{60}$ second. The equivalent aperture for this scene is f5.6 (the shutter is opening and closing four times slower than at $^1/_{250}$, so the aperture needs to be four times smaller than f2.8. The $^1/_{250}$ at f2.8 combination is the same as $^1/_{125}$ at f4 and $^1/_{60}$ at f5.6). Now it becomes possible to add the strobe to create the desired ratio—and a sense of direction to the light. The strobe was set at f5.6, creating a 2:1 lighting ratio, which looks natural given the cloudy conditions.

The key once again is to use a strobe to raise the light level in the shade to match the light illuminating the background. You are now in control over the balance between the combined light on your subject and your background. You can choose to have your subject in balance with the backdrop or render him or her lighter or darker than your backdrop.

There have been several examples so far that have shown that using a strobe and controlling your shutter speed can darken a too-bright backdrop. However, using your shutter speed to control the look of the background is not only important with a bright backdrop. Sometimes you'll have a darker backdrop that will go black if it is not carefully blended with the light from the strobe. Meter the scene behind your subject to determine what you will need to record detail behind your subject. At this point you have a reading of the ambient light alone, so you can choose an equivalent exposure that will suit your needs and will combine with your strobe to create a pleasant image. For example, if your ambient reading was f2.8 at $^1/_{250}$ and you wanted to shoot at f8, you would need to choose a different—but equivalent—ambient exposure. In order to obtain an exposure of f8 at $\frac{1}{250}$ second you would need to set your strobe at f8. Your strobe would be 3 stops brighter than the ambient light and would result in a harsh 9:1 ratio and a black background. However, working with equivalent exposures for the ambient light balances the equation, creating a more pleasing lighting ratio and maintaining detail in the background.

I often find it easier to understand the relationship between light sources by looking at the actual exposures rather than the ratios. In the example below, the strobe (tucked once again in the halo-style softbox) added about $\frac{2}{3}$ stop to the overall exposure, so the strobe was actually set less than the ambient light. In this case (below) the strobe is not quite a co-main light, so it acts as a fill light, even though it has an apparent impact on the image.

There are times when you will need to control a backlit scene, but you won't have the luxury of finding open shade. Jenny and her son (next page) were photographed on a west-facing beach on Oahu, Hawaii. The sun was beginning its decline, so it was well behind our subjects when we arrived at the shoot. As in the example on pages 82–83, a meter reading into the ocean read f11$\frac{7}{10}$ at $\frac{1}{250}$ second. The light metered

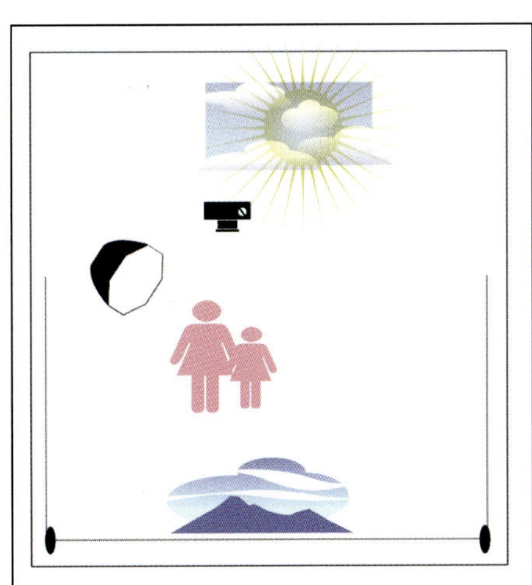

Nanette and Savannah were photographed under partly cloudy skies in a beautiful park on Oahu, Hawaii. The ambient light read f5.6$\frac{4}{10}$–f5.6$\frac{6}{10}$ at $\frac{1}{125}$ second, depending on the clouds. The combined exposure was f9, so the exposure of the strobe was just under f5.6. The strobe added the needed snap to the image but didn't overwhelm the background. The image was exposed at f8.

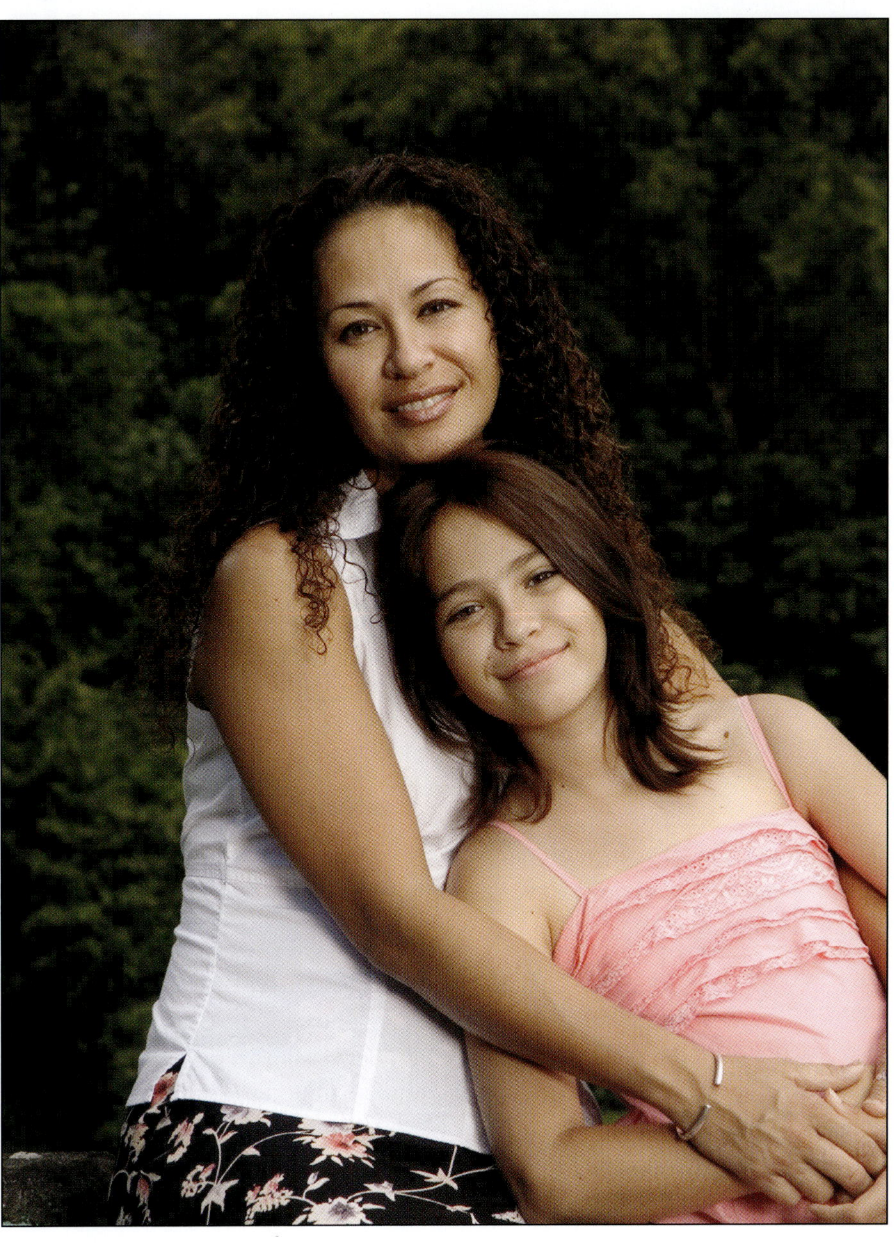

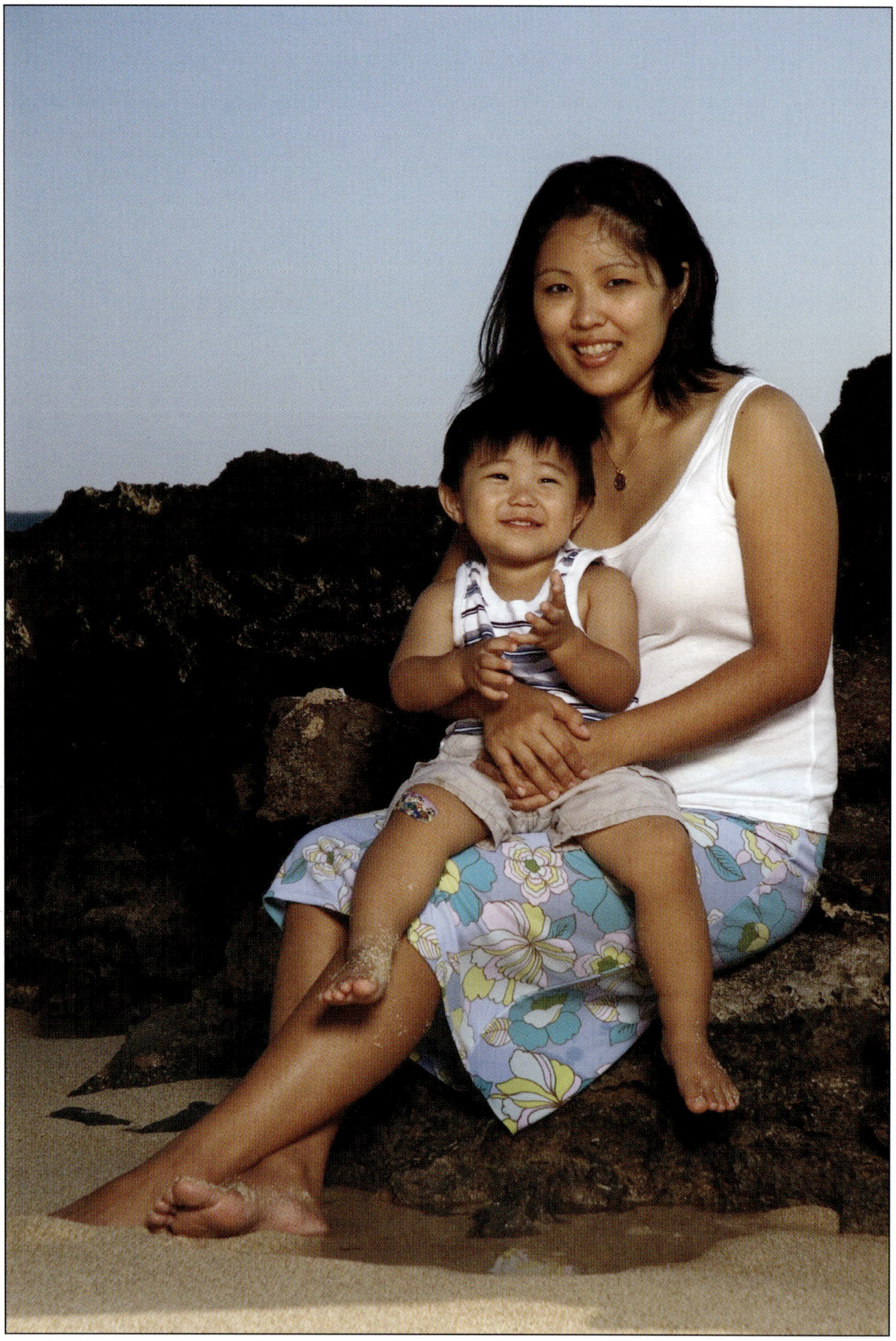

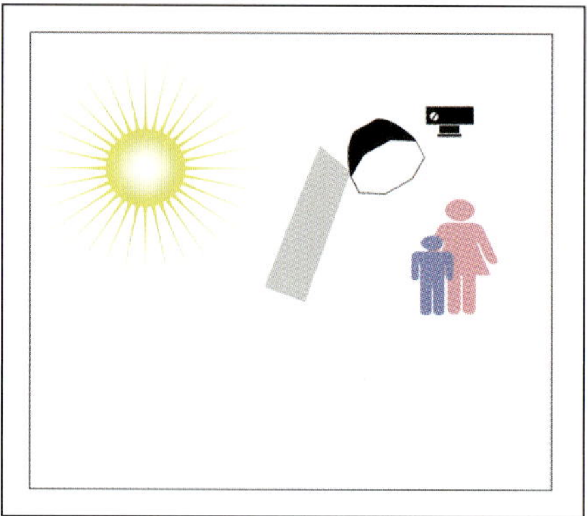

The main light for this "sun drenched" portrait is actually a strobe fit into a halo softbox. The sun was beginning to set behind Jenny and her boy. We used a scrim and a strobe to "switch" the direction of light. The strobe was carefully balanced with the backdrop to create the illusion of a sunlit beach scene!

toward the camera read about f5.6 4/10 or f5.6 5/10 tenths at 1/250 second. We would have gotten a similarly bad image if we set the camera at these values. A strobe would have helped, but the sun behind Jenny was still harsh and loaded with contrast, and it would have been extremely difficult to maintain the highlights in her white shirt with such a strong back light. We created our own open shade by using a scrim. My assistant (bravely) stood on some sharp (and wet) lava rocks behind Jenny. The large scrim softened the backlight beautifully but cut the light falling on our subjects by another stop or so. Now a strobe tucked into a halo-type softbox was introduced on the right side of the camera. At full power the strobe–ambient combination read f8 3/10 at 1/250 second—still 1 1/2 less than the light behind them. I simply changed the shutter speed to 1/500 second (which then gave me an aperture reading of f8 1/10) and shot the image. The backdrop is still about 1/2 stop overexposed, but the image now looks like the sun was in front of Jenny and her boy.

Earlier we looked at using a scrim to soften the light from the still too harsh afternoon sun. It was noted that scrims will have different effects depending on the fabric (or thickness of the fabric) used to make the scrim. One image of Brooke Tanaka (page 68) was acceptable and needed only the addition of a reflector to create a more pleasing image. The image of Cheryl (first seen on page 69 and repeated here for reference), however, is not acceptable for a location portrait—she may as well have been photographed against a seamless white background. A reflector would not bounce enough light back to bring up the washed-out background. A strobe was needed to bring back Diamondhead and Honolulu Harbor.

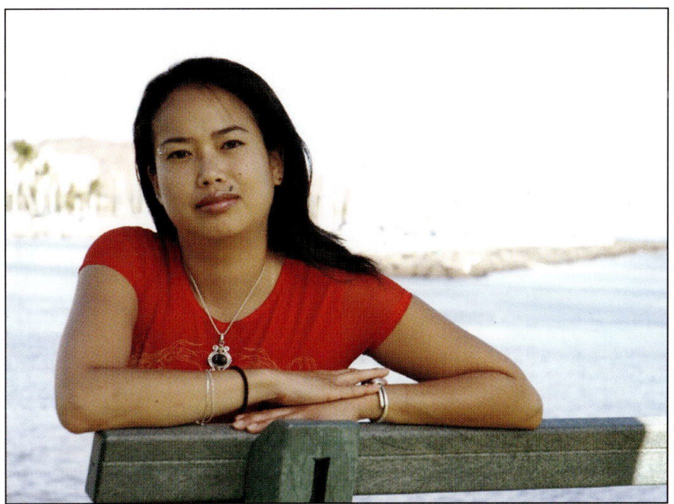

Right—The initial image was unacceptable. **Below—**A strobe was tucked into a halo-style softbox and positioned in line with the sun to match the shadows created by both light sources. My assistant held a 42-inch round scrim out of camera range. The exposure at Cheryl's cheek was f5 at $^{1}/_{250}$ while the background was around f11$^{1}/_{2}$! The light under the scrim is about 3 stops under the working aperture, so the ambient light would add a minimal amount to the exposure established by the strobe. We set the strobe at f11$^{1}/_{2}$, and suddenly we were back on location in Honolulu!

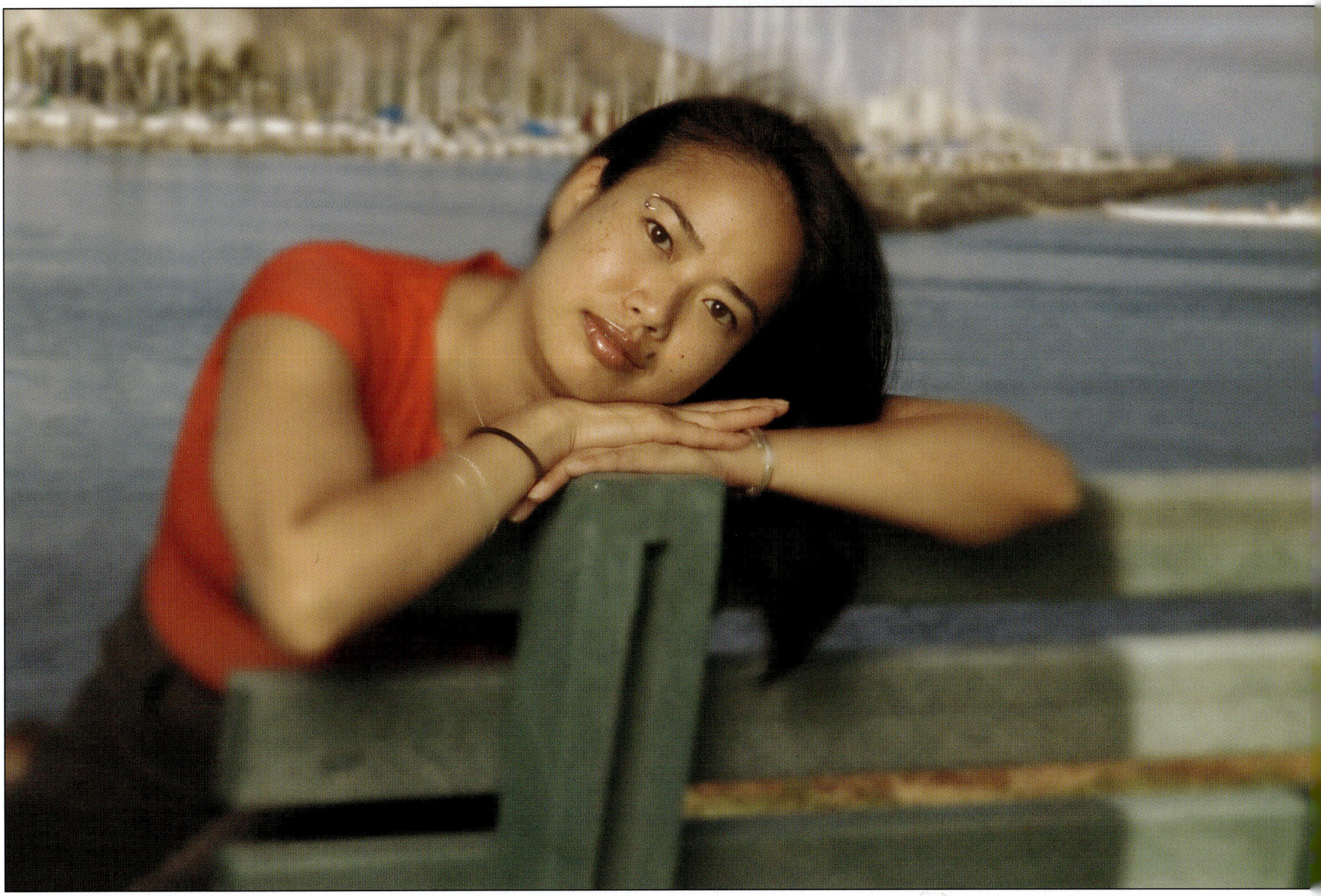

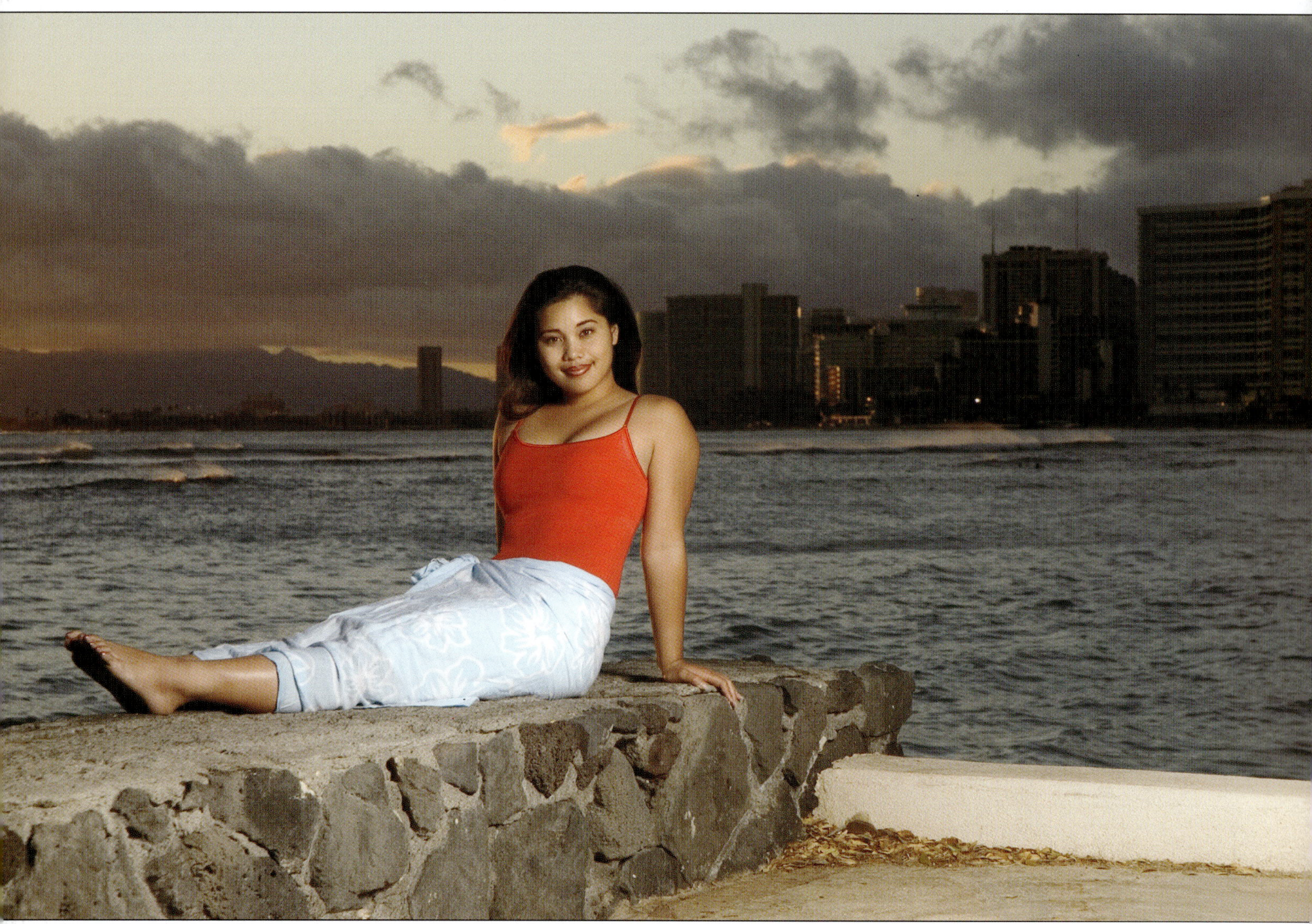

Above—The image of Debbie Brown, taken as the sun set by Waikiki, Hawaii, was created using a strobe to establish the main exposure while a slow shutter speed allowed enough detail to render the background recognizable. The amber hue of the whitecaps in the water was due to the low color temperature of the setting sun. **Facing Page—**Paul Gero expertly combined light and the lines in his location to draw us into this beautiful wedding portrait. What appears to be a formal, posed image actually occurred on the fly. The flash is the main light in this image and creates the lightest part of the image. Your eye is naturally drawn to the point of highest contrast in an image, which in this case is the couple. The flash is a great deal brighter than the ambient light surrounding the couple, and this could have easily resulted in an image with no detail in the background. Paul slowed the shutter speed to allow the ambient light to record and show the beautiful location. Dragging the shutter can create situations where the ambient light can add to the exposure established by the strobe, but this was probably not an issue for this shot. Paul used the LCD preview screen to judge when he had enough detail in the background. The image was shot at f2.8 at $^{1}/_{13}$ second with an ISO rating of 800.

Debbie Brown (above) was photographed as the sun set behind Waikiki, Hawaii. The light behind her was far less than what the strobe added to the scene, so without some care the backdrop would easily go black. The backdrop was brought back by "dragging the shutter," or shooting with a slow shutter speed. The slow shutter speed allowed some detail to show in the buildings of Waikiki, and the aperture controlled the exposure created by the strobe.

The following two images were created by Paul Gero and show the different effects that can be obtained by changing your shutter speed when com-

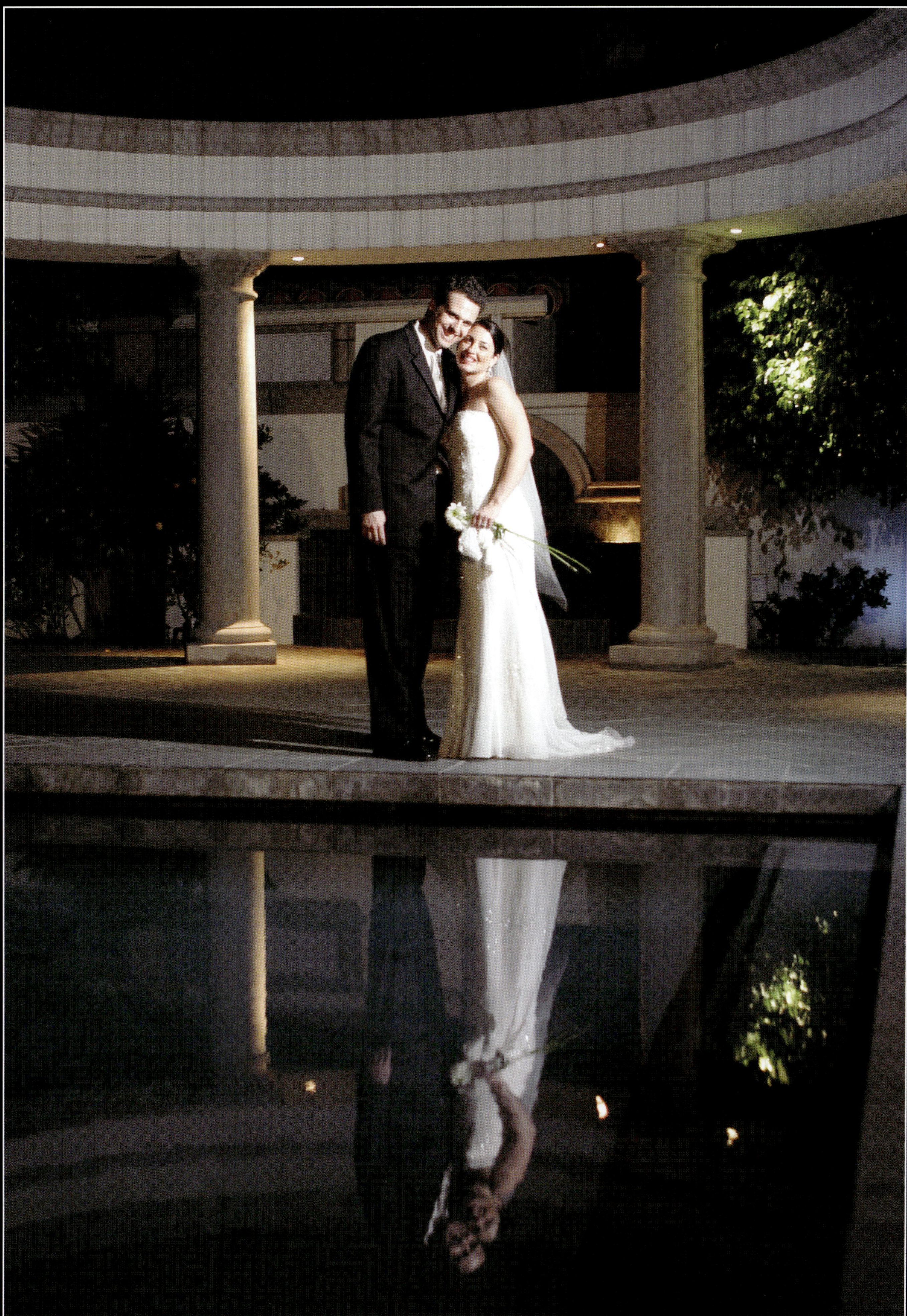

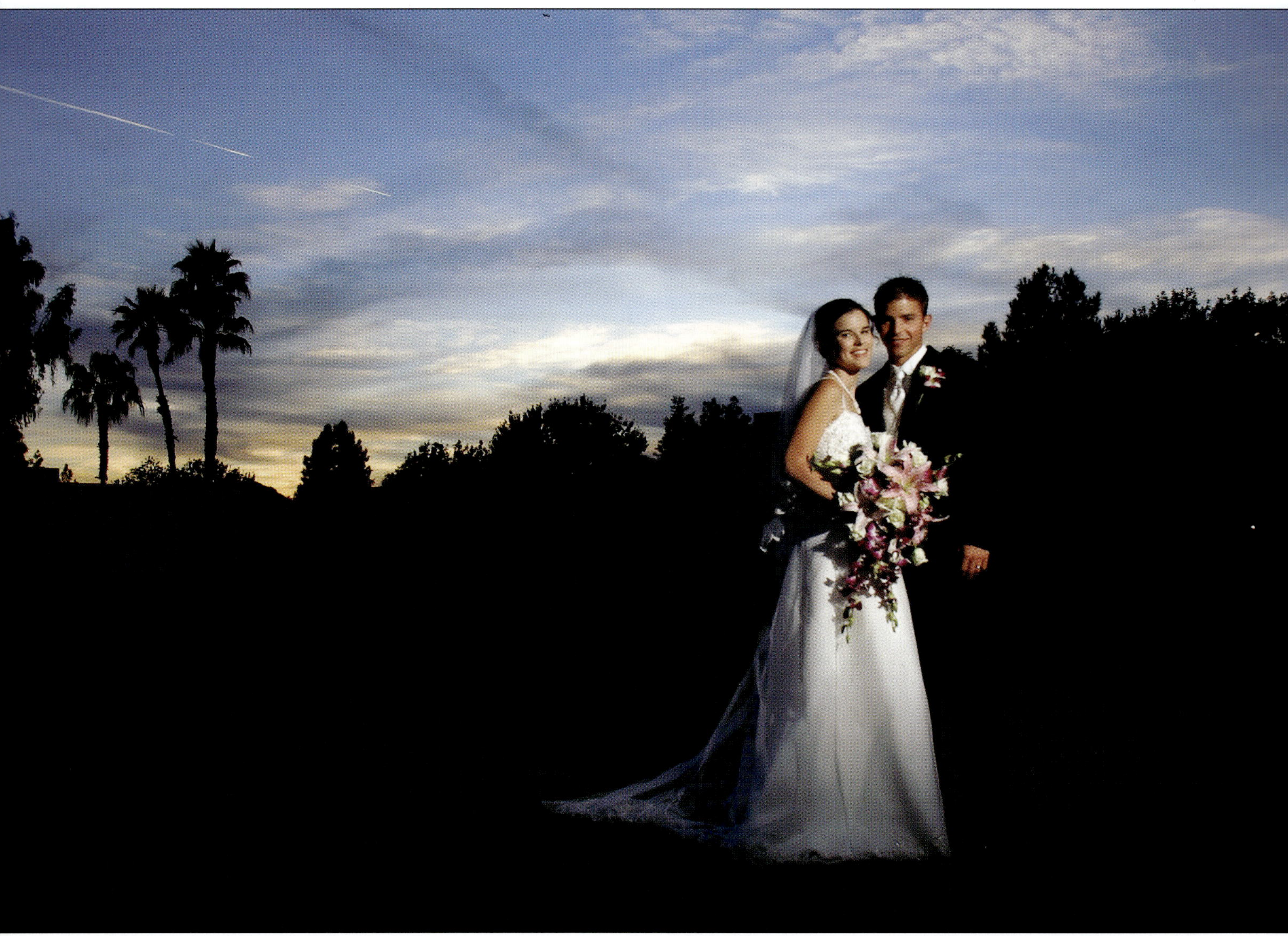

Paul Gero chose a faster shutter speed to ensure that the trees went dark without detail, creating a silhouette against the sky. Underexposing the backdrop also added some richness to the sky and helped bring out the clouds. The main light was a small handheld flash with a plastic diffuser. Paul likes the strong directional quality of the small light.

bining strobes with ambient light. Both images were created with a small handheld flash off camera and positioned on the right side of the camera. Paul's wife Nicki literally handheld the flash unit. The flash was modified with a small plastic diffuser but was still a harsh light source. Paul likes to use strong directional light when he can. He sees the diagonal pattern that the light creates as an important design element his images. The main exposure for both images was determined by a good camera-flash TTL system, but the background control was determined by what Paul previsualized and by modifying the shutter speed.

The first image (previous page) was created by "dragging" the shutter speed. A moderate to fast shutter would have created a black backdrop and would have resulted in a somewhat pleasing snapshot of the couple. Paul slowed the shutter speed down, allowing him to record detail behind the couple, creating the elegant wedding portrait. The couple is positioned in the middle of the scene, but the other design elements in the image keep it from becoming a static pose. A series of repeated patterns are held together by the sweeping arc of the building. The lines in this image could easily have become distracting but instead are used to lead the viewer's gaze to the couple. The pool is used to create a beautiful reflection—again creating repeated patterns—but is also used to draw us into the image. Paul allows us to explore the surroundings, but we ultimately wind up right where he wants us—looking at the couple.

The second image (facing page) was created not by dragging the shutter but rather by shooting with a fast shutter speed. In this case, detail in the background would have been distracting. Paul wanted the palm trees and the foliage to become silhouettes against the sky, but he also wanted to capture the mysterious sky.

Al Garcia used the shade of a tree to diffuse the bright sunlight in this portrait of the Donoher family. He used a fill flash to add a "pop" to his subjects' faces and to bring the background into a closer balance to the working aperture. The grass was still a bit hot, so I used the same layer blending mode technique shown in the introduction) to darken the grass a bit. This time, however, I changed the blending mode to Multiply, painted in the grass and the trees behind the family, and dropped the opacity of the masked layer to 30%. A few strokes with the healing brush and "voila!"

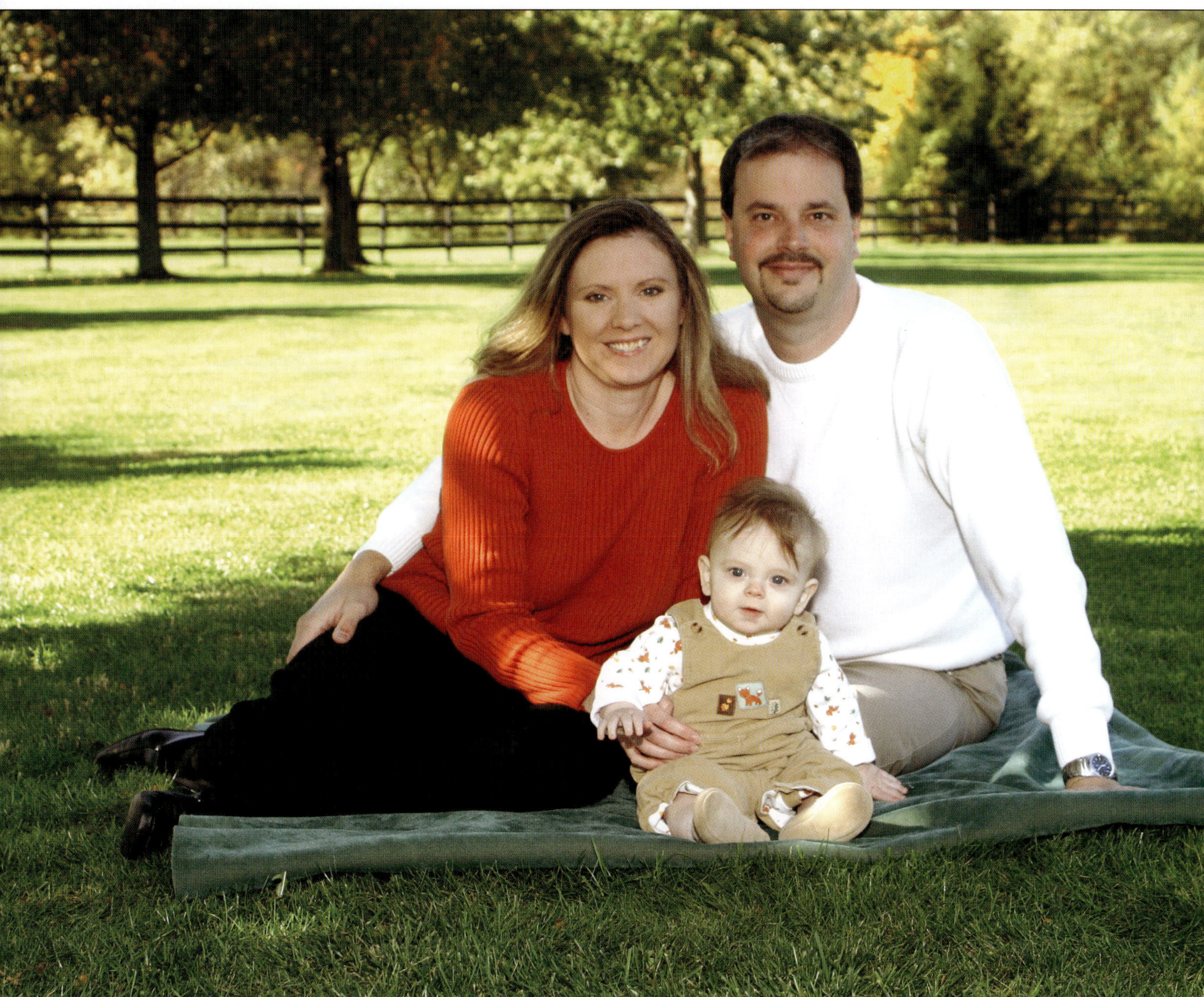

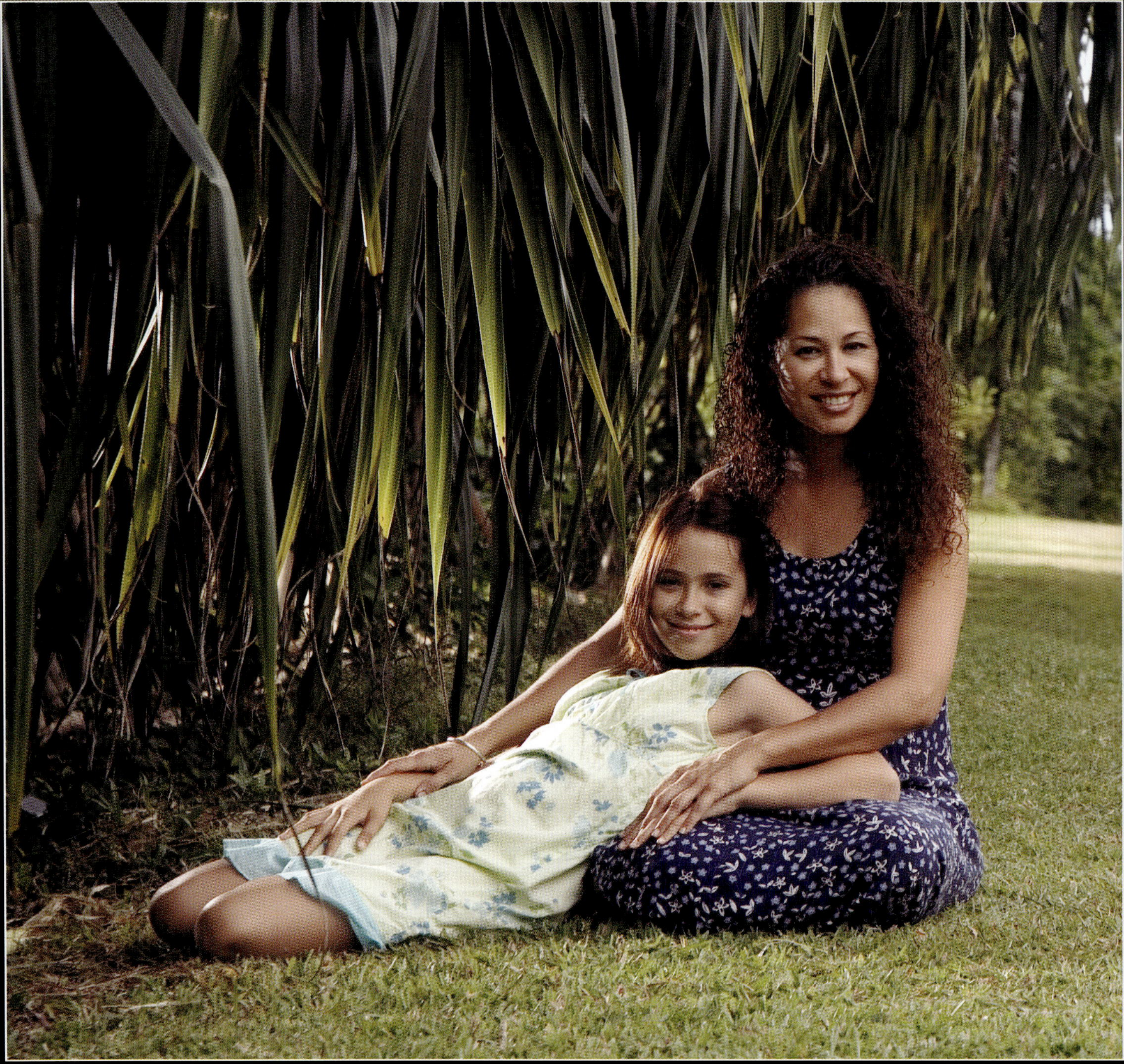

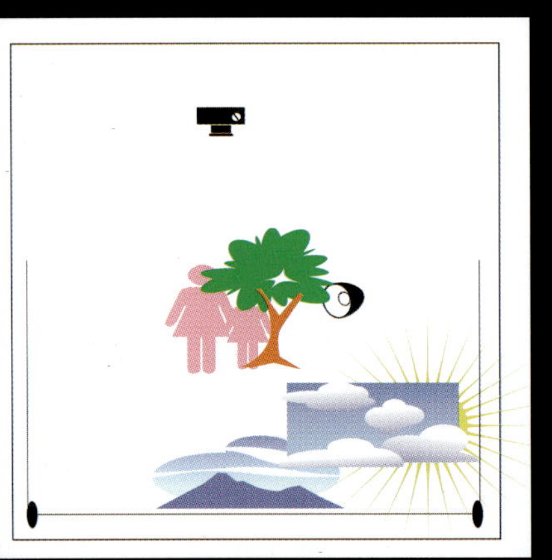

The exposure in the shade of the trees was f5.6 at 1/125 second. The lighting is consistent throughout the image because most of the scene was lit with the same light. There was a small section behind Nanette and Savannah where the light was more direct. However, a thick cloud cover also diffused that light, so it was not a great deal brighter than the open shade. The main source of contrast in the image came from a spotlight, fitted with a 20-degree gridspot, hidden behind the trees. The exposure at Nanette's hair was f5.6 and 1/10. The spotlight had so much more contrast than the surrounding light that we almost blew out the highlights even though it was only a 1/10-stop difference!

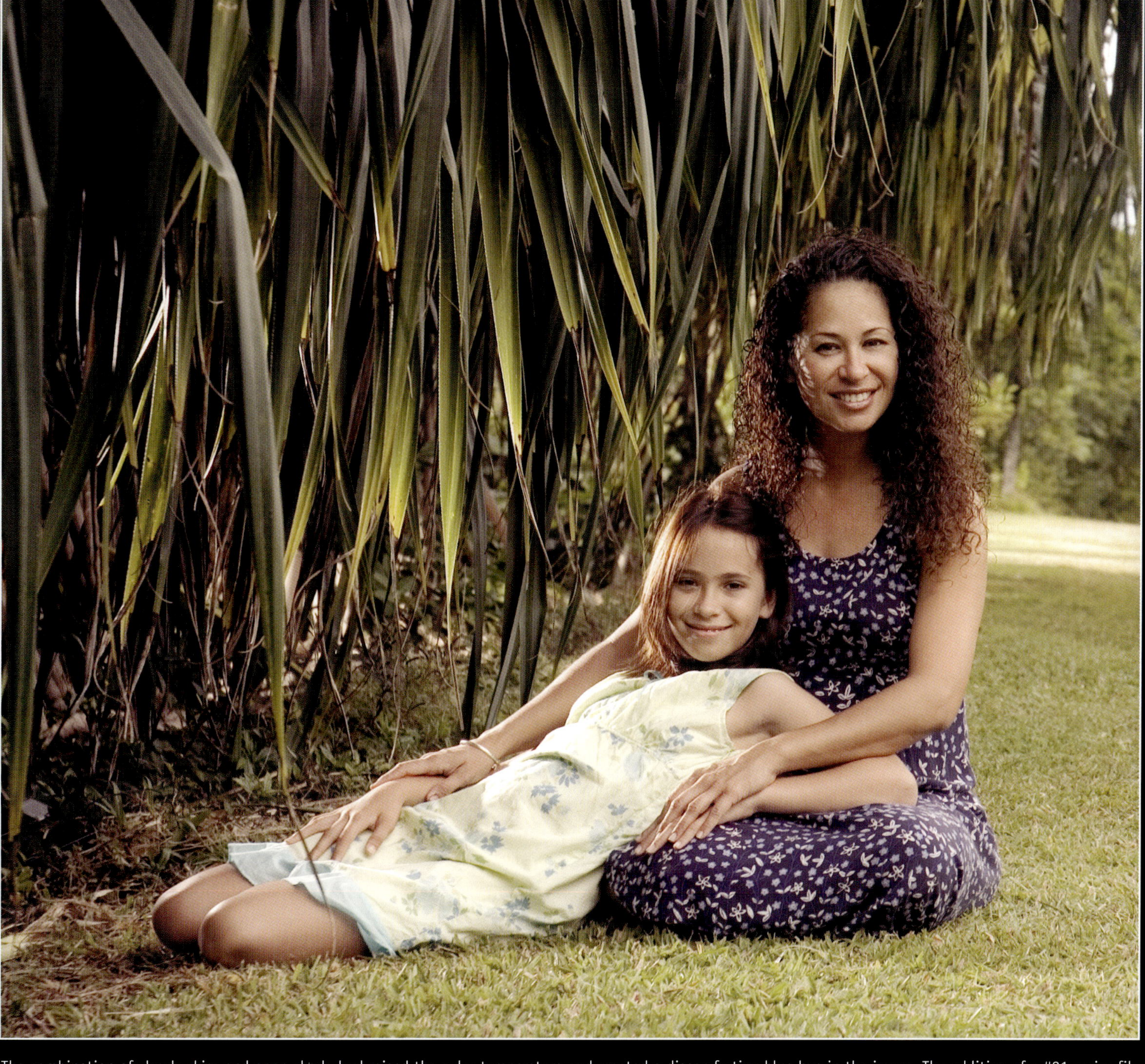

The combination of cloudy skies and open shade had raised the color temperature and created a discomforting blue hue in the image. The addition of a #81-series filter in Photoshop restores a nice healthy hue to Nanette and Savannah's skin tones.

This image was actually shot as a "digital Polaroid" to determine the proper balance for a shot recorded on film! Paul again used the preview mode to evaluate

THE VAST MAJORITY OF DIGITAL IMAGES NEED SOME COLOR CORRECTION.

when the image was getting close to what he had envisioned. He feels that the preview modes are useful but recommends exercising caution in using them to determine final exposure. He compares using a preview mode on a digital camera to when he used to develop and print black & white images. You get to a point where you know your darkroom well enough to be able to judge a black & white print under a safelight while it is still wet, but there is no comparison to switching on the overheads! He is even skeptical about relying on histograms and/or highlight clipping warnings on your camera because so many digital cameras are built to underexpose the image. Maintaining detail in the whites is certainly important to Paul, but he acknowledges that there will always be a tradeoff—especially with documentary wedding photography. His primary goal is to capture the moment and get good skin tones. He'll accept a little loss of detail in the dress as long as it is not too pronounced.

Strobes can be used to add a needed accent to an otherwise flat lighting scheme. The scene for the next image of Nanette and Savannah (previous two pages) was a beautiful park on the east side of Oahu, Hawaii. We liked the look of the trees in this section of the park. Positioning your subject within the shade of trees and bushes can be a very effective way to control harsh shadows from the direct sunlight. You do not need to worry about overexposing the background if what is behind your subject is lit with the same light that is illuminating your subject. The sun was behind a rather thick cloud cover by the time we got to the trees. However, there was still a sense of direction to the light coming in from their left. The addition of a hair/rim light helped provide the illusion of a bright sunny day and added the contrast needed to maintain visual interest.

Color temperature became an issue in this photograph for two reasons: (1) the family was positioned in open shade, a condition known to raise the color temperature of the light; and (2) the main source of light was cloudy skies, also known to raise the color temperature. The original image didn't look too bad, but the vast majority of digital images need some color correction. The photograph took on a nasty blue hue once the rest of it was color corrected. The fix was simple. I created a photo filter adjustment layer in Photoshop and chose a warming filter, in this case a #81, and set the density at 30%. Because the whole image needed to be warmed up, I did not erase any part of the adjustment layer.

FILL FLASH TECHNIQUES

The complex relationship between strobes and ambient light sources has been detailed thus far. However, there is a term that describes a commonly used technique. "Fill flash" techniques are often used to fill and soften shadows on sunny days and can be used to add light on cloudy days. By definition, any light source that adds less light than the main source of illumination is a fill source. While any size strobe/modifier can be used as a fill source, the term "fill flash" generally refers to using a handheld or on-camera flash unit.

Facing Page—This book has been about modifying and controlling light to fit your needs. Part of controlling the situation also lies in knowing your equipment well enough to know when it can provide you with a beautifully exposed image when it is not feasible to set up the shots as described above. Al Garcia relied on his camera's metering system and interface with the flash to capture a photograph that would have been lost if he had set up the scene. His engaging portrait of a young boy is a wonderful example of a photojournalistic approach to children's portraiture. As noted above, photojournalistic portrait artists do not necessarily have the luxury to set the lighting to the degree possible in a more formal portrait. Lighting concerns are still critical but play a secondary role to anticipating and "grabbing" the shot as it unfolds. Understanding light and knowing how to set your camera—and knowing when to trust your equipment—is an essential component in the photojournalist's ability to control the lighting.

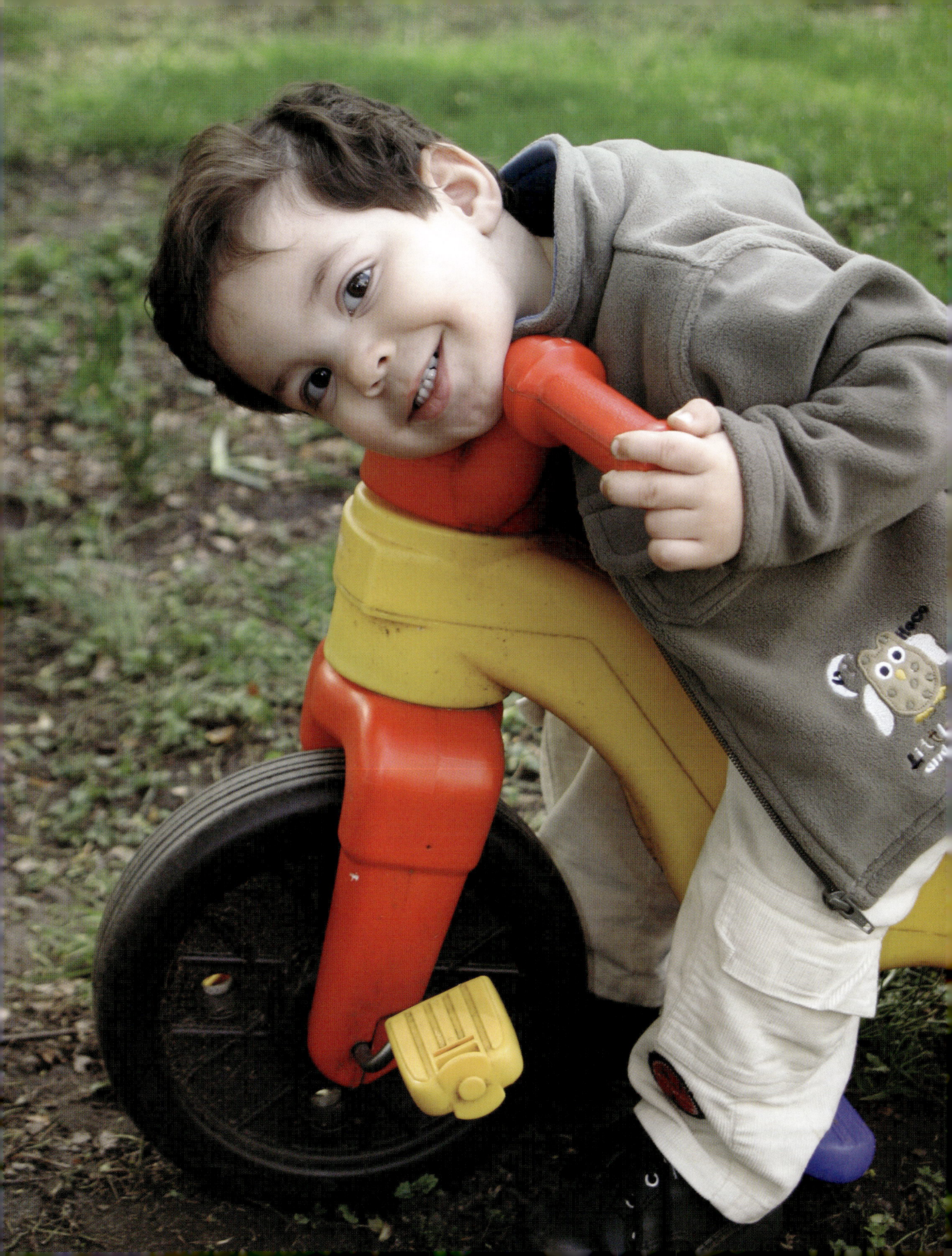

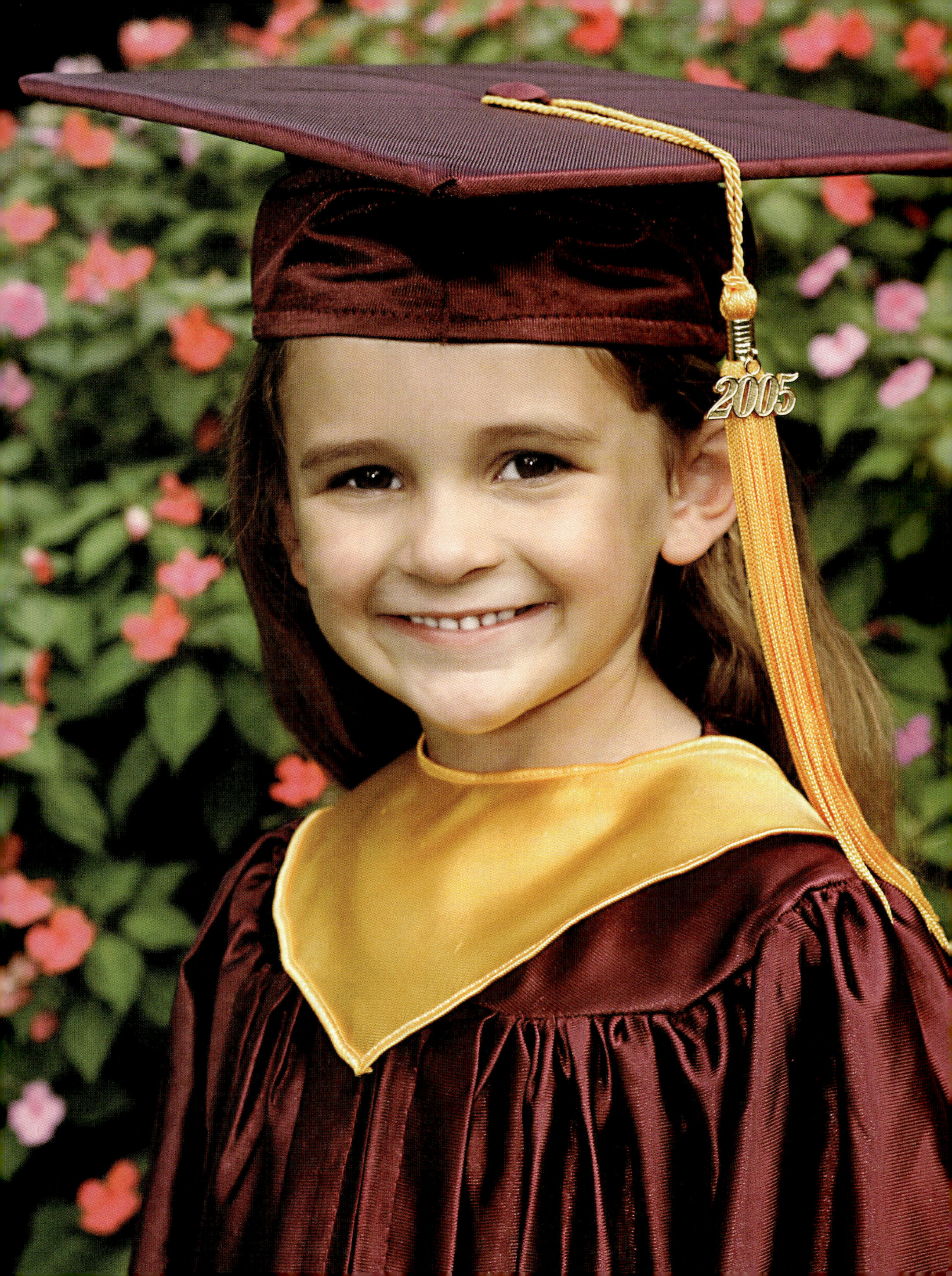
2005

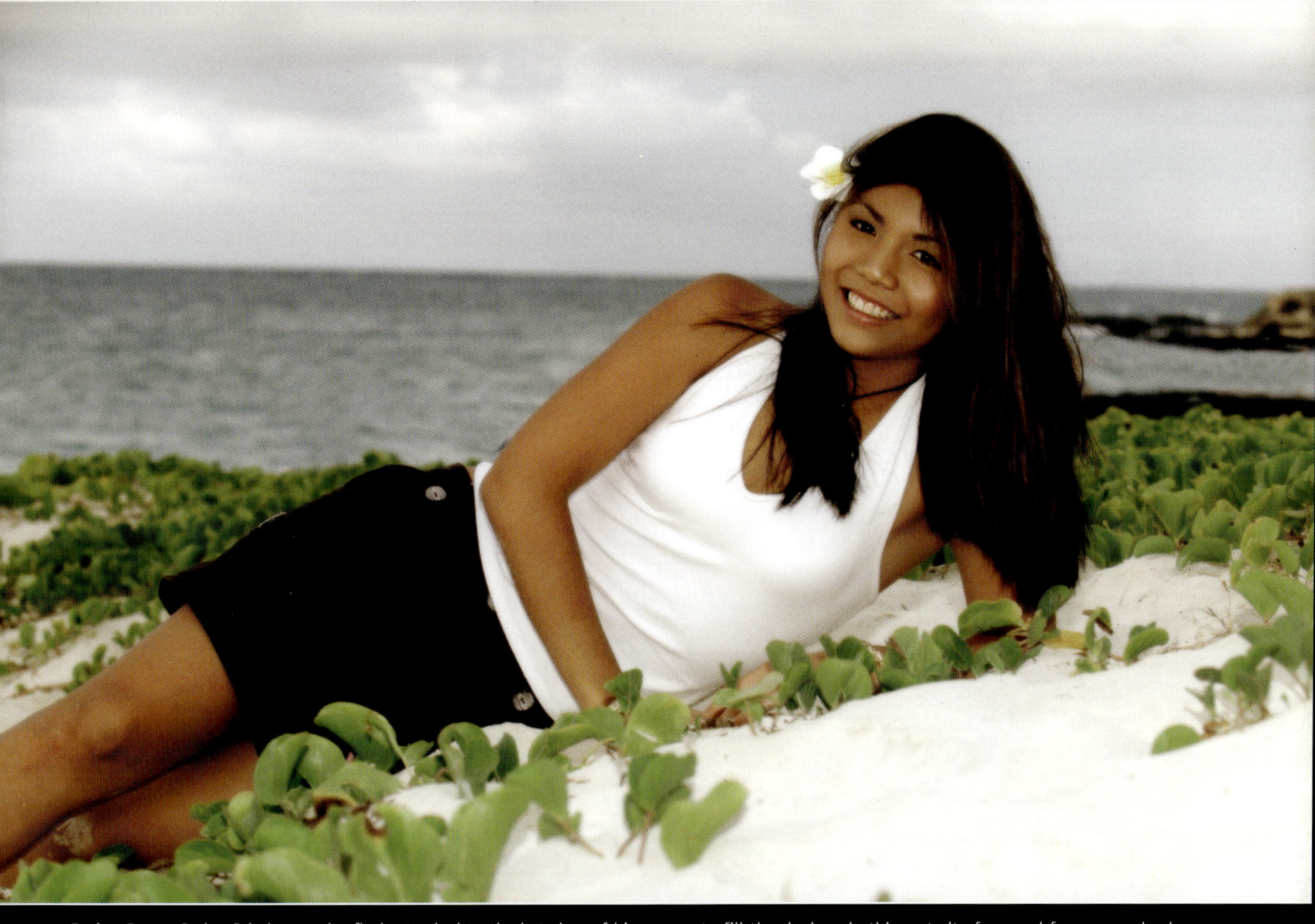

Facing Page—Parker Pritcher used a flash attached to the hot shoe of his camera to fill the shadows in this portrait of a proud former preschooler. He diffused the light from the flash with a plastic diffuser. **Above—**David Taylor used a similar technique at the opposite end of the school spectrum to capture this endearing senior portrait.

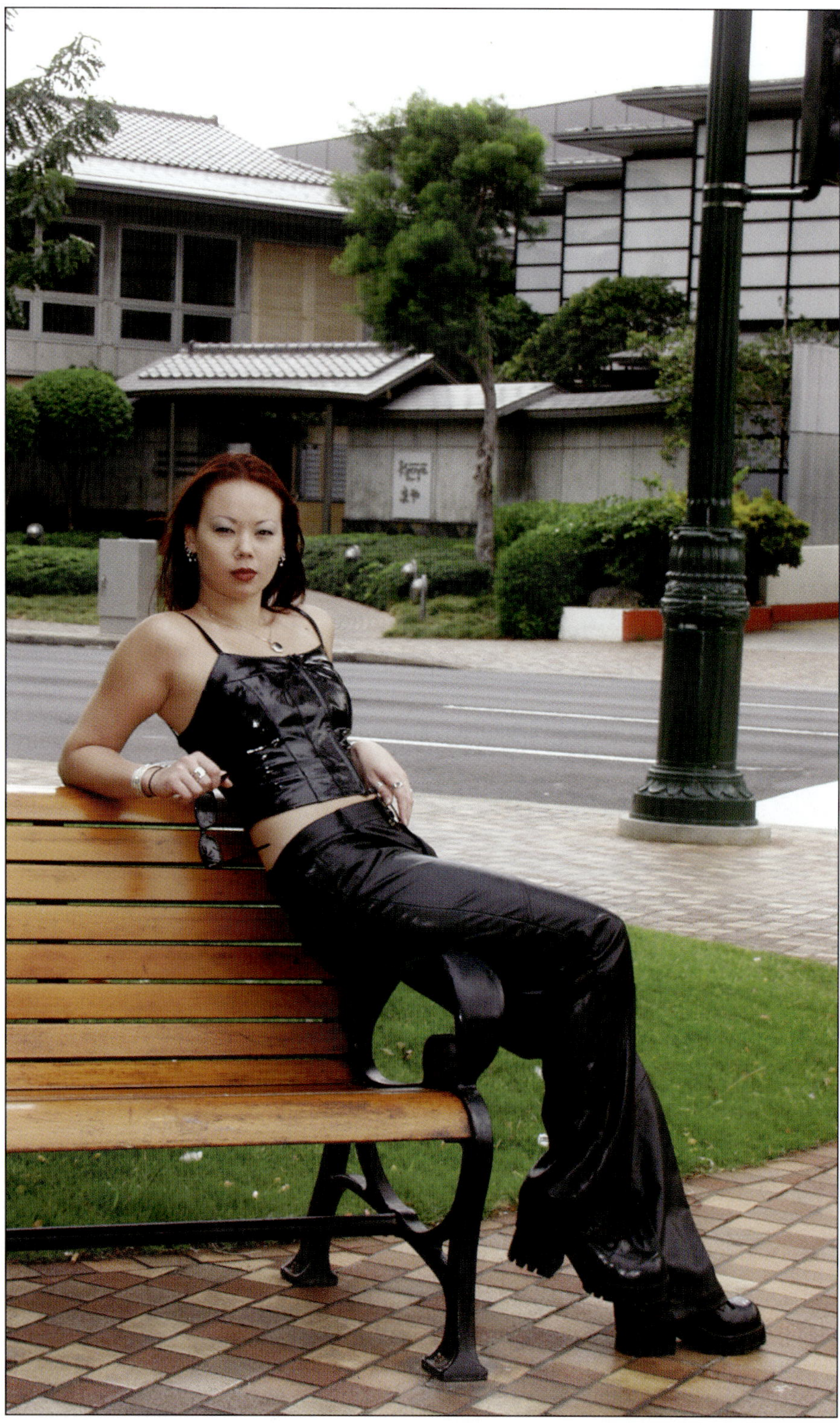

There may be times when you have no choice but to trust your equipment to get you out of a jam. Understanding the factors that might fool your system will help you decide to put the control in the "hands" of your equipment. Tanya was photographed on a flat, cloudy day, and the light behind her was no different from the light in front of her, so I knew that the camera's metering system would not be fooled. I set the camera's flash mode to between -1 and -2 stops and let the machine take over.

The on-camera flash is either supported off of the lens plane by using a bracket, or directly on or built into the camera. In other words, sources of fill flash tend to be very small light sources. Small light sources produce more contrast than larger light sources, so the balance between the fill and main light needs to be carefully controlled or the impact of the small flash will overpower the larger main light. However, the primary benefit of fill flash is the ease and portability of its use.

The examples in this chapter show some of the many applications of fill flash techniques. Many of the better digital cameras have controls to set the output of their built-in flash units, and other, more sophisticated handheld flashes operate in manual mode or in conjunction with the camera to output a specific ratio of light. Check your camera and flash manuals to determine how to set the desired output on your system.

The increased mobility that using a fill flash affords can be a great help when photographing young children, especially when you are taking a photojournalistic approach.

Al Garcia used the program mode with fill flash to create the absolutely charming portrait of a young boy shown on page 95. He offers these wise words: "When photographing children, you have to work fast! Therefore, I like to keep my lighting simple and extremely portable. Also, small children have a hard time keeping their eyes open, even in indirect sunlight. For this reason, I like to place them in the shade and rotate them as the sun comes around. I usually get my best results when the sun ducks behind a cloud and produces nice even light in the background . . . while I'm carrying on like a clown (to get the kids to look and sometimes smile). I change my shutter speed to control the brightness of my background as the sun goes in and out of the clouds."

However, fill flash can be used effectively in formal portraiture as well. Parker Pritcher used fill flash to soften the shadows in his adorable portrait of a young graduate (page 96). The light from the flash was set at ½ stop less than the ambient light. A flash that is set at 1 stop less than the ambient light would add ½ stop to the exposure, so Parker's system added ¾ stop to the equation. The flash is technically still a fill flash, but the increased contrast of the small light source makes it appear to be more of a co–main light. Parker softened the contrast of the small light by placing a plastic diffuser over the strobe.

Built-in "pop-up" strobes can even be used in a pinch to create effective portraits. In this case the fashionable portrait of Tanya (left) was created on a cloudy day with flat light. The full set of "location" gear was 3000 miles away, so it was time to improvise. This was one of those times to trust the equipment! The flat lighting would not create many difficulties for the camera's metering system, and the camera had settings that controlled the output of the built-in flash. The flash was set between -1 and -2 stops to provide less light than the ambient light, and the camera was set to program mode.

BARE BULB

Bare bulb is a technique that is often successful in a fill flash situation. The best source for a fill is one that does not alter the impact or direction of the main light. When used properly, barebulb flash fits this definition perfectly. A bare bulb is one where the light is completely unmodified and extends evenly from the light source in 360 degrees. It is, however, a very small light source and produces light with a lot of contrast, so it should be used with caution; on page 34 we saw an example in which the light from the bare bulb had too much contrast for the scene and overpowered the softer light from cloudy skies. For another example of this technique, see pages 100–101.

SHOOTING SUNSETS

Sunsets often provide beautiful backdrops for outdoor portraits. Balancing the light illuminating your subject and getting a rich, colorful sunset is not as difficult as it may seem. The way to obtain rich, deep colors in your sunset is to underexpose the background.

GETTING A RICH, COLORFUL SUNSET IS NOT AS DIFFICULT AS IT MAY SEEM.

Therefore, the spill and wraparound light from the setting sun will not be much of a factor in your main exposure. Your main exposure will need to come from a strobe because there will not be enough light to bounce back with a reflector—especially when shooting at the shutter speeds you'll need to capture the sunset. A larger light source (e.g., a strobe in a softbox or halo) will provide a more natural look, but these images will almost always appear to be lit by a strobe.

Your main exposure will be based on the output of your strobe. Your strobe will set the f-stop. The colors of the sunset are controlled by the shutter speed. Changing the shutter speed will affect the amount of ambient light that will be added to the strobe to produce the actual main exposure. However, in practice, the amount of light added by the ambient source will be minor. You might see a slight difference in the shadows, but it is unlikely that there will be a noticeable difference in the skin tones. The images shown on pages 102–3 demonstrate the effects of changing your shutter speed to obtain sunsets of different saturations.

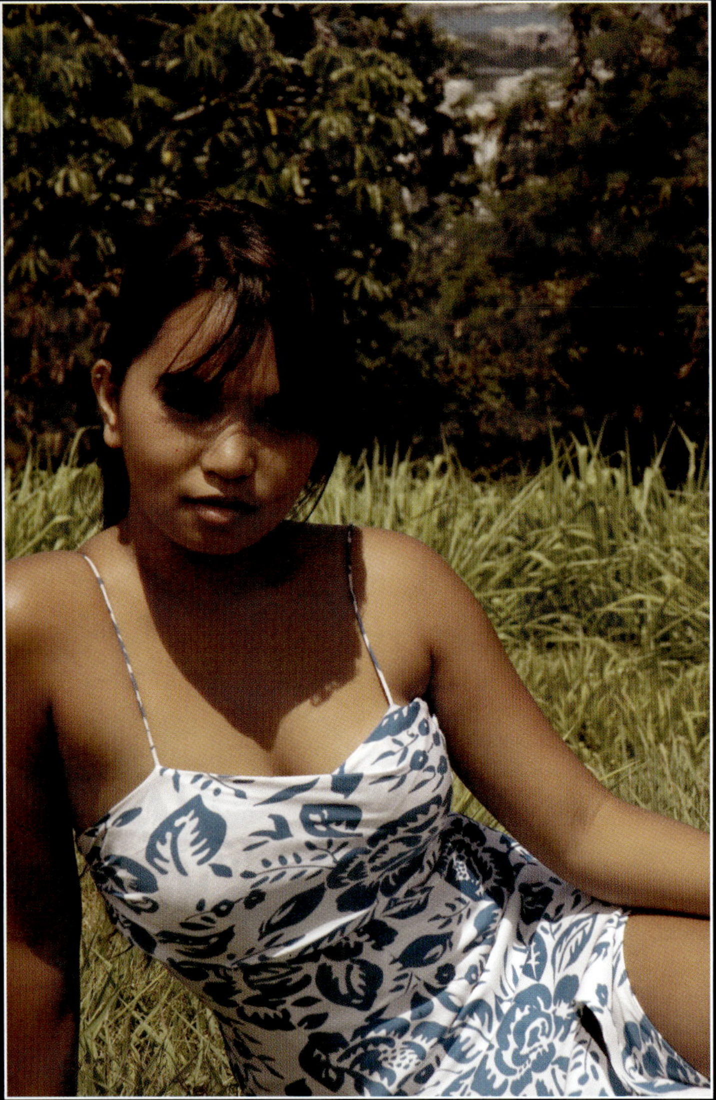

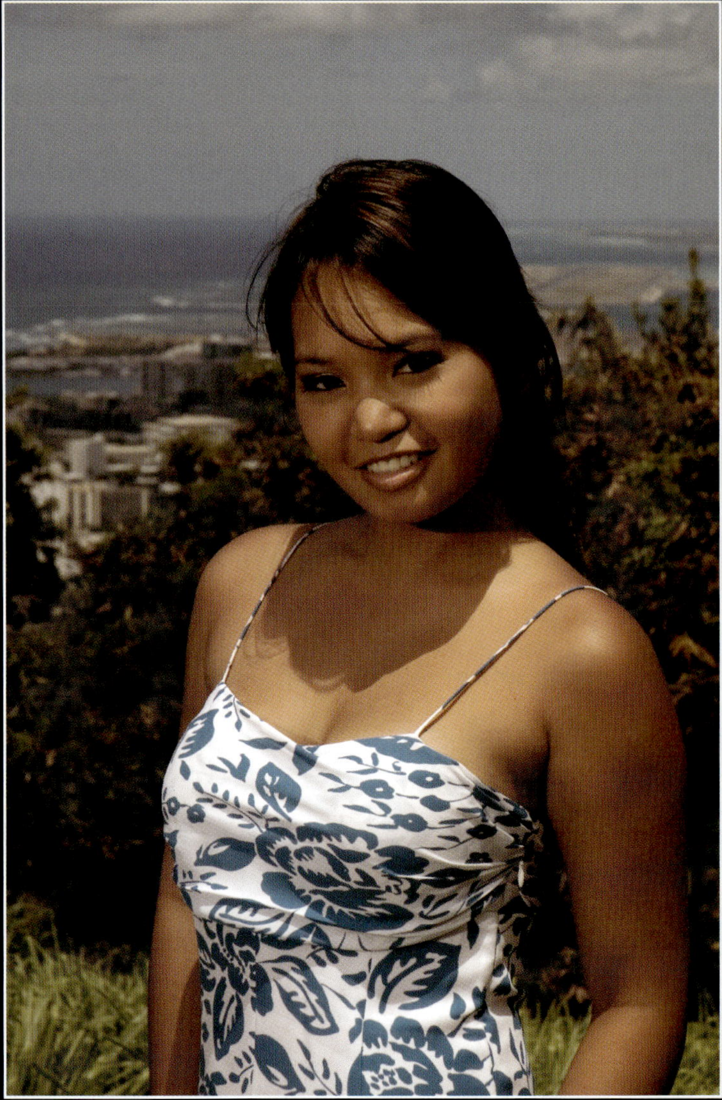

Here is yet another example of the ugly effects of overhead sunlight (left). This time we modified the situation by adding light to fill the shadows via a bare-bulb strobe (we pointed the monohead I was using straight up in the air and left the flash tube unobstructed). The flash added $^{1}/_{2}$ stop to the equation, so it was 1 stop less than the ambient light. The addition of the strobe makes this a decent photograph that was made better with some simple retouching in Photoshop (right). However, the best solution to creating a pleasing photograph of Teresa Bringas at this problematic location (facing page) was to put the strobes away and bring out a silver/gold reflector!

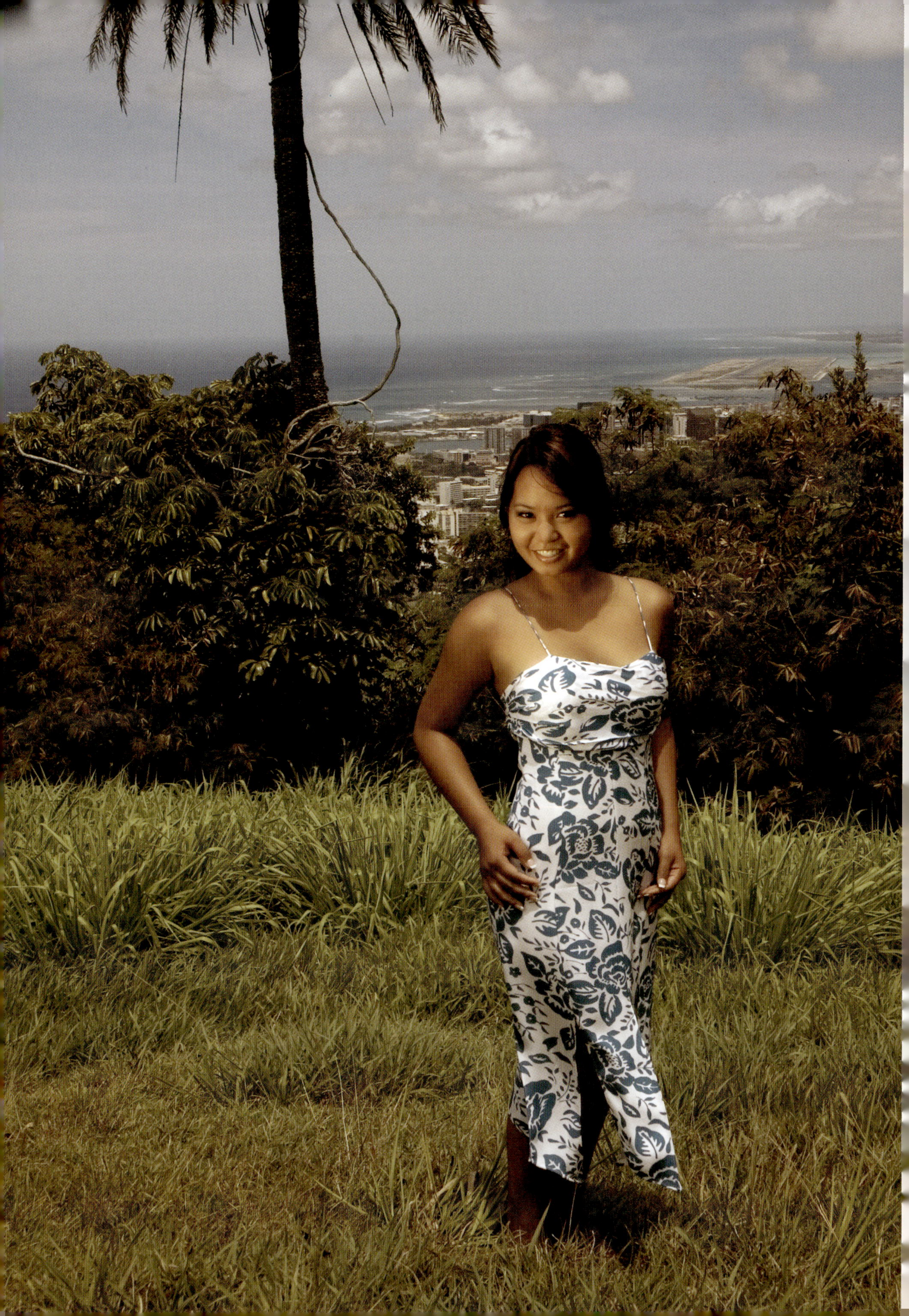

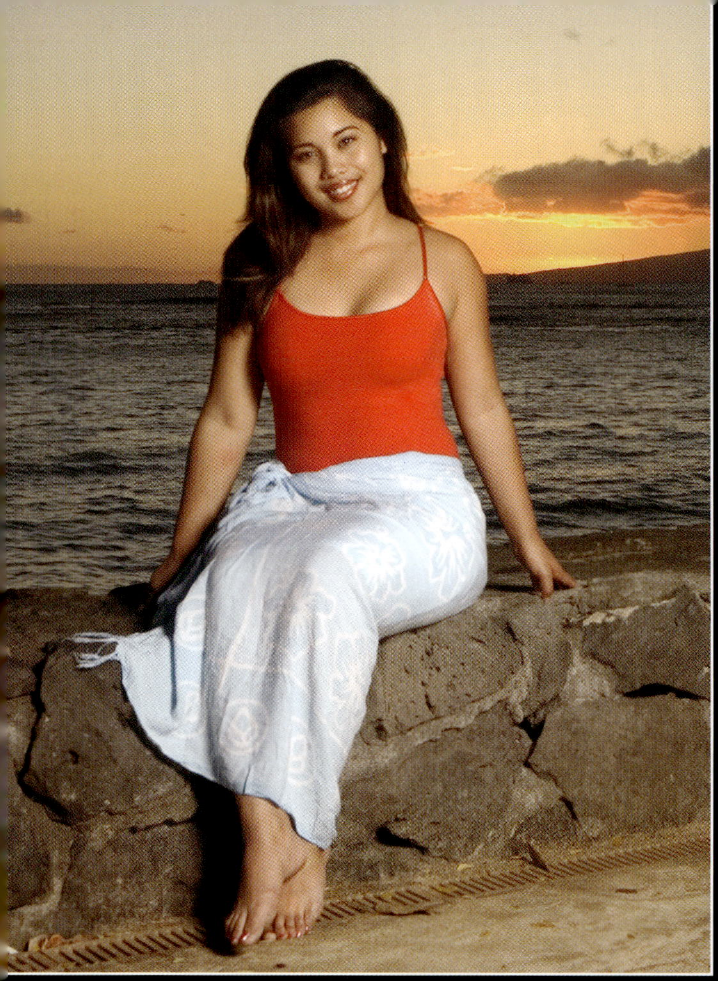

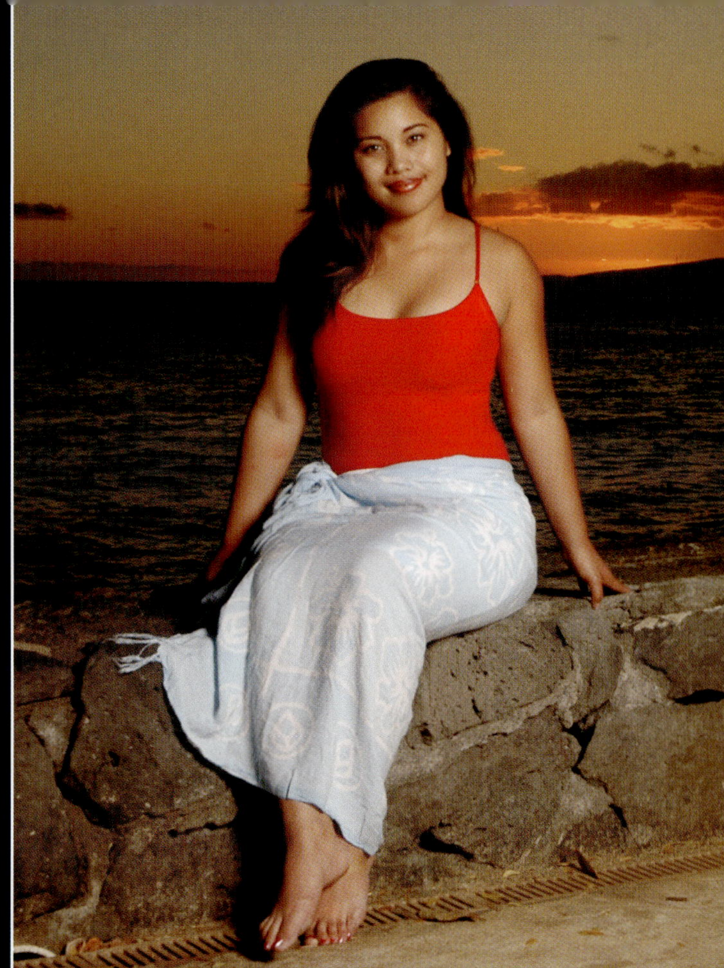

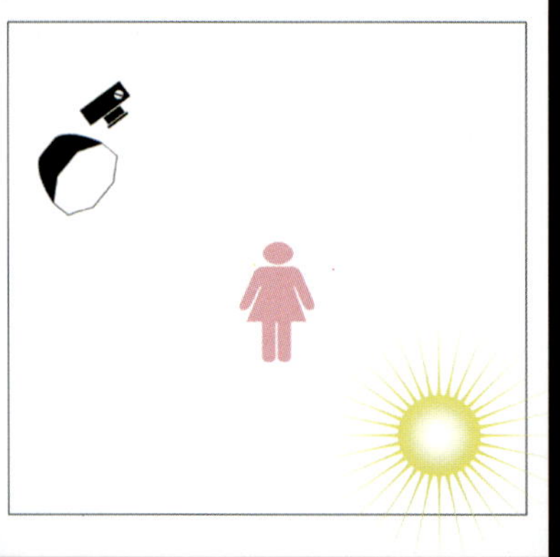

Top Left—Debbie Brown was photographed for this series on a southwest-facing shore on Oahu. The first image shows the portrait shot at $^1/_{125}$ second at f8. **Top Right—**The second image was photographed at $^1/_{400}$ second at f8, and I feel the sunset is too dark. The shadows leading into Debbie's hair are also darker than in the previous image. **Right—**The third image was photographed at $^1/_{250}$ second to lighten the background again. The light was falling off dramatically by now, so we had to open the aperture $^2/_3$ stop (f5.6$^1/_3$ or f6.3). Your actual image will change according to your preference. **Facing Page—**This is my favorite image from the series. It was shot at $^1/_{125}$ second at f8.

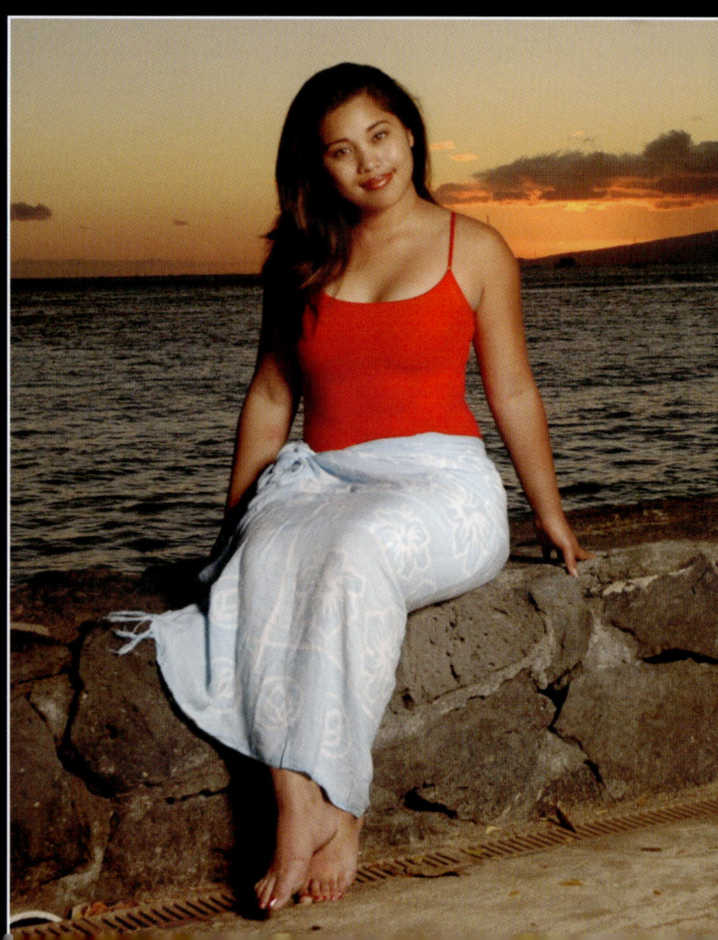

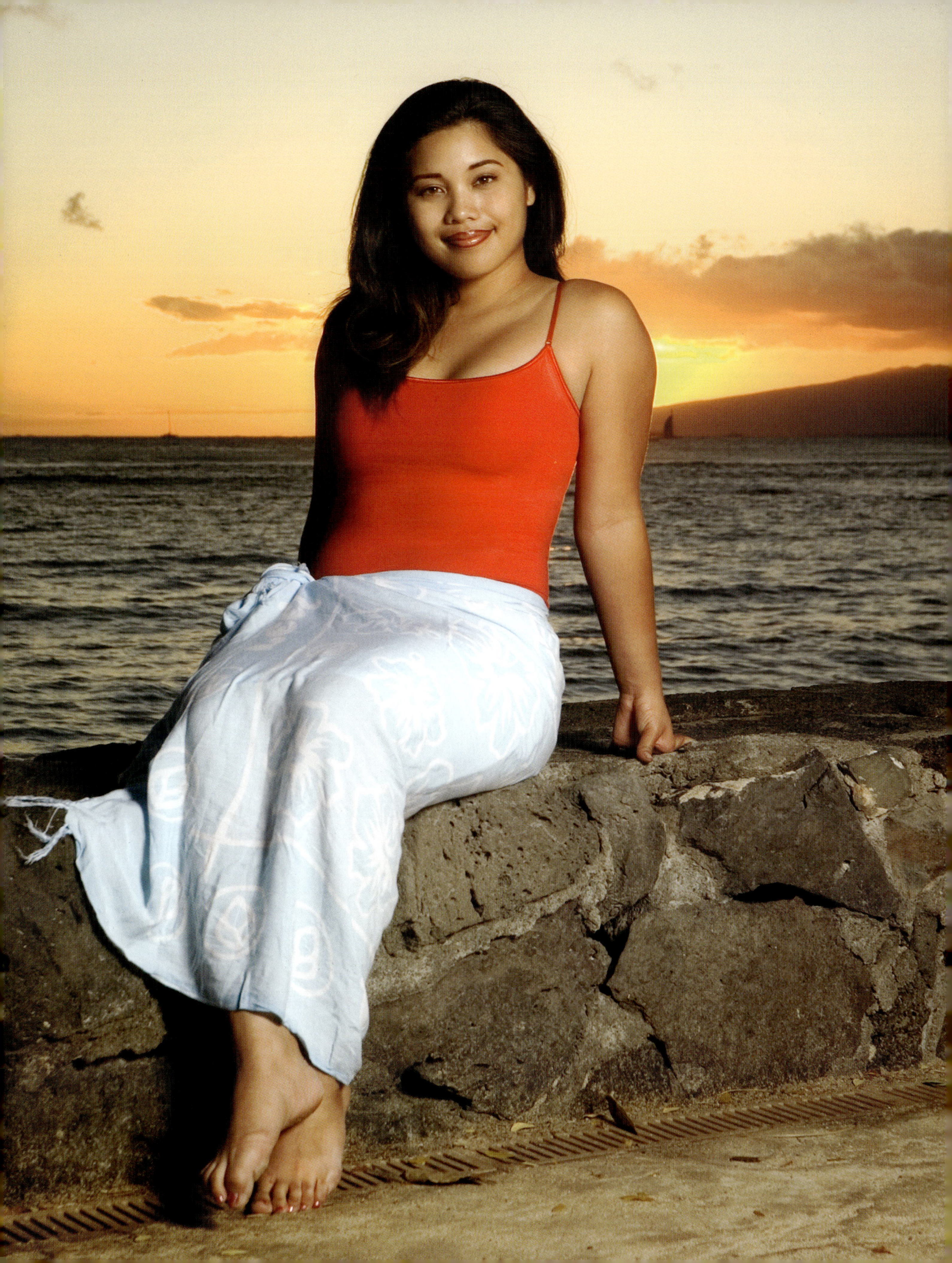

CHAPTER 4

BASIC RETOUCHING TECHNIQUES

There have been several Photoshop tips throughout this book showing specific ways to improve or play with your images. As a general rule, every digital image will require some retouching. Some images will require a lot more retouching than what is described below. Presented in this chapter are a couple of retouching strategies that you may want to apply to almost all of your images. They are meant solely as a starting point and not in any way as an inclusive set of retouching techniques. There are many books available that are devoted to retouching your portraits, and a detailed look at the topic is beyond the scope of this volume.

AS A GENERAL RULE, EVERY DIGITAL IMAGE WILL REQUIRE SOME RETOUCHING.

Color correction issues are a given regardless of how carefully you apply the principals detailed in this book. You will probably need to set the white and black points in your images, even with a perfectly exposed photograph. How your images print depends upon how closely your monitor is calibrated to your printer. Complex color management issues are well beyond the scope of this book, but you still need to start with a basically color corrected image. Color correction "by the numbers" is a technique that was described briefly earlier in this volume (see chapter 1) and will "fix" most of the color issues you will face. It is also fairly simple. The key is to determine what part of your image falls within the black and white ranges and set those spots to a predetermined value that corresponds to black without detail and white without detail. The range of values is currently on a numeric scale from 0 to 256. Zero is black without detail and 256 is white without detail. However, many people who work with digital images recommend setting the black value to 10 and the white value to 245 to compensate for printing issues. I use 10 and 245, but you'll have to experiment with the values. The image used to demonstrate the technique did not require much color correction, so the differences will be subtle. There will be times, however, when the differences before and after color correction are quite dramatic.

FINE-TUNING THE IMAGE

This image of Rachael Regina (*image 1*) was imported into Photoshop as it was shot. The white balance was set for daylight, and the image was created with a scrim–strobe–ambient combination described in chapter 3. The strobe was positioned along the same axis as the sunshine to keep the specular highlights and shadows looking natural. The image was captured in RAW, but no post-production RAW conversions were done. The image has a nice range from highlights to shadows

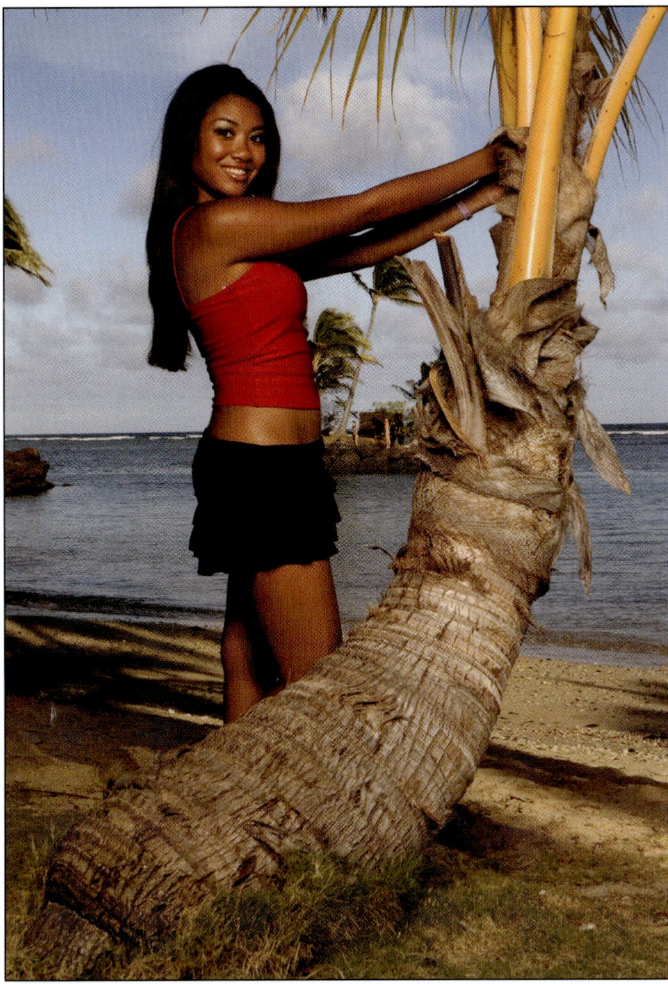

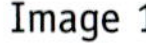

Image 1

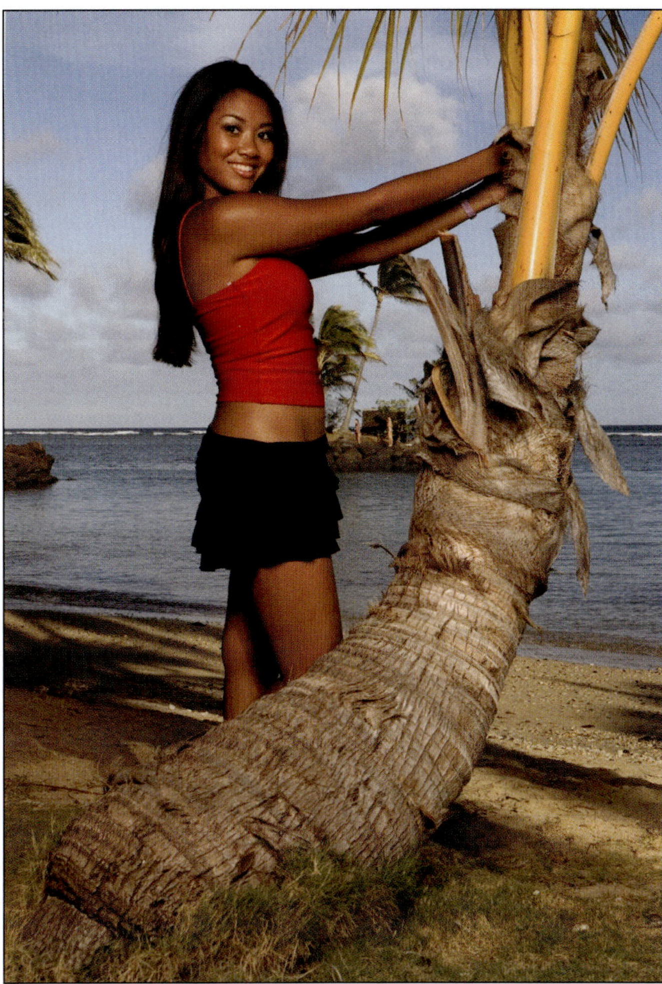

Image 2

and is certainly "passable" as is, but like most digital images, it could use a little adjusting.

The first thing I did was straighten the horizon line (*image 2*). I selected the measure tool (it's hidden in the color sampler toolbox) and clicked on a spot on the horizon where the water met the sky. Dragging the measure tool along the horizon line will act as a level and will establish how much you need to rotate the canvas to straighten the horizon. Next, I went to the image drop-down menu and selected Rotate Canvas> Arbitrary. The amount of rotation that is needed is automatically included. I hit OK and achieved a straight horizon. (A new white border will be created when you straighten the horizon this way. There will be times when you will have to crop the image to get rid of this border. In this case, however, the white areas were small enough for me to use the clone tool to fix the image.)

Let's get back to color correction. Open the information palette. This is an extremely useful palette because it tells you the color values for every spot in your image: simply move your cursor around the image and read the values. I was looking for the black spot, so I searched for the lowest numbers I could find. The circle in the image identifies the darkest points of the photograph (*image 3*). Some of the values in Rachael's shorts were all under 10, so I chose one of those spots as my black point.

The next step is to open the layers palette and click on the adjustment layers icon at the bottom of the layers palette (or choose New Adjustment Layer from the layer drop-down menu on the toolbar.) Using adjustment layers allows you to make changes to the way your image looks without actually changing the values of the original pixels. You can make modifications to these changes or even delete them and start over, and

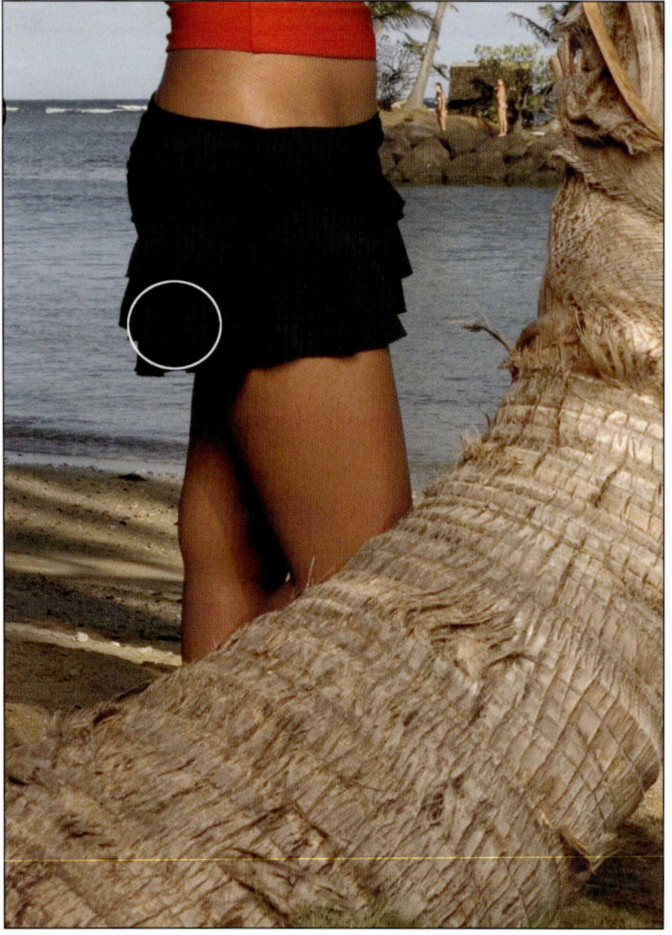
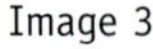

Image 3

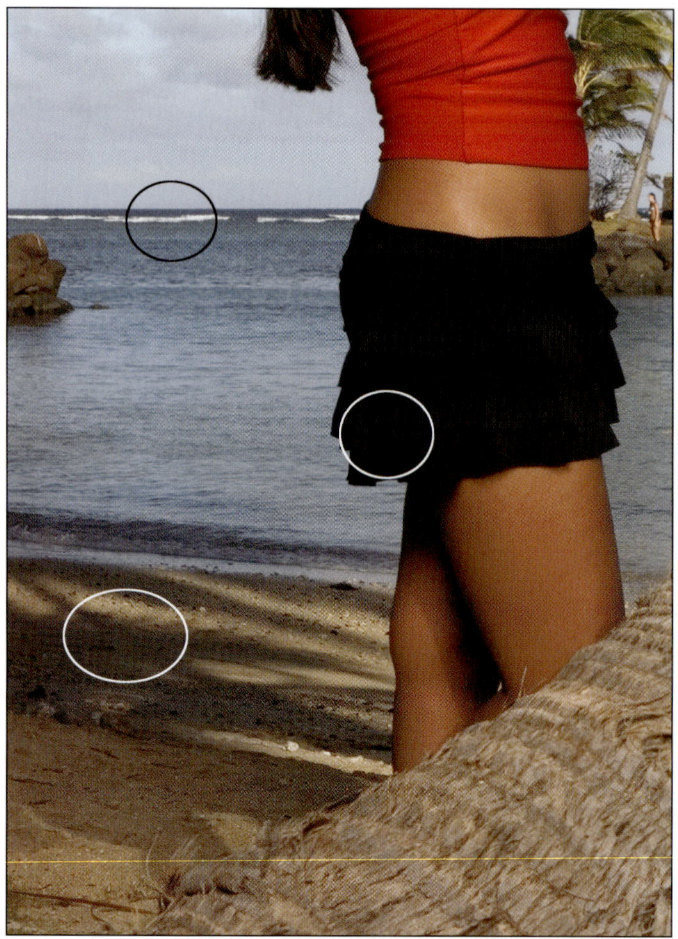

Image 4

you still have all of the original data. *If* you make changes to the original layer and save the changes, then you cannot undo it. Always do your retouching on duplicate or adjustment layers (save one version with all the layers intact and save a flattened version for output purposes). Next, complete the following steps:

1. Choose Curves from the pop-up menu. A curves dialog box will open, and you will see three eyedroppers in the lower-right corner: one to set the black point, one for the white point, and one for the gray point.
2. Double click the black eyedropper and set the values you want. I work in RGB mode, so I set each RGB value to 10. Click OK.
3. Double click the white eyedropper. I set each of the RGB values to 245. Click OK.
4. The gray eyedropper is used to correct any color cast not "fixed" by the adjustments you will make with the black eyedropper and white eyedropper. The value for each of the RGB settings is usually in the middle of the range, perhaps 128 each.
5. Click on the black eyedropper and move it through the image, watching the numbers in the information palette change. Find the spot that is as close as possible to the values you set in step 2. Click the spot that has the lowest numbers. This will force the red, blue, and green values for that spot to the number you have set—in this case, 10. Any color shifts in the black zone are now adjusted.
6. The whitecaps in the ocean provide a reference for the white point. I had to enlarge the image on my screen to find the lightest area. Click on the white eyedropper and find the spot in your image that is closest to the values you set in the white eyedropper. Click on this spot to set your white point.
7. There wasn't any point in this image where the three values were close to 128 each (gray point),

but the gray eyedropper seems to adjust the values of the selected spot regardless of the values. I looked around for a spot where the RGB values were close to each other. The darker shadows on the sand seemed to hover around 79, so I clicked on a spot within the new circle. This adjustment corrected any remaining color shift (*image 4*).

The image of Rachael did not change that much with the color correction. Some images, like the one of Manu and her family (*images 5 and 6*), will show a dramatic change.

Keep in mind that setting white and black points will only adjust the information that is captured. It will not add detail where detail doesn't exist. So, color correction techniques will help a properly exposed image but will not fix a badly exposed photograph. There may be some images that simply do not have a black or white point (such as high and low key portraits). You cannot force a white or black point in these cases. Work within the range you have and use either the black or white eyedropper in conjunction with the gray eyedropper. Also, if you want a little more control over color correction, you can use the color sampler tool to lock in a number of values and manually adjust each of the color channels.

THE ETHICS OF RETOUCHING

Retouching portraits always has some degree of controversy attached to it. The question has less to do with whether to retouch or not but how much retouching should be done. Generally speaking, the portrait that

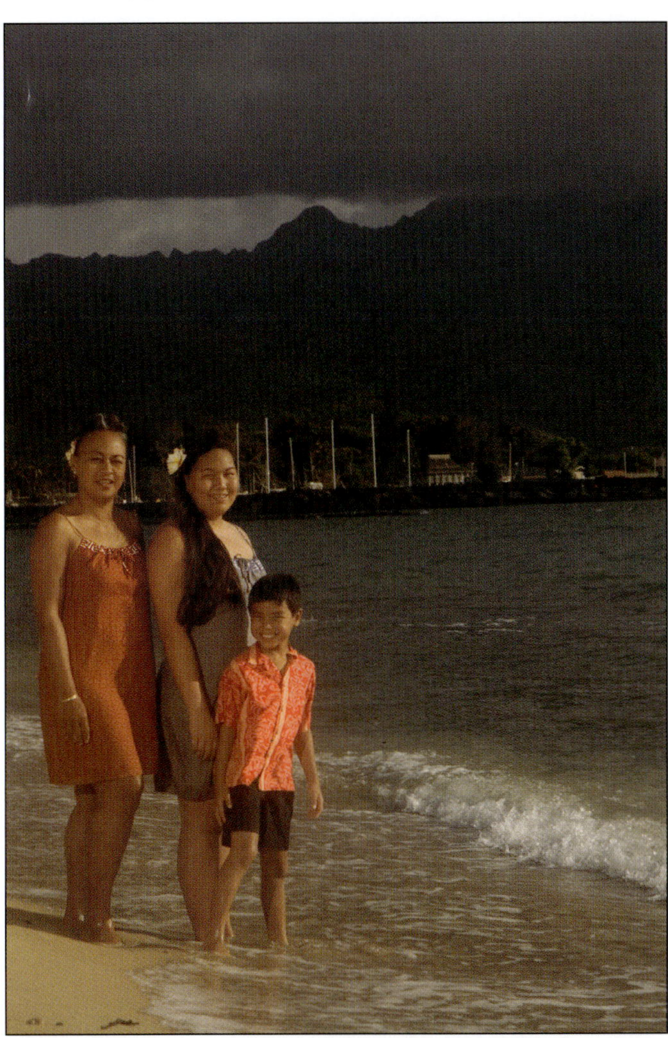

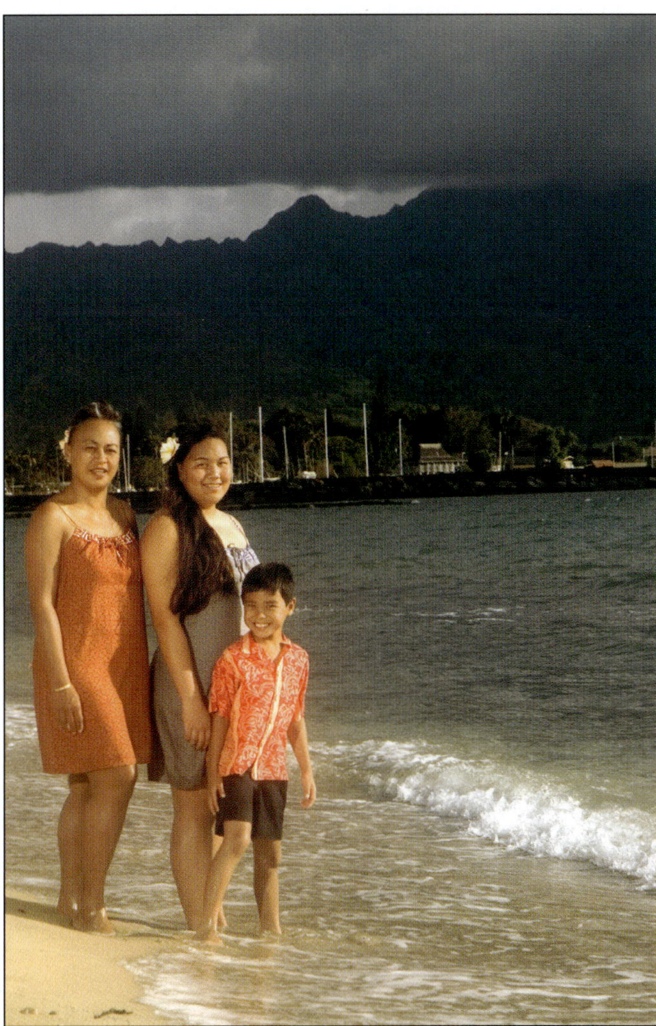

Image 5 (Left) and Image 6 (Right)—The image of Manu and her kids was exposed properly but still imparted a flat, dull image. The simple color correction technique just described brought the image to life!

has been retouched should maintain the essence of the person in the photograph. Facial lines may be softened somewhat, but removing them completely often looks fake. The extent to which a portrait is retouched is a very personal decision that needs to be made on a portrait-by-portrait basis.

THE VAST MAJORITY OF IMAGES I CREATE ARE RETOUCHED TO SOME DEGREE.

The vast majority of images I create are retouched to some degree. There are many ways to retouch images and many Photoshop tools that can be used to complete the task—and everyone seems to have their favorites.

The Basic Tools. From my perspective, the basic tools to master are the healing brush (and its patch tool partner) and the clone tool. The healing brush and clone tools work in similar ways. A section of the image is "selected" by alt/opt clicking part of your image and then moving your cursor to the part of the image that you wish to replace. The clone tool replaces the target area with the selected information. The healing brush is a "smarter" version of the clone tool and serves most of your simple retouching needs. The selected information is blended with the information around the target and the texture of the target area is maintained (please note: this was a very simplistic explanation of how the healing brush works—please see a Photoshop manual for a better and more detailed explanation). However, the healing brush still has some trouble with sharp color transitions, so you need to learn how the clone tool works, as well. Also there is no way (at this time) to lower the opacity of the healing brush while you are using it, but you can fade each stroke by going to the edit drop-down menu and choosing the Fade Healing Brush option. If I am using the healing brush to lighten lines or soften the area under my subject's eyes, then I will fade each stroke to 40% (*image 7*).

Rachael's portrait did not need any retouching, but for the sake of demonstration, the healing brush was used to remove most of the straggling and flyaway hairs, and the area under her eyes was slightly lightened by using the healing brush and fading these strokes to 40% of the original opacity. Next, I used the healing brush to tone down the hot spots on her cheek from the strobe. I also took out most of the wrinkles in her shirt—just for fun!

The remaining flyaway hairs were "erased" using the clone tool in areas where the healing brush would have problems. I also removed the tag from Rachael's shirt and smoothed remaining wrinkles that were too close to the trees behind her for the healing brush to handle. Furthermore, I removed the two people from the island behind her and removed her bracelet. It is important to pay close attention to your sample point to keep your "cloning" from becoming obvious. A few more strokes with the healing brush on her shirt, and I was finished (*image 8*).

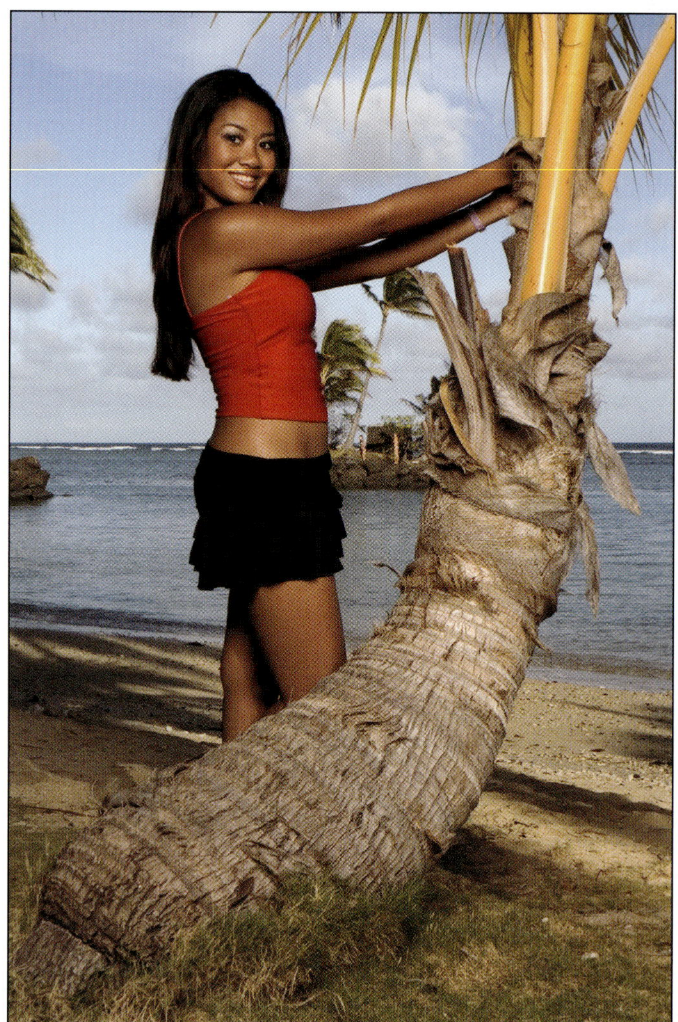

Image 7 (above), Image 8 (facing page)

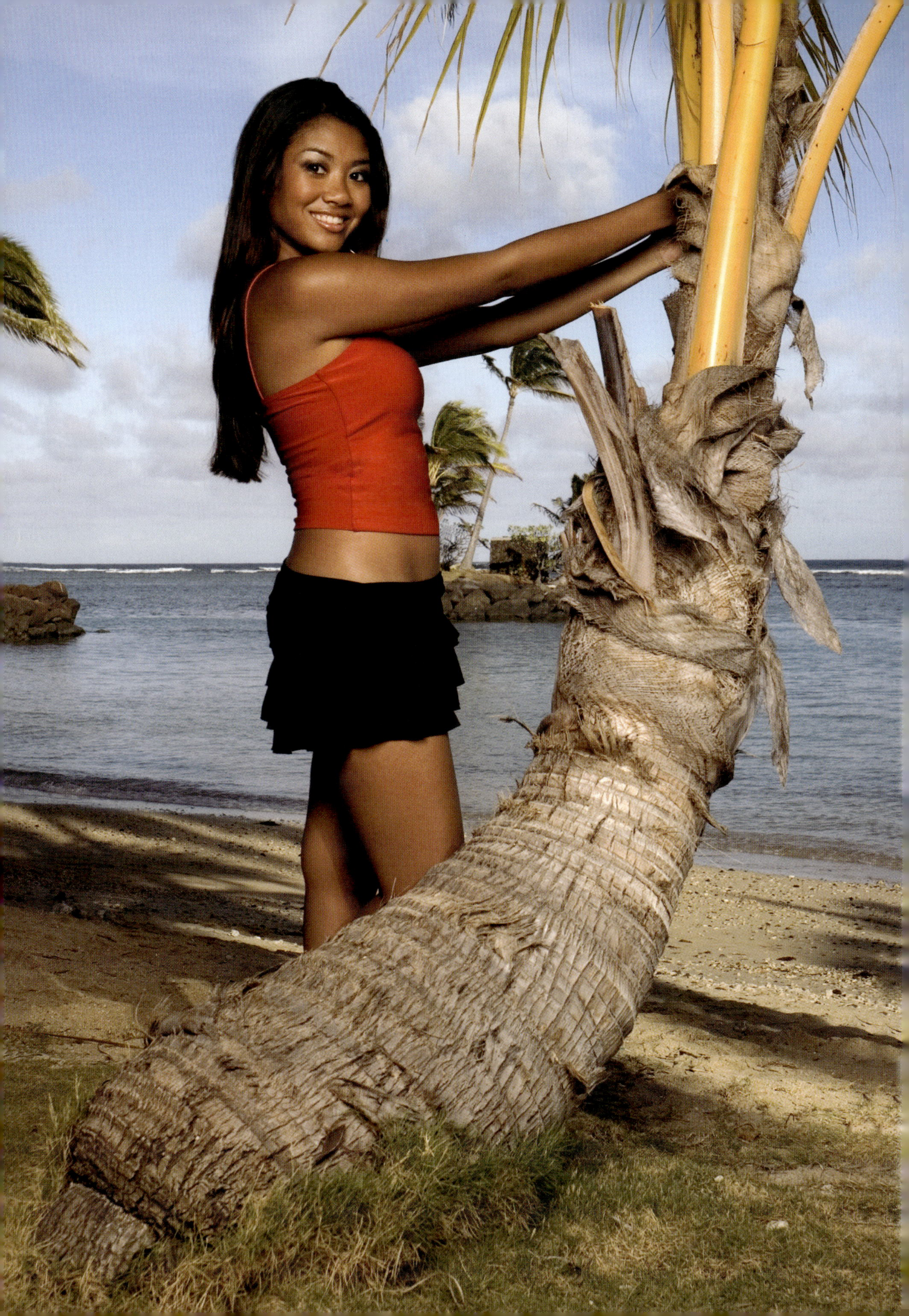

CHAPTER 5

THE BUSINESS OF DIGITAL PORTRAITURE

THE PROS AND CONS OF DIGITAL CAPTURE

Photographer Paul Gero, like the other photographers I spoke with in writing this book, feels strongly that "digital has changed the business in a monumental way." His comment, "There is an immediacy with photography now that never existed" is echoed by Stan Cox II, who states that as soon as you can get the image into a computer you can enjoy the photograph, share it, or begin to work on it. Don Herzig takes the idea of immediacy even further: "In an ever-increasing 'I need it now' society, it has become an absolute necessity. If you cannot produce timely results, your clients will go elsewhere." Al Garcia adds that aside from the immediate gratification of being able to show a client *exactly* what the image is going to look like without having to wait for the "Polaroid to develop" and having to explain to the client that the Polaroid is much "contrastier" than the final image on film, digital has given the photographer an extra edge of confidence. Al says, "Although, back in the days of shooting film, we were very meticulous about checking out our equipment before a big shoot and metering constantly during the shoot to ensure that we were doing everything right and that everything was working as it should, we were literally working in the dark until that beautiful little LCD screen was invented. Even though we are experts in our craft, there were still numerous variables beyond our control. Concerns such as, 'did we get a bad batch of film?', 'did my new assistant load my film backs incorrectly?', 'did the lab screw up while loading our 4x5 chromes into the processor?', etc., were completely eliminated by digital but replaced by others (such as a corrupted memory card that played back fine during the shoot, but when you inserted it into a cheap card reader all the files were rendered unopenable)! However, unlike film, a corrupted memory card can often be salvaged."

IF YOU CANNOT PRODUCE TIMELY RESULTS, YOUR CLIENTS WILL GO ELSEWHERE.

For Paul, the benefits of digital capture also include being able to change the color temperature or set a custom color balance on the fly and "to use RAW software to create different looks for the same image and then align them in Photoshop to create a truly amazing print . . . it's possible to do that with film, but much trickier and more time consuming." Stan also loves being back in the "darkroom" again and finds the creative benefits of digital capture invigorating.

Digital capture seems to be a double-edged sword in many respects. The immediacy and increased creativity has come at a cost. Each photographer I spoke with has commented that digital capture has changed their workflow and in many cases has resulted in more work.

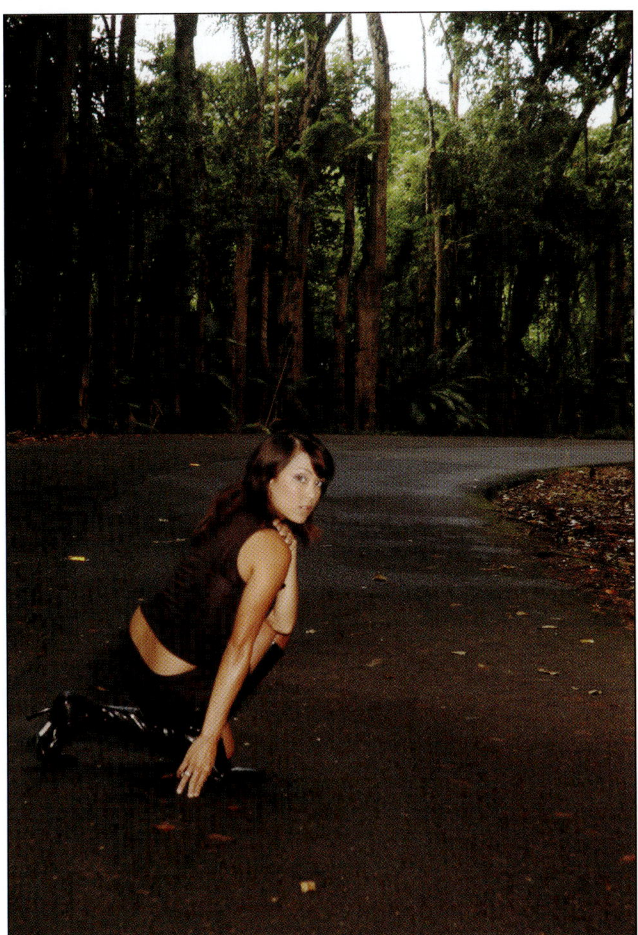

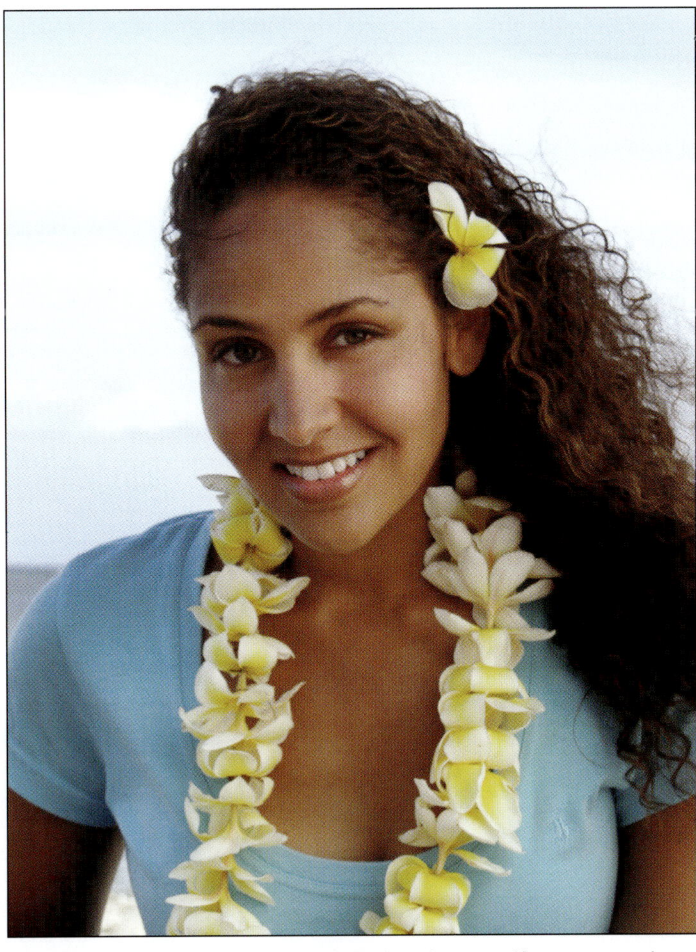

The immediate feedback of digital photography allows you to preview the shoot before you leave the location. It doesn't matter if you are creating a fashion image or a beach-side portrait; it is nice to know that you have the shot "in the can" before loading the gear and leaving the set. Kathryn was photographed in-land on the East Coast of Oahu while Anja Lee posed on a beach on the Southeast corner of Oahu.

Paul states, "Digital has also shifted the entire business because labs are going away and the onus of production is now on the shoulders of photographers. I suspect the labs that do survive will do so because they have adapted to the digital environment and help photographers manage their digital work." Al states, "It has definitely increased the amount of post-production work I have to do. Now, I have to edit, color balance, enhance, and correct many images after a shoot. However, oftentimes I don't *need* to manipulate them, but in the never-ending quest for 'wow!' images, I do it *because I can!*" Stan agrees that the workflow has increased dramatically from the "shoot, rewind, and drop off at the lab" days, but, like Al, he finds the process very rewarding—and the never-ending learning curve stimulating. Paul puts the workflow issue into perspective, saying, "It's just different. While it's sometimes easier to just take your film to the lab, have them process and scan it, and then pick it up, you're very dependent on the lab's commitment to quality and the level of skill of the scanner operator. When you are working on your own digital files, the results can be more controlled to your precise tastes than is possible even with the best custom lab. Over time, your increased skill in working with the RAW images and learning to use batch processing can make it easier and faster. The burn-in time to get to that point can be long, though."

David Taylor used to spend hours in the darkroom but now he spends hours bouncing between three computers! "When we shot film, the lab took care of the color management and retouching, tasks we now complete ourselves. So we had to learn new techniques, and we are now responsible for the color and quality of our final images. This is great but very time consuming."

David and Paul both see a potential drawback to the immediacy of digital capture. David states, "Being able to see your images *now* is the photographers' ultimate dream come true—however, the art of previsualization is very important and something newer photographers may be missing out on." Paul feels that there is a risk of relying on the preview screen too much, which can lead to "less concentration on the subjects and capturing moments." There may actually have been some benefit to "having a disciplined approach through having only thirty-six shots and having to make them work" to get *the* moment.

Digital capture has had a profound effect on how photographers shoot and conduct business—with associated pros and cons. On the one hand, digital capture has freed the photographer from "counting shots" and has allowed him or her to keep shooting if *the* shot is not in the first batch. Immediate previewing has also helped sales.

Digital capture has helped Al in both the portrait and commercial aspects of his business: "The ability to show your clients their 'proofs' at the point of sale while they are still excited about the shoot leads to many impulse orders. Also, digital, with its ability to be sent to a client across the country almost immediately, has allowed us to take on assignments that before were not possible because the lab could not do it in time or because the rush charges would blow the budget for the shoot." Stan's sales from his promotional specials have quadrupled. He states, "A lot of people come in thinking they're just going to pick up a free 8x10-inch print, but after having fun in the studio and then see-

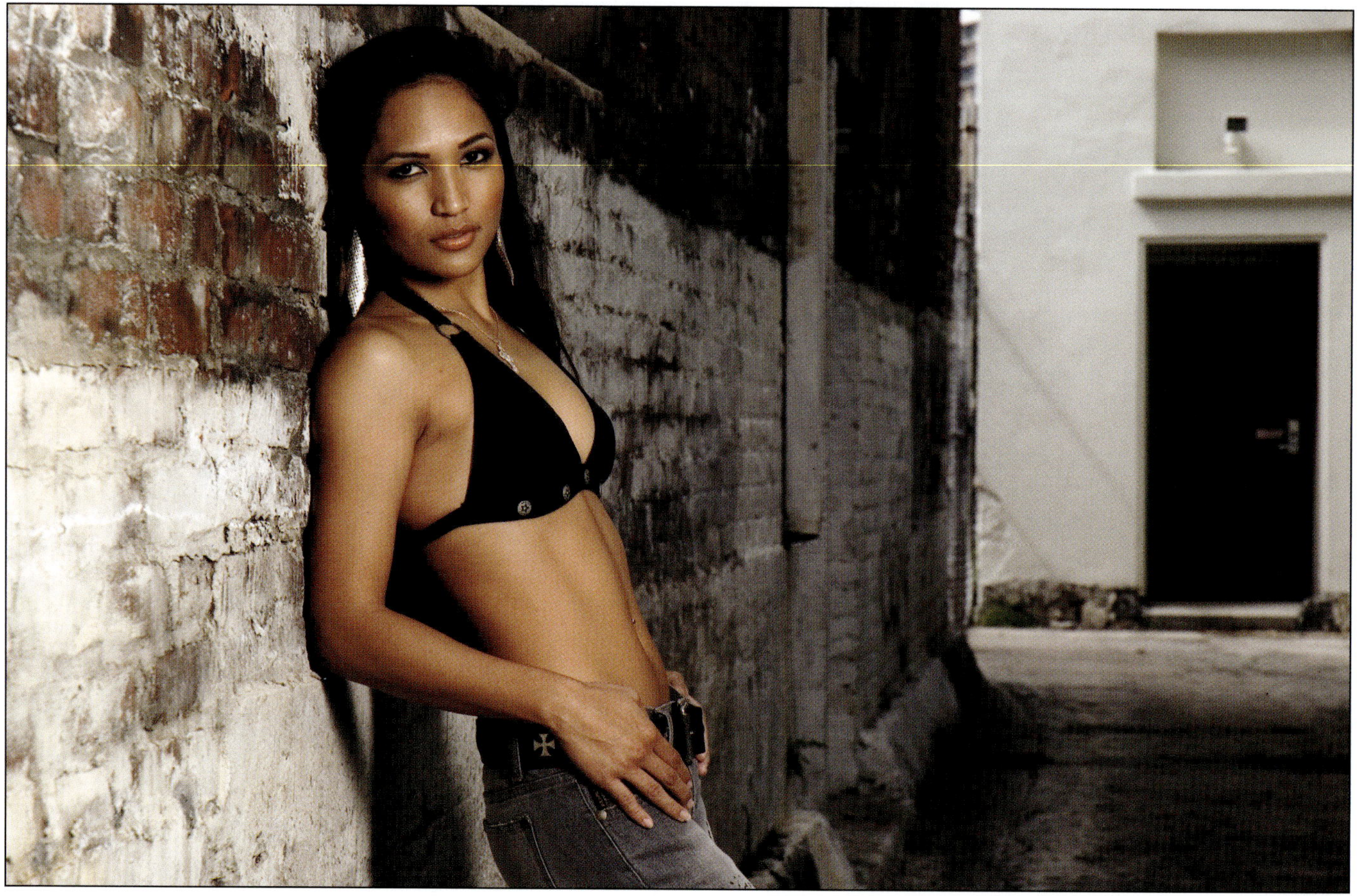

Digital photography has shifted the post-production work from the lab to the photographer. Studying the techniques—and mistakes—detailed in this book will help keep your post-production work to a minimum. The post-production work for this fashionable portrait was minimal because the flash–ambient ratio was carefully controlled to illuminate Tishanna while making sure that detail was not lost either down the alley or in the white door in the background.

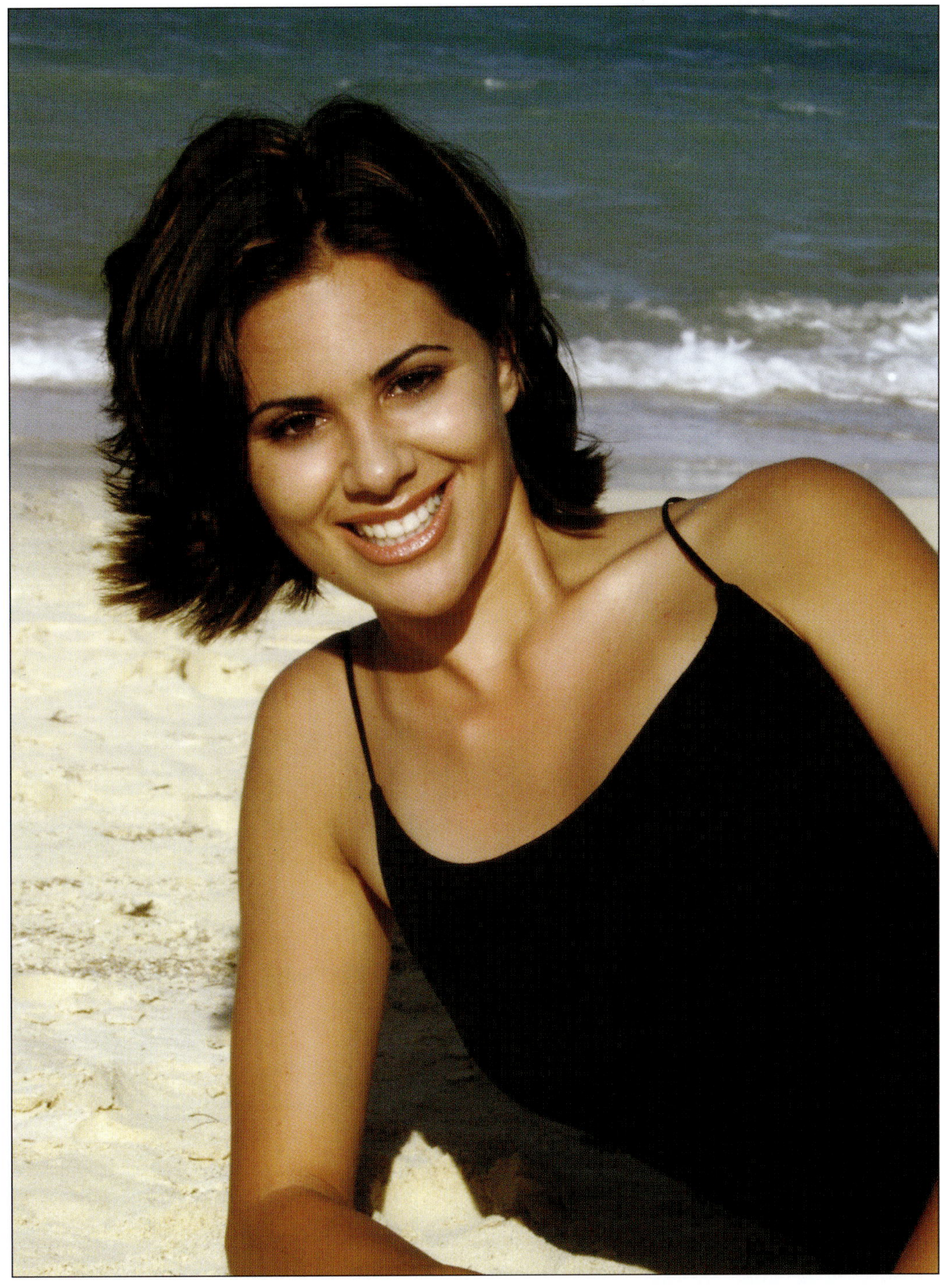

Kristina Poulos was photographed on an East Coast beach on Oahu. The natural light was beautiful. However, the bright light made it very difficult to see the LCD screen to preview the images as they were shot. This was a throwback to the film days that Paul Gero talked about—even with a "preview" I still had to "work the shoot" to get *the* shot.

ing the images right there and then, the excitement level is very high, and the impulse buy plays into the experience." Stan says, prior to digital capture, "the client went home and came back in a week or so to view the images, but often the whole family wouldn't show up, the excitement wasn't the same, priorities shifted, etc." Paul adds that digital has helped sales because "it allows quicker turnover with lower costs. For example, I can take a RAW file and create print sizes from 4x6 through 20x30 inches from the same file. With film I would have to get a higher-resolution scan done for that large size (or do it myself), which takes time. I think we can now easily share our images online . . . and that opens up sales opportunities. We can more easily create DVDs and slideshows. Of course, these can be done from scanned film, but the

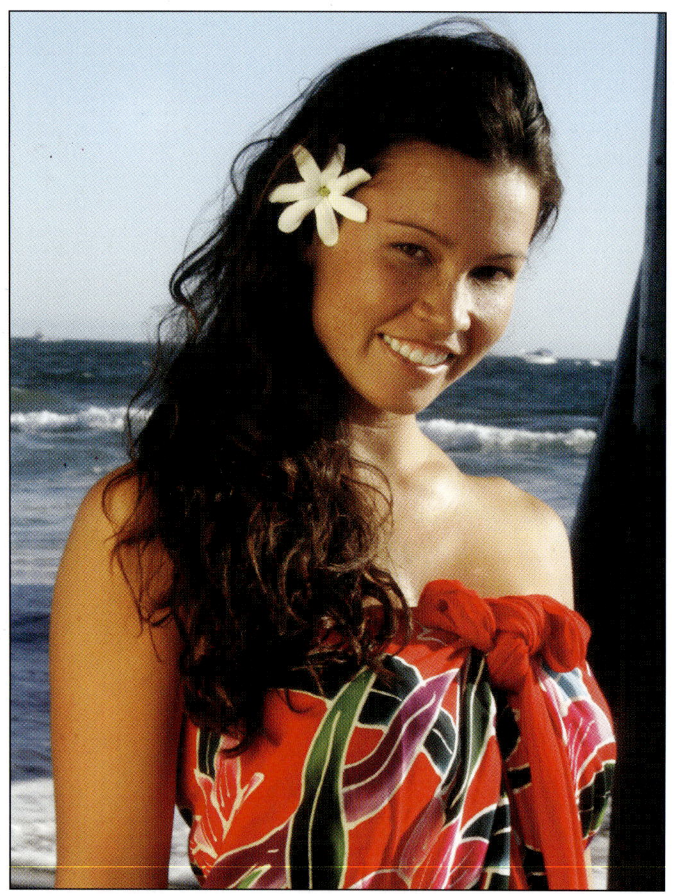

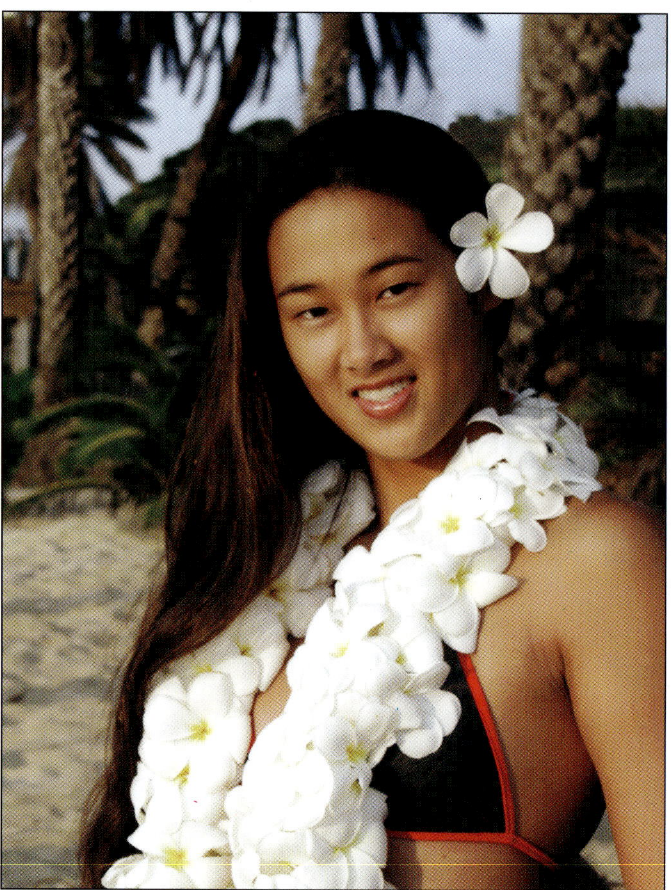

Left—One ironic consequence of the digital revolution is the proliferation of mediocre photos gaining acceptance in both the portrait and commercial worlds. The antidote is to make sure that your images are so much better than mediocre that your client *has* to hire you. Sanna Dioso was photographed on a beach in Los Angeles. The sun was setting to camera right and a pier was casting a shadow. Handling these types of difficult situations will help you stand out. A gold reflector and some minor Photoshop work were used to fill the shadows and even the light for this portrait. **Right and Facing Page—**Image theft and unauthorized printing of your images have become greater threats in the digital world. The internet has literally opened your studio doors to the world. It has also opened the door to people "right-clicking" [on a PC] and taking your image. Embedding your name and/or copyright information in your image can deter would-be thieves. Returning to the fun part of this saga, we have Midori Every beautifying a construction scene in downtown Honolulu (facing page) and Tianne overshadowing some of Hawaii's gorgeous flowers (above right)!

downside is the wait to get it shipped, processed, and returned, and then hoping everything survives the shipping."

Another benefit of the immediate nature of digital capture is the ability to keep shooting if you have to. Don states, "That is the beauty of digital. You know immediately if you have the shot or not." Stan has occasionally had to return to the studio and says that each time resulted in a better sale. David says, "There have been a number of times when, after viewing the images I had just shot, I knew I did not have what I needed and continued the shoot. Being able to shoot an unlimited number of images is great, but be prepared to spend lots of time editing." Paul also appreciates being able to return to the studio to keep shooting but once again cautions that "it can also be a crutch in letting you just get the 'expected' shot rather than just shooting, looking, and pushing to go beyond as you might do when shooting film without the camera screen to preview."

Digital capture has also resulted in an extremely odd dichotomy between people's expectations and reality. The reality, as we have seen, is that it is extremely difficult to create beautiful digital portraits. At the same time, however, many people are growing more and more "content" with mediocre images that they shoot

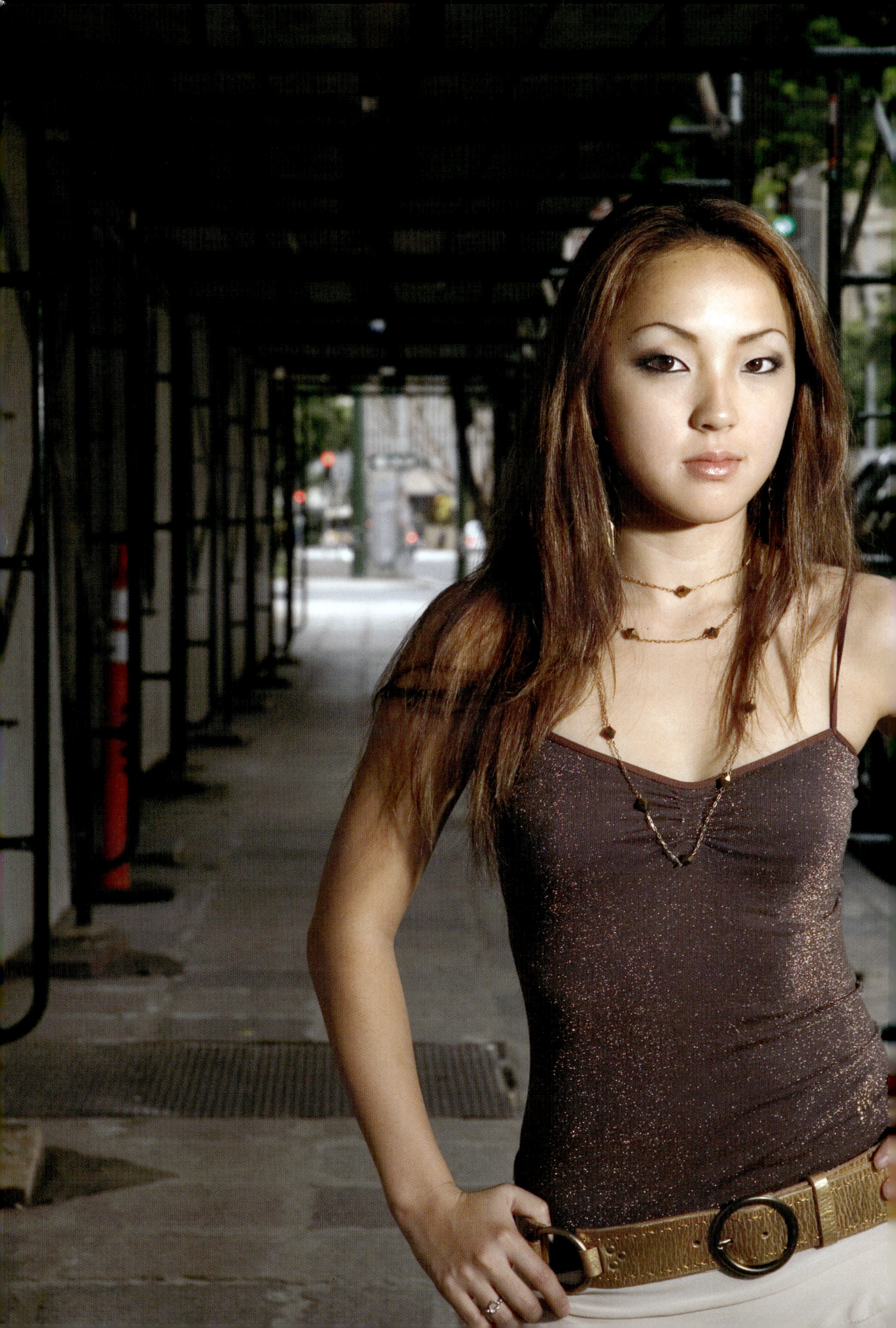

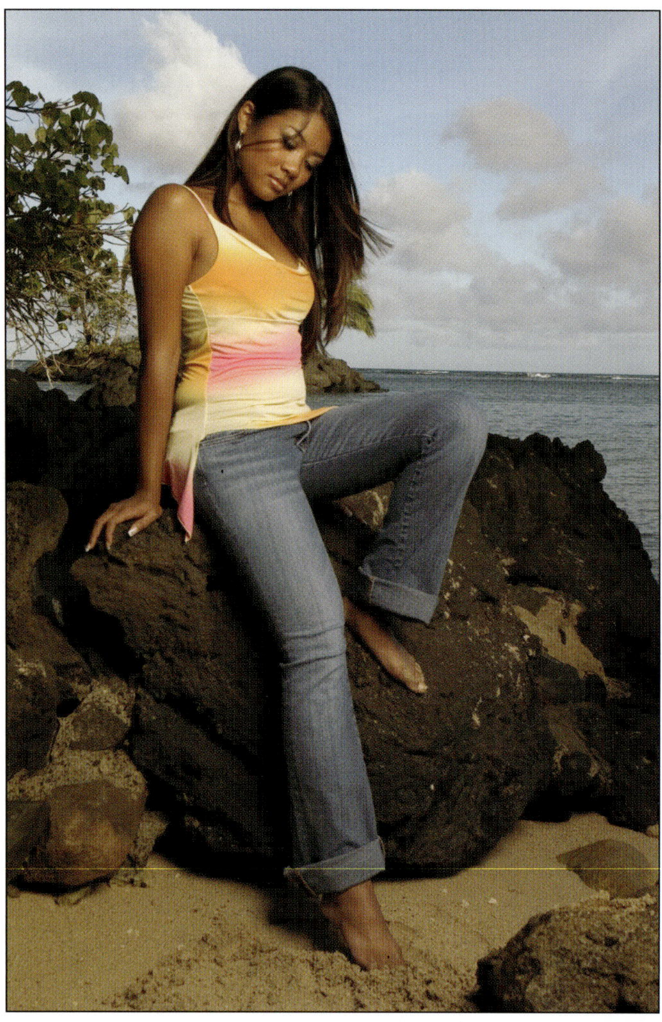

You, the photographer, own the copyright to your image the second you click the shutter. Copyright protection was granted to artists by the founders of the United States of America [*Note:* copyright laws and the associated rights vary from country to country]. However, you are not guaranteed the full weight of the law unless your images are registered with the US copyright office. This gentle portrait of Rachael Regina is one of thousands of images of mine that are registered with the United States Library of Congress Copyright Office.

and manipulate. The need for professional photographers has never been greater, and yet the perception is that digital is easy. In both the portrait and commercial world, there is a danger that "good enough" will become the norm. Don sadly states that he knows "a lot of very talented photographers who are retiring from the business due to an increasingly savvy clientele who accept less professional results at a significant savings." Al's comments are profound: "Digital changed everything. Digital has changed the industry completely. The magic genie that somehow created and printed these beautiful images on paper has been let out of the bottle. Today, many companies are producing their own in-house images. Just about every major company today has their own in-house marketing team that, through the use of their high-resolution point & shoot digital camera and a competent person in Photoshop, can produce a very nice marketing piece. Although the really elaborate high-end, point-of-sale pieces still need to be photographed by us, the simplicity and [perceived] forgiving nature of digital is taking work away from us and devaluing the precision that we so often put into our craft." I believe that the key here is to study the concerns and lighting issues that have been discussed in this book and create photographs that are so much better than "good enough" that your client will have to come to you time after time for their important images.

File sharing and the many self-printing kiosks also pose risks to the digital photographers' business. The best way to prevent your clients from printing their own images from digital proofs is to not provide them! Your sales will likely increase if you proof the session with your client right after the shoot. However, there are times when this is not possible. The consensus of the photographers I spoke with is that you should provide small images at low enough resolution that the print quality of the images would be lousy. Most of the photographers I spoke to provide image that are 5 or 6 inches at 70 to 72dpi. Paul says that he actually expects some clients to print their own images. He states that he tries to price his services so that he is adequately compensated. He says, "Any additional print sales are icing on the cake. Besides, they can copy a proof all they want, but it won't be quite the same as a fine-tuned, custom print for an album or enlargement that I would create. Being able to sell a client on your vision and skill in creating that album or final wall-sized print is where I want to take my business, and I want to find clients who *get* that distinction." Stan does his best to maintain control over the printing of his images but will charge the full price per print in the rare situation when the client needs a high-resolution CD. Another protective technique is to make sure that your copyright is embedded in each image. This will not guarantee that your client will not be able to print the images, but it will help. Many retail stores are becoming more aware of the federal laws about printing or copying copyrighted materials.

The same advice holds for posting images on the Internet. You could password-protect your web pages, but you could also make sure that every posted image has your copyright notice embedded in it. Someone would then need to open your image in a photo editing program and actively remove your © in order to use the image. Editing your image to use without your permission is considered "willful infringement," and such a violation makes it much easier for you to win a copyright infringement lawsuit.

U.S. federal law states that we own the copyright to an image at the exact moment it is created. This statement is true for every image that is not created as a "work for hire." A detailed discussion of copyright and work-for-hire issues is well beyond the scope of this book. However, it is important to note that although we own the copyrights to each image we create as freelance photographers, we are not fully protected and are not afforded all the possible statutory damages in a willful infringement case unless our images are registered with the U.S. Copyright Office. Digital capture has made the process of registering your images easy! You can register a group of unpublished images as one set. Simply burn a CD or DVD with all the images from one or more shoots, download and fill out the proper form from the U.S. copyright website, and send the discs, forms, and whatever fees are involved (cheap!) to the copyright office. Go to www.copyright.gov for many more details about copyright issues and how to register your images.

So, it is much harder to control the lighting with digital, the workflow and time in post-production has increased dramatically, and it has become extremely difficult to avoid the unauthorized printing/use of your images. The question becomes: is digital capture worthwhile? Each of the photographers whose work and comments appear in this book would respond that digital capture is *absolutely* worth it!

Sunset over Western Oahu seems like a fitting way to say "Aloha!" Many mahalos ["thanks"] to all who participated in this book—in this case it's my friend Teresa Bringas.

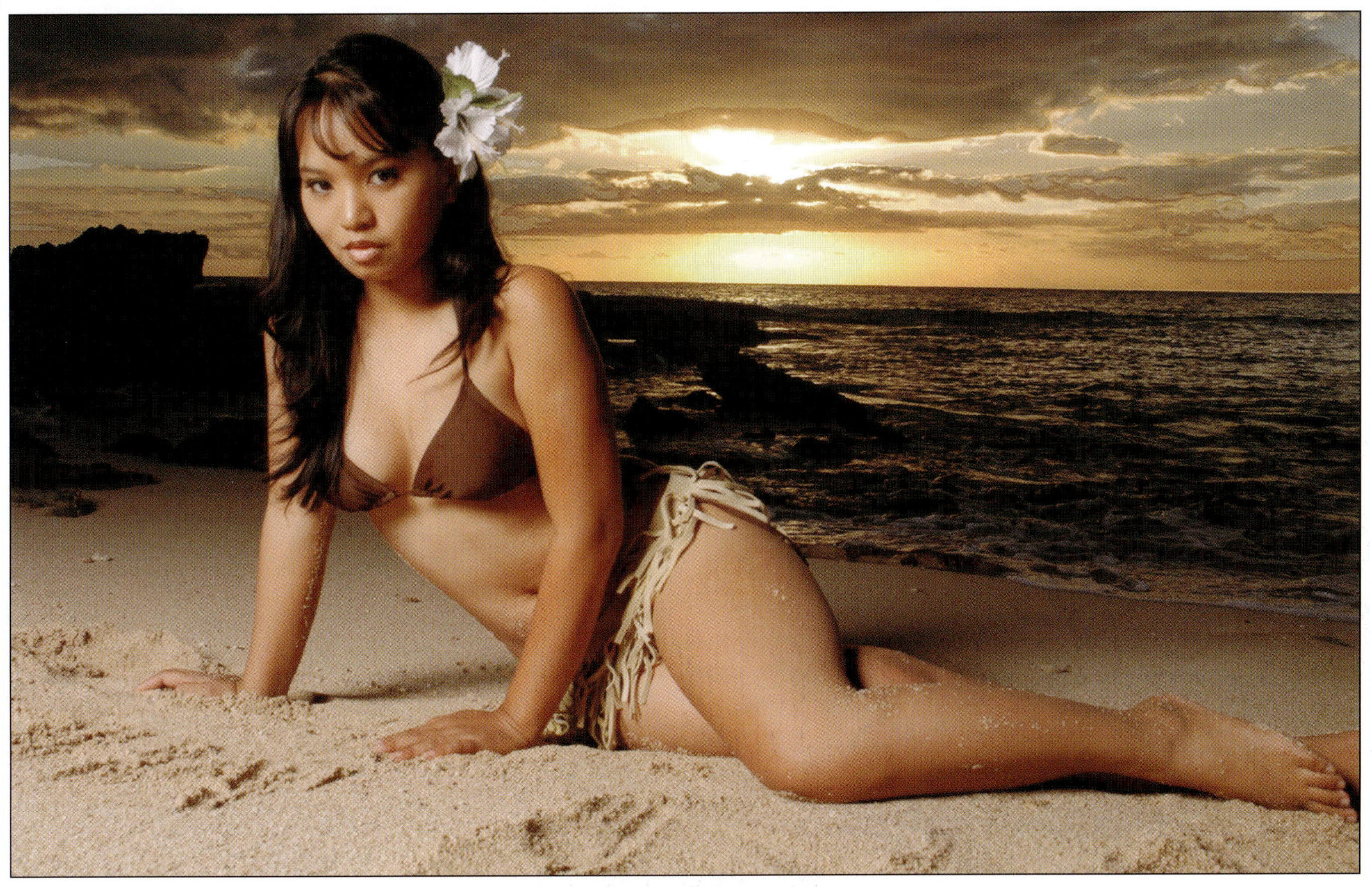

ABOUT THE AUTHOR

Stephen Dantzig is the author of *Lighting Techniques for Fashion and Glamour Photography* (Amherst Media) and more than thirty articles and lessons on photographic lighting and ethics. He is a frequent contributor to *Rangefinder*, and his lessons have appeared in *Professional Photographer*, *PC Photo*, *Studio Photography & Design*, ProPhoto West, and the Photoflex Web Photo School and www.shootsmarter.com. His work has appeared on more than twenty-two magazine covers including local, regional, and national markets. Some of his published works have appeared in *Portrait Photographer's Handbook*, *Group Portrait Photography Handbook*, *The Best of Portrait Photography*, and *The Best of Photographic Lighting* (all from Amherst Media), and *This Week Magazine* (Hawaii), *Pleasant Hawaii Magazine*, *Doll Reader*, *Studio City Lifestyles Magazine*, *Santa Clarita Valley Living*, and *The Los Angeles Times*. Stephen is a twenty-one-time Award of Merit recipient from the Professional Photographers of Los Angeles County and has received two Awards of Merit from the Professional Photographers of Hawaii. His specialties include fashion, beauty, and corporate photography. Stephen also holds a Doctor of Psychology degree from the Rutgers University Graduate School of Applied and Professional Psychology. He now works and resides in Honolulu, Hawaii.

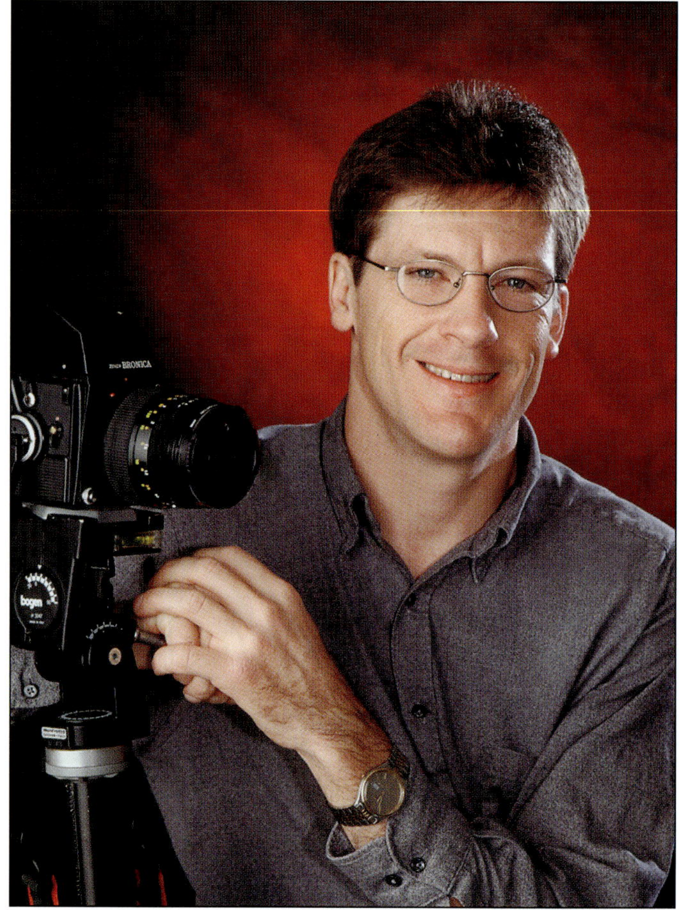

Photo by Harry Lang.

CONTRIBUTORS

Stan P. Cox II is president and director of photography for Paramount Photography Hawaii. He is a self-taught artist and began his career in art in Santa Barbara, California, by illustrating a book of human anatomy at age eight. His preferred medium gradually shifted from watercolors to painting with light and shadows. A native Californian, Stan moved to Kaua'i, Hawaii, in 1976, and has lived on all the major Hawaiian Islands over the last thirty years. He completed the New York Institute of Photography curriculum in 1982 and has been creating portraits all over Hawaii ever since. His clientele include a number of Hawaiian celebrities who devote much of their time and resources to local charities. Stan's "Local Heroes" exhibit was a great success. He is also known for his scenes of the Hawaiian landscape, flora, and "cloudscapes," capturing the unique beauty of the Hawaiian sky. Website: www.paramountphotography.com.

Al Garcia is a commercial photographer based in New Jersey. He attended the University of California at Los Angeles and Rutgers University for photography. His first "professional" (translated as "paid") job came at the age of seventeen when he photographed his first wedding. He worked in local camera stores during college and later became a studio manager/photo assistant for a very busy commercial studio. The studio handled numerous national accounts, ranging from Mont Blanc pens to Mercedes. At age twenty-three, along with two partners, Al opened the first of two Photo Studio, Lab and Camera stores. For fifteen years they serviced clients from Revlon to JVC and did both in-studio and on-location custom portraits. Al has since sold his retail camera stores and works as a freelance commercial photographer. He lives on the Delaware River, in New Jersey, with his wife and two children.

Paul F. Gero has been a working photographer since 1983, when he graduated from Marquette University with a degree in journalism. Paul immediately started as an intern for the *Chicago Tribune*. Six months later, the paper made him a full-time staff photographer. In 1985, the paper reassigned him to their Washington, DC bureau. In 1989, Paul left the *Tribune* for a contract position with the French agency Sygma, based in Washington, and then ventured west for a newspaper staff position, this time at the Arizona Republic in Phoenix. Paul's photojournalism career has seen some vastly different and intriguing assignments. He has covered the second term of the Reagan administration, the 1988 political campaigns and conventions, as well as political unrest in Haiti, the NBA Finals (featuring Charles Barkley versus Michael Jordan), the Super Bowl, the aftermath of the Colossio assassination in Mexico, and created a commemorative panorama poster of the first pitch of the Arizona Diamondbacks baseball team. His work has been published worldwide in *Time, People, Sports Illustrated,* and *US News & World Report.* Paul has studied with Will Crockett and William Albert Allard.

In the late 1990s, Paul began investigating the world of wedding photojournalism and started to consider doing this work. In 2000, he photographed the weddings of three of his photographer friends and discovered that he loved documenting weddings. The jobs renewed his love of documentary photography in general. He also met his future wife, Nicki, who was the maid of honor at the third wedding. They were married within a year. In March of 2002, Paul and Nicki decided to leave Phoenix for the cooler climate of California, and he began his freelance career at that time. He now divides his time between documenting weddings, creating documentary children's photography, writing, and teaching. Paul is the author of *Digital Wedding Photography* (Muska & Lipman/ Premier Trade, 2004). Paul and Nicki are expecting their first child in January, 2006. Website: www.paulfgero.com.

Don Herzig has been around photography since childhood, watching his father, for hours on end, develop images in the bathtub of a makeshift darkroom. Unlike most photographers, however, Don's photography took an unusual turn, when part of his duties as a detective for a police department included recording homicide scenes. Things have changed significantly for Don, who now specializes in children's photography, a subject that he freely admits is "a far cry from photographing the 'darker side' of life." He is a member, past president, and past Photographer of the Year for the Professional Photographers of Los Angeles County. Don has had prints go national, has his fellowship from the Professional Photographers of California, and has been profiled in *Rangefinder* magazine. His photographs have been published in the Kodak Gallery Award Collection Album, the PPA Loan Collection, and Showcase books, and he has received the Kodak Gallery Award.

Harry Lang has been a photographer all his life but has seriously pursued and honed his craft within the last seven years. He is influenced by a number of fashion photographers including Patrick Demarchelier, Stephen Meisel, and Bruce Weber. Harry is mostly self-taught but also served as an assistant to Stephen Dantzig for several years. Harry prefers a more "edgy" style, choosing to break convention and try something new. When not shooting, Harry enjoys time with his family and playing video games. He currently lives in Los Angeles with his wife Elise and son Griffin.

Lieutenant-Colonel Parker Pritchard is a Texas native and career Army Officer who has served on Active Duty in both Military Intelligence and the Field Artillery Corps. He has served in many positions and in many parts of the world including Hawaii and Baghdad, Iraq. He holds a Bachelor's Degree in Criminal Law from Sam Houston State University and a Masters of Administration from Central Michigan University. His awards include the Bronze Star Medal, Meritorious Service Medal (2 OLC), Joint Service Achievement Medal, Army Commendation Medal, Army Achievement Medal (4 OLC), Iraq Campaign, Global War on Terrorism Service Medal, and the Humanitarian Service Medal. He has also been awarded the Parachutist and the Air Assault badges. He has been an amateur photographer for years and has a love for all aspects and types of digital imagery. He is married to the former Julie Croskey of Huntington, New York, and they have two daughters, Taylor, age seven, and Emily, who is five years old.

David Taylor graduated with a bachelor's degree from Southern Illinois University at Carbondale, Department of Cinema and Photography in 1985. He paid for his education by photographing weddings. After college he moved to Chicago where he worked as a commercial photographer from 1985 to 1992. In 1992, David returned to his roots to photograph weddings and portraits. In 1998, David joined the Professional Photographers of America, and by 2003 had earned the degree Master of Photography. He has had three prints and a wedding album accepted to the PPA Loan Collection and, according to the PPA, had the best wedding album in the nation in 2001. His work has been seen on the cover of *Rangefinder* and inside *Professional Photographer* magazine. In 2001, he moved his family and business to Hawaii where he creates beautiful timeless images of children, families, high school seniors, and weddings. Website: www.photokailua.com.

T. J. Walker founded Command Z, a fully integrated graphic design and corporate branding firm, in 1991 with a solid foundation in graphic design and corporate identity. Terry brought his experiences as senior designer of Delahoussaye Design, a large New York City–based organization, with him as he founded Command Z. It was his intent from the start to build a small firm where he could personally oversee every project. Command Z emphasized quality control with a commitment to command performance and cutting-edge conceptualizations that ensure client satisfaction. His client list includes some of the biggest names in the entertainment industry as well as privately owned companies. His record of repeat business speaks to his success. With the combined efforts of one of his longtime clients, Terry now serves as creative director for the Hopper Group, an advertising agency that specializes in entertainment venues throughout the country. Website: www.hopper-group.com.

INDEX

OTHER BOOKS FROM

Amherst Media®

Also by the Same Author . . .

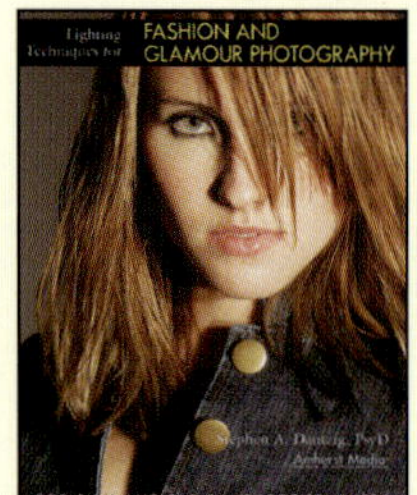

LIGHTING TECHNIQUES FOR
FASHION AND GLAMOUR PHOTOGRAPHY

In fashion and glamour photography, light is the key to producing images with impact. With these techniques, you'll be primed for success! $29.95 list, 8½x11, 128p, over 200 color images, index, order no. 1795.

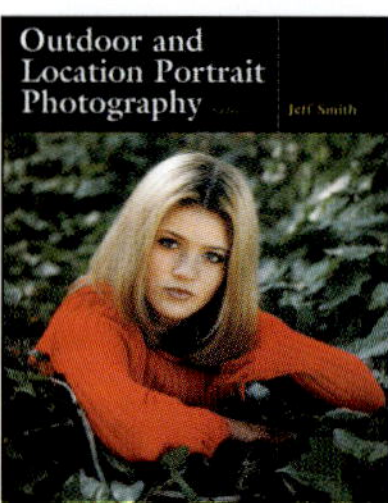

OUTDOOR AND LOCATION PORTRAIT PHOTOGRAPHY, 2nd Ed.

Jeff Smith

Learn to work with natural light, select locations, and make clients look their best. Packed with step-by-step discussions and illustrations to help you shoot like a pro! $29.95 list, 8½x11, 128p, 80 color photos, index, order no. 1632.

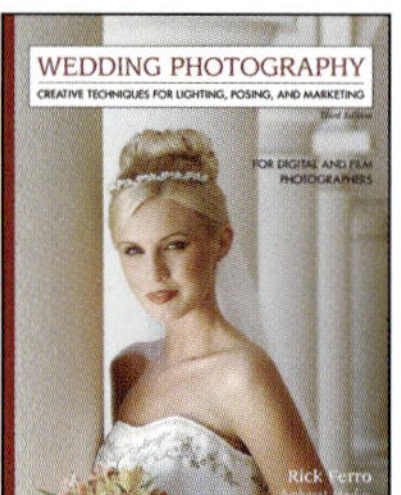

WEDDING PHOTOGRAPHY

CREATIVE TECHNIQUES FOR LIGHTING, POSING, AND MARKETING, 3rd Ed.

Rick Ferro

Creative techniques for lighting and posing wedding portraits that will set your work apart from the competition. Covers every phase of wedding photography. $29.95 list, 8½x11, 128p, 125 color photos, index, order no. 1649.

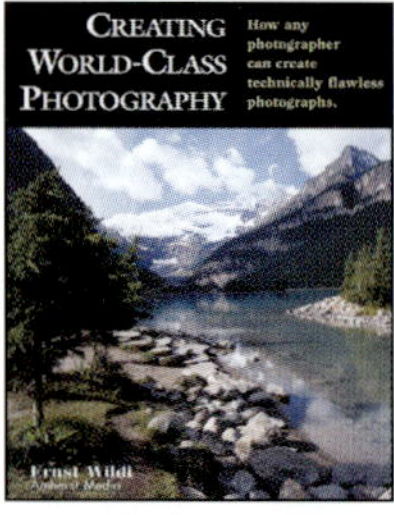

CREATING WORLD-CLASS PHOTOGRAPHY

Ernst Wildi

Learn how to create technically flawless photos. Features techniques for eliminating technical flaws in all types of photos—from portraits to landscapes. Includes the Zone System, digital imaging, and much more. $29.95 list, 8½x11, 128p, 120 color photos, index, order no. 1718.

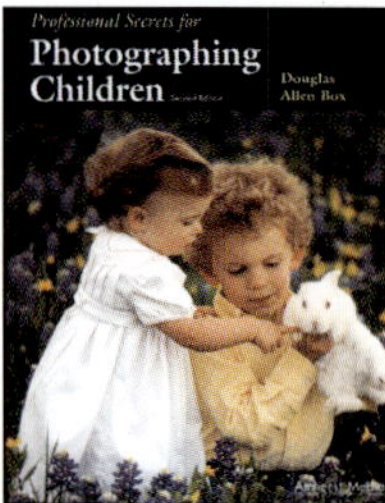

PROFESSIONAL SECRETS FOR PHOTOGRAPHING CHILDREN

2nd Ed.

Douglas Allen Box

Covers every aspect of photographing children, from preparing them for the shoot, to selecting the right clothes to capture a child's personality, and shooting storybook themes. $29.95 list, 8½x11, 128p, 80 color photos, index, order no. 1635.

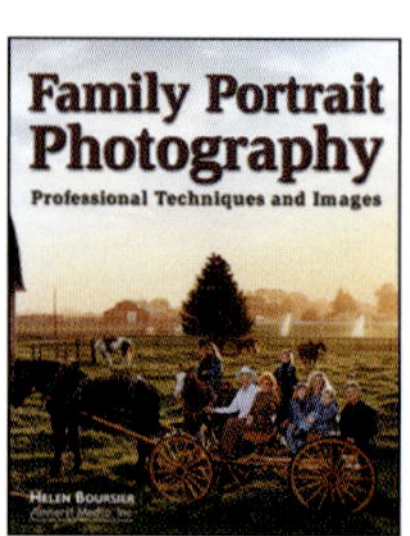

FAMILY PORTRAIT PHOTOGRAPHY

Helen Boursier

Top professionals teach you how to operate a successful studio. Includes marketing family portraits, working with clients, posing, lighting, selection of equipment, and images from a variety of top portrait shooters. $29.95 list, 8½x11, 120p, 120 b&w and color photos, index, order no. 1629.

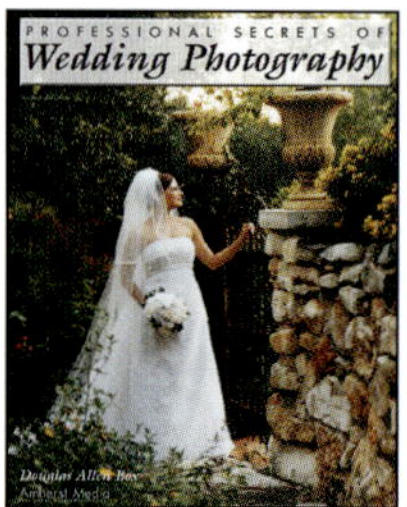

PROFESSIONAL SECRETS OF WEDDING PHOTOGRAPHY, 2nd Ed.

Douglas Allen Box

Top-quality portraits are analyzed to teach you the art of professional wedding portraiture. Lighting diagrams, posing information, and technical specs are included for every image. $29.95 list, 8½x11, 128p, 80 color photos, order no. 1658.

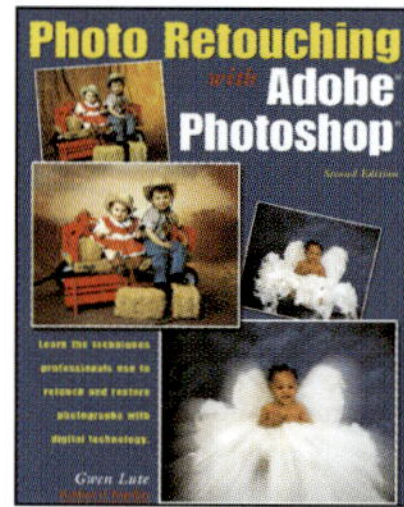

PHOTO RETOUCHING WITH ADOBE® PHOTOSHOP®, 2nd Ed.

Gwen Lute

Teaches every phase of the process, from scanning to final output. Learn to restore damaged photos, correct imperfections, create realistic composite images, and correct for dazzling color. $29.95 list, 8½x11, 120p, 100 color images, order no. 1660.

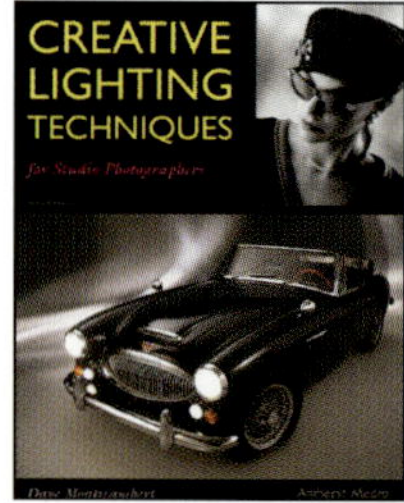

CREATIVE LIGHTING TECHNIQUES FOR STUDIO PHOTOGRAPHERS, 2nd Ed.

Dave Montizambert

Whether you are shooting portraits, cars, tabletop, or any other subject, Dave Montizambert teaches you the skills you need to take complete control of your lighting. $29.95 list, 8½x11, 120p, 80 color photos, order no. 1666.

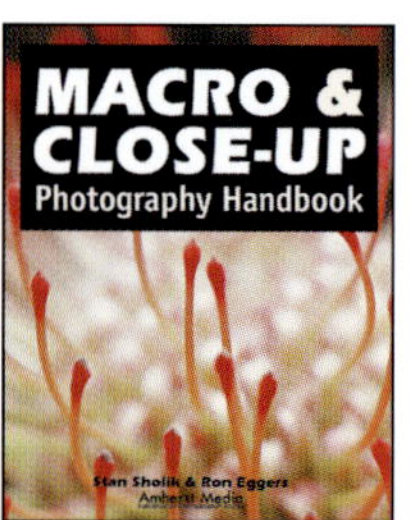

MACRO & CLOSE-UP PHOTOGRAPHY HANDBOOK

Stan Sholik and Ron Eggers

Learn to get close and capture breathtaking images of small subjects—flowers, stamps, jewelry, insects, etc. Designed with the 35mm shooter in mind, this is a comprehensive manual full of step-by-step techniques. $29.95 list, 8½x11, 120p, 80 b&w and color photos, order no. 1686.

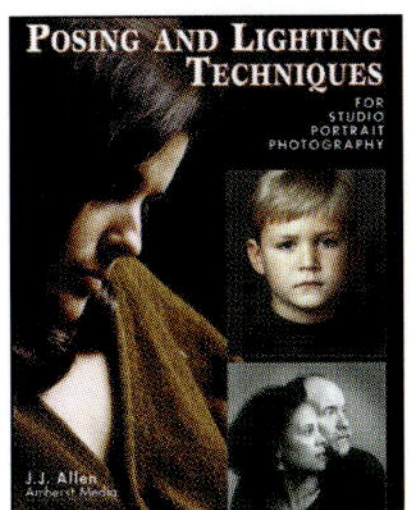

POSING AND LIGHTING TECHNIQUES FOR STUDIO PHOTOGRAPHERS

J. J. Allen

Master the skills you need to create beautiful lighting for portraits. Posing techniques for flattering, classic images help turn every portrait into a work of art. $29.95 list, 8½x11, 120p, 125 color photos, order no. 1697.

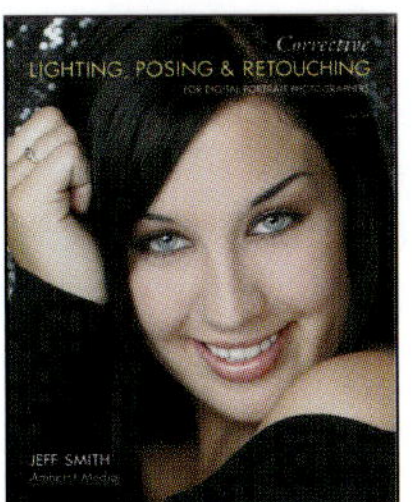

CORRECTIVE LIGHTING, POSING & RETOUCHING FOR DIGITAL PORTRAIT PHOTOGRAPHERS, 2nd Ed.

Jeff Smith

Learn to make every client look his or her best by using lighting and posing to conceal real or imagined flaws—from baldness, to acne, to figure flaws. $34.95 list, 8½x11, 120p, 150 color photos, order no. 1711.

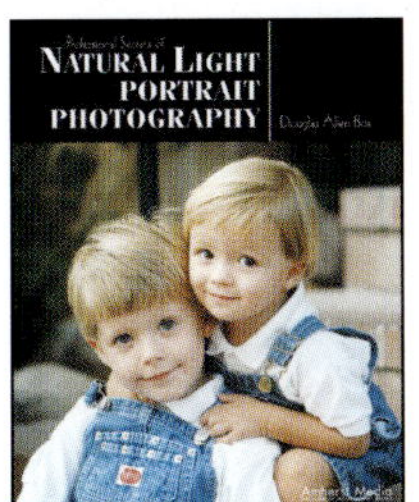

PROFESSIONAL SECRETS OF

NATURAL LIGHT PORTRAIT PHOTOGRAPHY

Douglas Allen Box

Use natural light to create hassle-free portraiture. Beautifully illustrated with detailed instructions on equipment, lighting, and posing. $29.95list,8½x11, 128p, 80 color photos, order no. 1706.

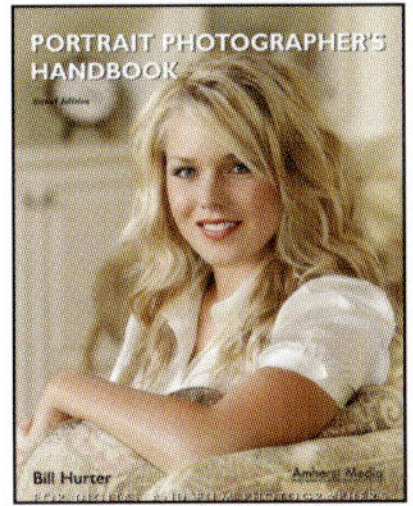

PORTRAIT PHOTOGRAPHER'S HANDBOOK, 2nd Ed.

Bill Hurter

Bill Hurter has compiled a step-by-step guide to portraiture that easily leads the reader through all phases of portrait photography. This book will be an asset to experienced photographers and beginners alike. $29.95 list, 8½x11, 128p, 175 color photos, order no. 1708.

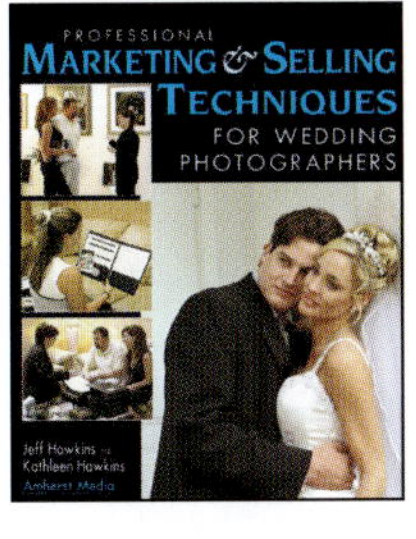

PROFESSIONAL MARKETING & SELLING TECHNIQUES FOR WEDDING PHOTOGRAPHERS

Jeff Hawkins and Kathleen Hawkins

Learn the business of wedding photography. Includes consultations, direct mail, advertising, internet marketing, and much more. $29.95 list, 8½x11, 128p, 80 color photos, order no. 1712.

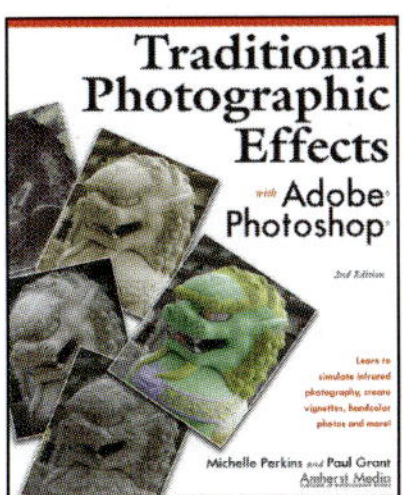

TRADITIONAL PHOTOGRAPHIC EFFECTS WITH ADOBE® PHOTOSHOP®, 2nd Ed.

Michelle Perkins and Paul Grant

Use Photoshop to enhance your photos with handcoloring, vignettes, soft focus, and much more. Step-by-step instructions are included for each technique for easy learning. $29.95 list, 8½x11, 128p, 150 color images, order no. 1721.

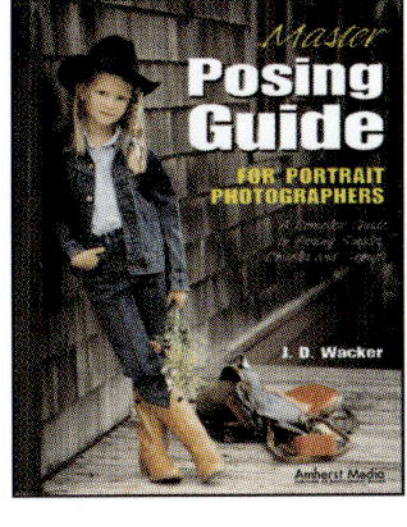

MASTER POSING GUIDE FOR PORTRAIT PHOTOGRAPHERS

J. D. Wacker

Learn the techniques you need to pose single portrait subjects, couples, and groups for studio or location portraits. Includes techniques for photographing weddings, teams, children, special events, and much more. $29.95 list, 8½x11, 128p, 80 photos, order no. 1722.

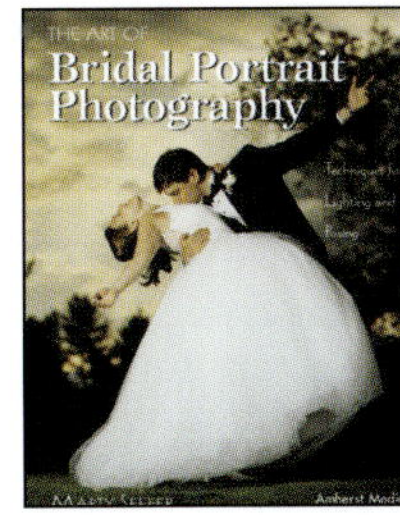

THE ART OF BRIDAL PORTRAIT PHOTOGRAPHY

Marty Seefer

Learn to give every client your best and create timeless images that are sure to become family heirlooms. Seefer takes readers through every step of the bridal shoot, ensuring flawless results. $29.95 list, 8½x11, 128p, 70 color photos, order no. 1730.

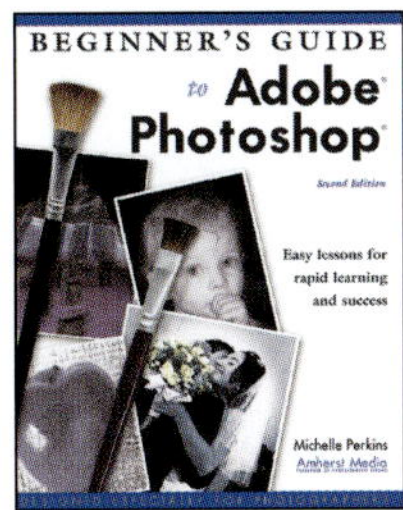

BEGINNER'S GUIDE TO ADOBE® PHOTOSHOP®, 2nd Ed.

Michelle Perkins

Learn to effectively make your images look their best, create original artwork, or add unique effects to any image. Topics are presented in short, easy-to-digest sections that will boost confidence and ensure outstanding images. $29.95 list, 8½x11, 128p, 300 color images, order no. 1732.

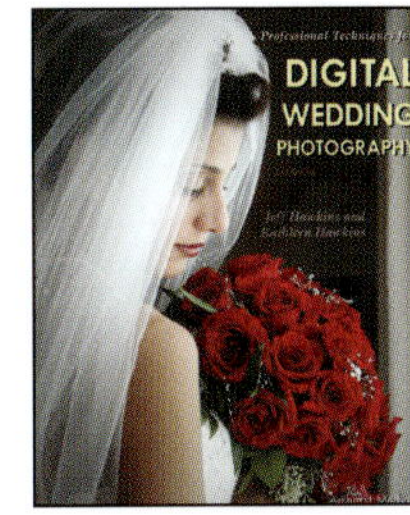

PROFESSIONAL TECHNIQUES FOR

DIGITAL WEDDING PHOTOGRAPHY, 2nd Ed.

Jeff Hawkins and Kathleen Hawkins

From selecting equipment, to marketing, to building a digital workflow, this book teaches how to make digital work for you. $29.95 list, 8½x11, 128p, 85 color images, order no. 1735.

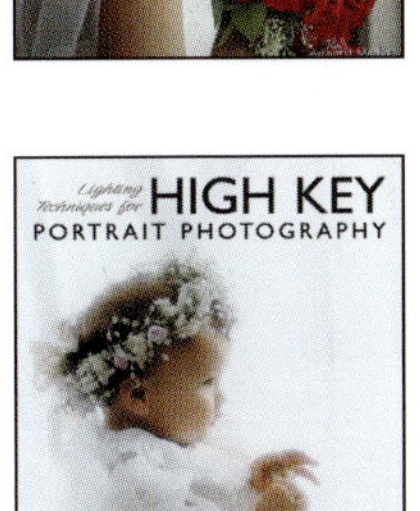

LIGHTING TECHNIQUES FOR

HIGH KEY PORTRAIT PHOTOGRAPHY

Norman Phillips

Learn to meet the challenges of high key portrait photography and produce images your clients will adore. $29.95 list, 8½x11, 128p, 100 color photos, order no. 1736.

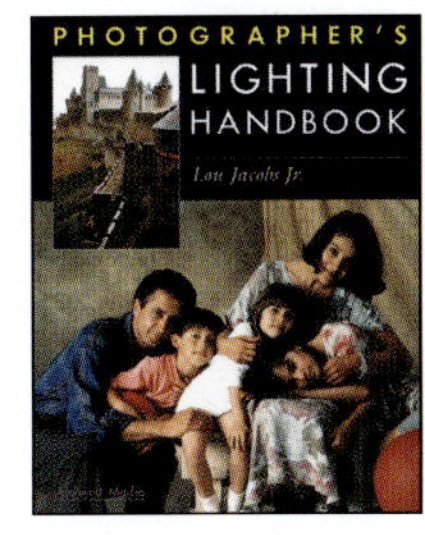

PHOTOGRAPHER'S LIGHTING HANDBOOK

Lou Jacobs Jr.

Think you need a room full of expensive lighting equipment to get great shots? With a few simple techniques and basic equipment, you can produce the images you desire. $29.95 list, 8½x11, 128p, 130 color photos, order no. 1737.

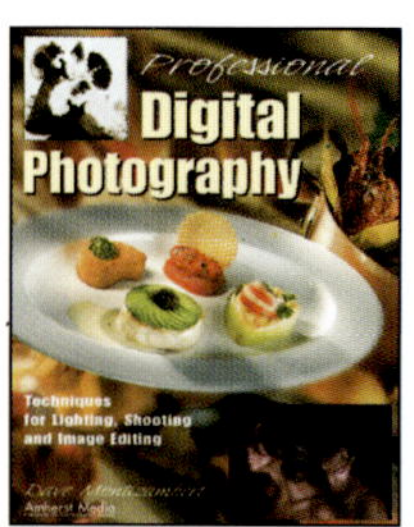

PROFESSIONAL DIGITAL PHOTOGRAPHY

Dave Montizambert

From monitor calibration, to color balancing, to creating advanced artistic effects, this book provides those skilled in basic digital imaging with the techniques they need to take their photography to the next level. $29.95 list, 8½x11, 128p, 120 color photos, order no. 1739.

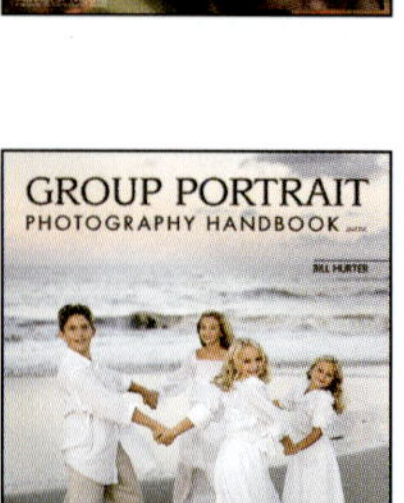

GROUP PORTRAIT PHOTOGRAPHY HANDBOOK, 2nd Ed.

Bill Hurter

Featuring over 100 images by top photographers, this book offers practical techniques for composing, lighting, and posing group portraits—whether in the studio or on location. $34.95 list, 8½x11, 128p, 120 color photos, order no. 1740.

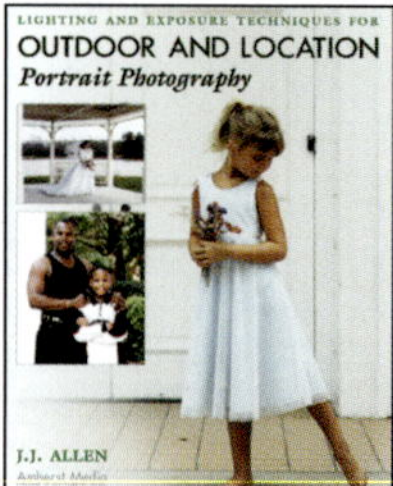

LIGHTING AND EXPOSURE TECHNIQUES FOR OUTDOOR AND LOCATION PORTRAIT PHOTOGRAPHY

J. J. Allen

Meet the challenges of changing light and complex settings with techniques that help you achieve great images every time. $29.95 list, 8½x11, 128p, 150 color photos, order no. 1741.

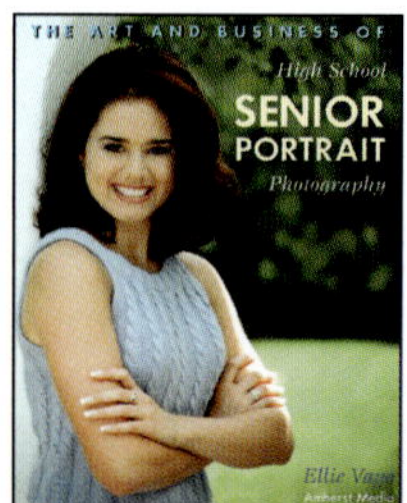

THE ART AND BUSINESS OF HIGH SCHOOL SENIOR PORTRAIT PHOTOGRAPHY

Ellie Vayo

Learn the techniques that have made Ellie Vayo's studio one of the most profitable senior portrait businesses in the U.S. $29.95 list, 8½x11, 128p, 100 color photos, order no. 1743.

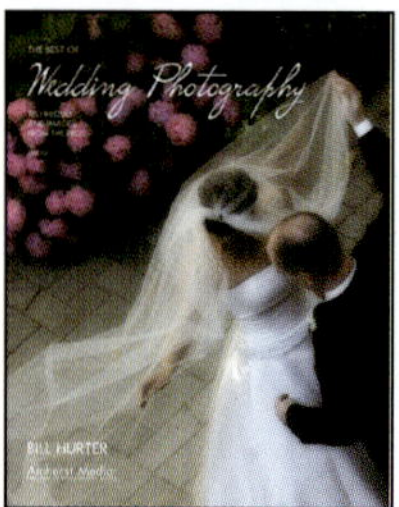

THE BEST OF WEDDING PHOTOGRAPHY, 2nd Ed.

Bill Hurter

Learn how the top wedding photographers in the industry transform special moments into lasting romantic treasures with the posing, lighting, album design, and customer service pointers found in this book. $34.95 list, 8½x11, 128p, 150 color photos, order no. 1747.

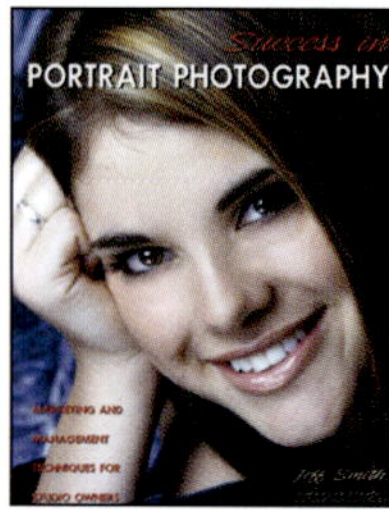

SUCCESS IN PORTRAIT PHOTOGRAPHY

Jeff Smith

Many photographers realize too late that camera skills alone do not ensure success. This book will teach photographers how to run savvy marketing campaigns, attract clients, and provide top-notch customer service. $29.95 list, 8½x11, 128p, 100 color photos, order no. 1748.

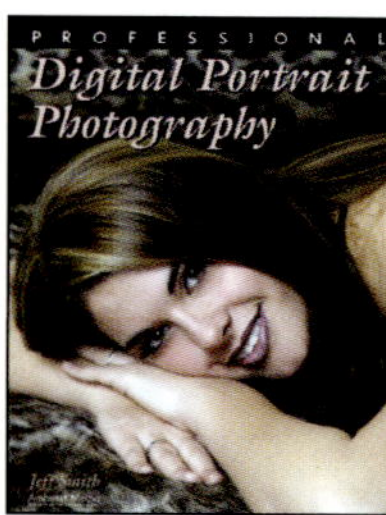

PROFESSIONAL DIGITAL PORTRAIT PHOTOGRAPHY

Jeff Smith

Because the learning curve is so steep, making the transition to digital can be frustrating. Author Jeff Smith shows readers how to shoot, edit, and retouch their images—while avoiding common pitfalls. $29.95 list, 8½x11, 128p, 100 color photos, order no. 1750.

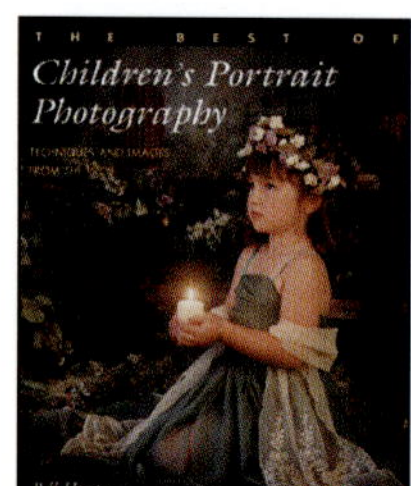

THE BEST OF CHILDREN'S PORTRAIT PHOTOGRAPHY

Bill Hurter

Rangefinder editor Bill Hurter draws upon the experience and work of top professional photographers, uncovering the creative and technical skills they use to create their magical portraits of these young subejcts. $29.95 list, 8½x11, 128p, 150 color photos, order no. 1752.

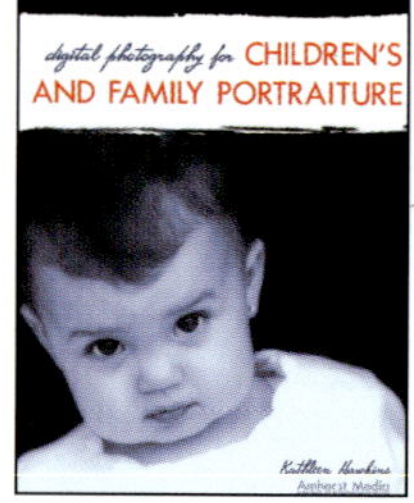

DIGITAL PHOTOGRAPHY FOR CHILDREN'S AND FAMILY PORTRAITURE

Kathleen Hawkins

Discover how digital photography can boost your sales, enhance your creativity, and improve your studio's workflow. $29.95 list, 8½x11, 128p, 130 color images, index, order no. 1770.

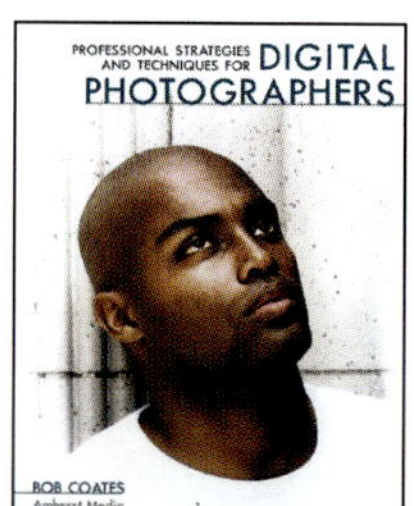

PROFESSIONAL STRATEGIES AND TECHNIQUES FOR DIGITAL PHOTOGRAPHERS

Bob Coates

Learn how professionals—from portrait artists to commercial specialists—enhance their images with digital techniques. $29.95 list, 8½x11, 128p, 130 color photos, index, order no. 1772.

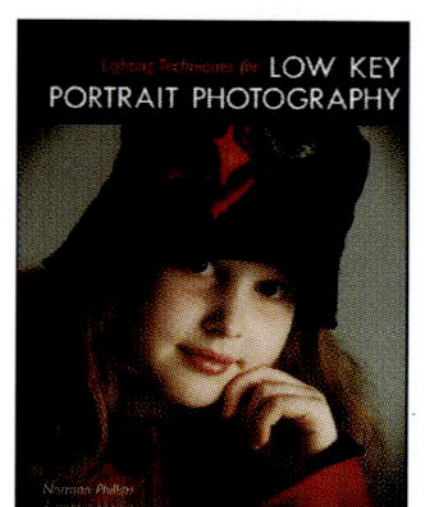

LIGHTING TECHNIQUES FOR LOW KEY PORTRAIT PHOTOGRAPHY

Norman Phillips

Learn to create the dark tones and dramatic lighting that typify this classic portrait style. $29.95 list, 8½x11, 128p, 100 color photos, index, order no. 1773.

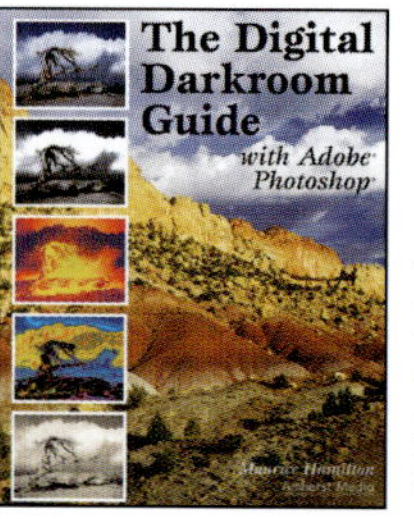

THE DIGITAL DARKROOM GUIDE WITH ADOBE® PHOTOSHOP®

Maurice Hamilton

Bring the skills and control of the photographic darkroom to your desktop with this complete manual. $29.95 list, 8½x11, 128p, 140 color images, index, order no. 1775.

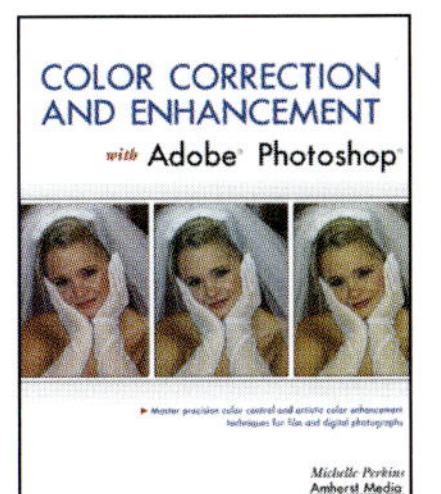

COLOR CORRECTION AND ENHANCEMENT WITH ADOBE® PHOTOSHOP®

Michelle Perkins

Master precision color correction and artistic color enhancement techniques for scanned and digital photos. $29.95 list, 8½x11, 128p, 300 color images, index, order no. 1776.

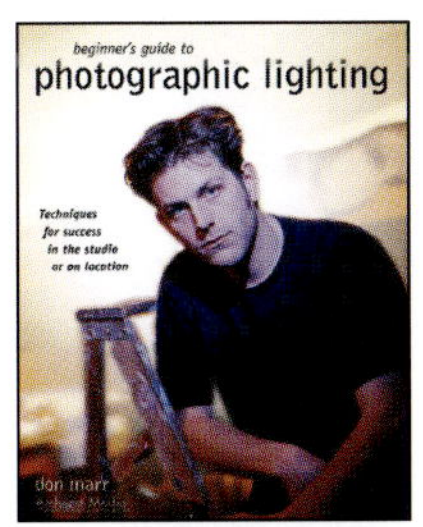

BEGINNER'S GUIDE TO PHOTOGRAPHIC LIGHTING

Don Marr

Create high-impact photographs of any subject with Marr's simple techniques. From edgy and dynamic to subdued and natural, this book will show you how to get the myriad effects you're after. $29.95 list, 8½x11, 128p, 150 color photos, index, order no. 1785.

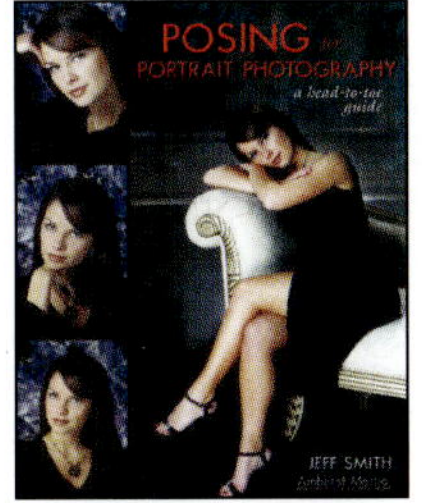

POSING FOR PORTRAIT PHOTOGRAPHY

A HEAD-TO-TOE GUIDE

Jeff Smith

Author Jeff Smith teaches surefire techniques for fine-tuning every aspect of the pose for the most flattering results. $29.95 list, 8½x11, 128p, 150 color photos, index, order no. 1786.

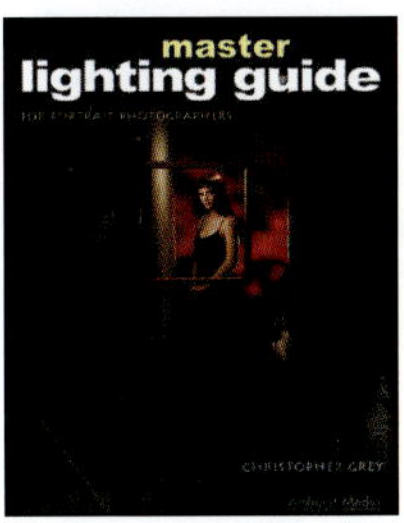

MASTER LIGHTING GUIDE

FOR PORTRAIT PHOTOGRAPHERS

Christopher Grey

Efficiently light executive and model portraits, high and low key images, and more. Master traditional lighting styles and use creative modifications that will maximize your results. $29.95 list, 8½x11, 128p, 300 color photos, index, order no. 1778.

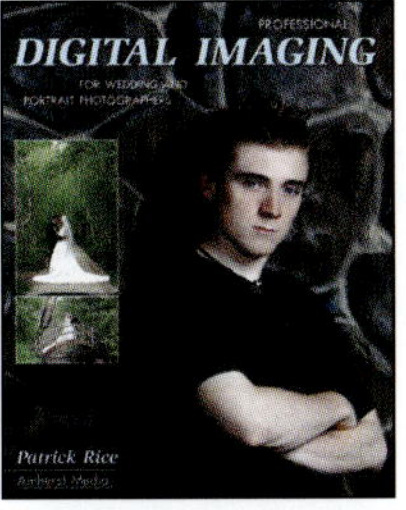

PROFESSIONAL DIGITAL IMAGING FOR WEDDING AND PORTRAIT PHOTOGRAPHERS

Patrick Rice

Build your business and enhance your creativity with practical strategies for making digital work for you. $29.95 list, 8½x11, 128p, 200 color photos, index, order no. 1780.

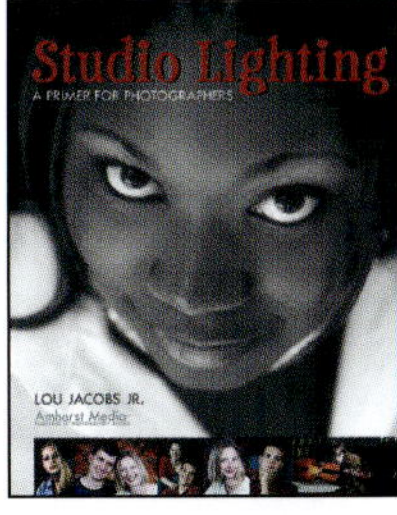

STUDIO LIGHTING

A PRIMER FOR PHOTOGRAPHERS

Lou Jacobs Jr.

Get started in studio lighting. Jacobs outlines equipment needs, terminology, lighting setups and much more, showing you how to create top-notch portraits and still lifes. $29.95 list, 8½x11, 128p, 190 color photos index, order no. 1787.

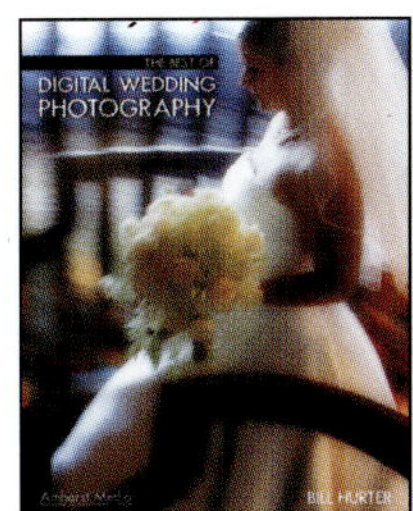

THE BEST OF DIGITAL WEDDING PHOTOGRAPHY

Bill Hurter

Explore the groundbreaking images and techniques that are shaping the future of wedding photography. Includes dazzling photos from over 35 top photographers. $29.95 list, 8½x11, 128p, 175 color photos, index, order no. 1793.

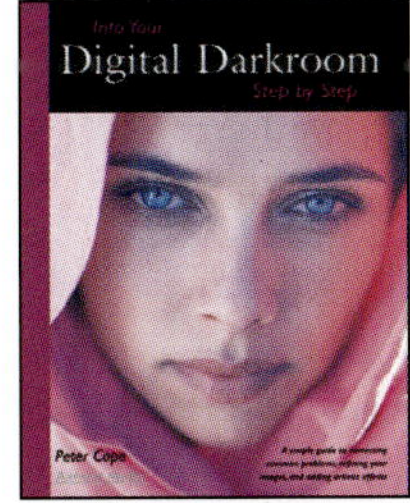

INTO YOUR DIGITAL DARKROOM STEP BY STEP

Peter Cope

Make the most of every image—digital or film—with these techniques for photographers. Learn to enhance color, add special effects, and much more. $29.95 list, 8½x11, 128p, 300 color images, index, order no. 1794.

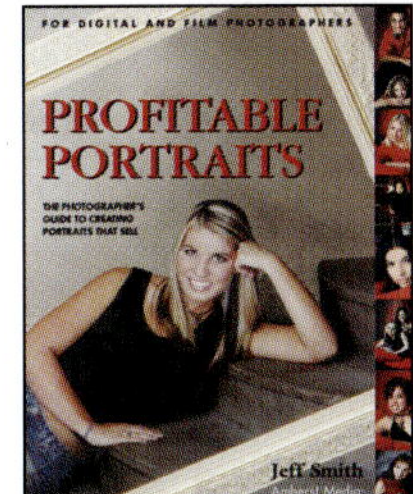

PROFITABLE PORTRAITS

THE PHOTOGRAPHER'S GUIDE TO CREATING PORTRAITS THAT SELL

Jeff Smith

Learn how to design images that are precisely tailored to your clients' tastes—portraits that will practically sell themselves! $29.95 list, 8½x11, 128p, 100 color photos, index, order no. 1797.

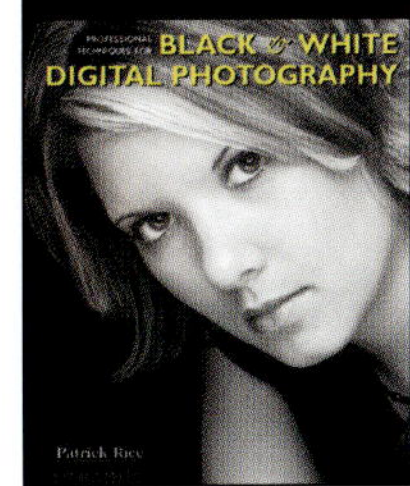

PROFESSIONAL TECHNIQUES FOR BLACK & WHITE DIGITAL PHOTOGRAPHY

Patrick Rice

Digital makes it easier than ever to create black & white images. With these techniques, you'll learn to achieve dazzling results! $29.95 list, 8½x11, 128p, 100 color photos, index, order no. 1798.

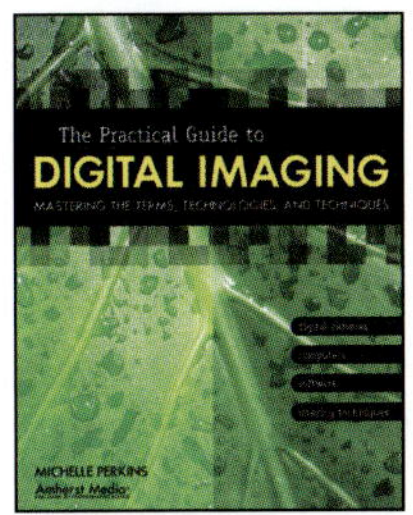

THE PRACTICAL GUIDE TO DIGITAL IMAGING

Michelle Perkins

This book takes the mystery (and intimidation!) out of digital imaging. Short, simple lessons make it easy to master all the terms and techniques. $29.95 list, 8½x11, 128p, 150 color images, index, order no. 1799.

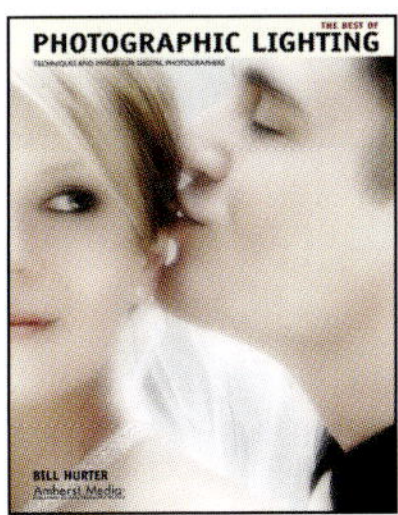

THE BEST OF PHOTOGRAPHIC LIGHTING

Bill Hurter

Top professionals reveal the secrets behind their successful strategies for studio, location, and outdoor lighting. Packed with tips for portraits, still lifes, and more. $34.95 list, 8½x11, 128p, 150 color photos, index, order no. 1808.

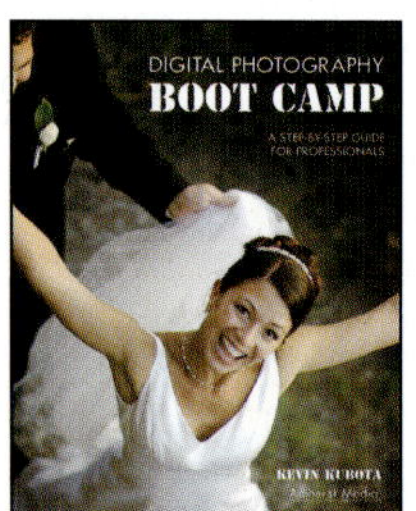

DIGITAL PHOTOGRAPHY BOOT CAMP

Kevin Kubota

Kevin Kubota's popular workshop is now a book! A down-and-dirty, step-by-step course in building a professional photography workflow and creating digital images that sell! $34.95 list, 8½x11, 128p, 250 color images, index, order no. 1809.

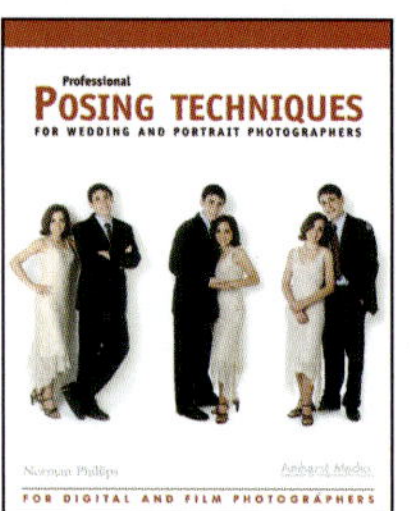

PROFESSIONAL POSING TECHNIQUES FOR WEDDING AND PORTRAIT PHOTOGRAPHERS

Norman Phillips

Master the techniques you need to pose subjects successfully—whether you are working with men, women, children, or groups. $34.95 list, 8½x11, 128p, 260 color photos, index, order no. 1810.

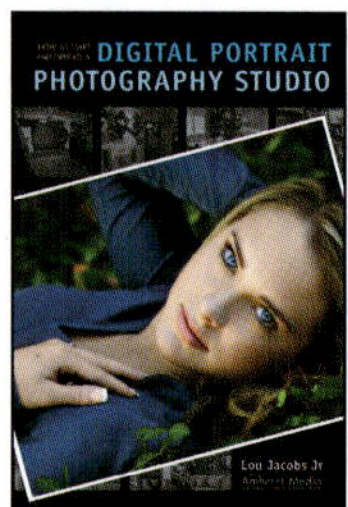

HOW TO START AND OPERATE A

DIGITAL PORTRAIT PHOTOGRAPHY STUDIO

Lou Jacobs Jr.

Learn how to build a successful digital portrait photography business—or breathe new life into an existing studio. $39.95 list, 6x9, 224p, 150 color images, index, order no. 1811.

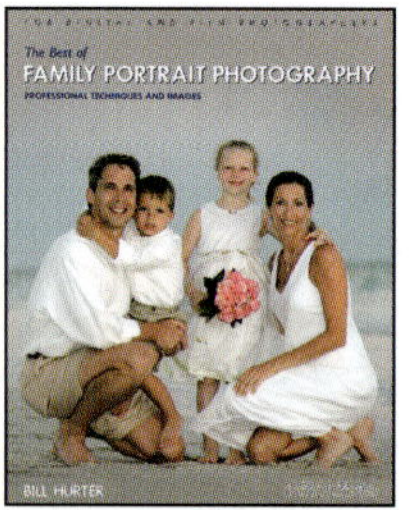

THE BEST OF FAMILY PORTRAIT PHOTOGRAPHY

Bill Hurter

Acclaimed photographers reveal the secrets behind their most successful family portraits. Packed with award-winning images and helpful techniques. $34.95 list, 8½x11, 128p, 150 color photos, index, order no. 1812.

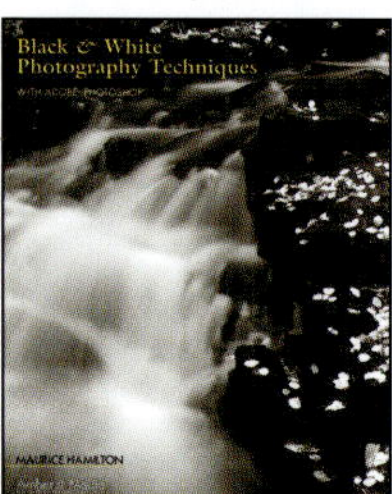

BLACK & WHITE PHOTOGRAPHY TECHNIQUES WITH ADOBE® PHOTOSHOP®

Maurice Hamilton

Become a master of the black & white digital darkroom! Covers all the skills required to perfect your black & white images and produce dazzling fine-art prints. $34.95 list, 8½x11, 128p, 150 color/b&w images, index, order no. 1813.

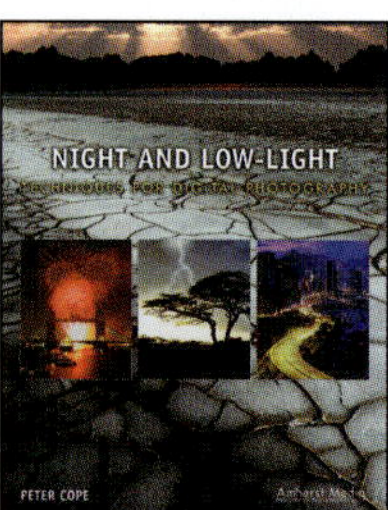

NIGHT AND LOW-LIGHT TECHNIQUES FOR DIGITAL PHOTOGRAPHY

Peter Cope

With even simple point-and-shoot digital cameras, you can create dazzling nighttime photos. Get started quickly with this step-by-step guide. $34.95 list, 8½x11, 128p, 100 color photos, index, order no. 1814.

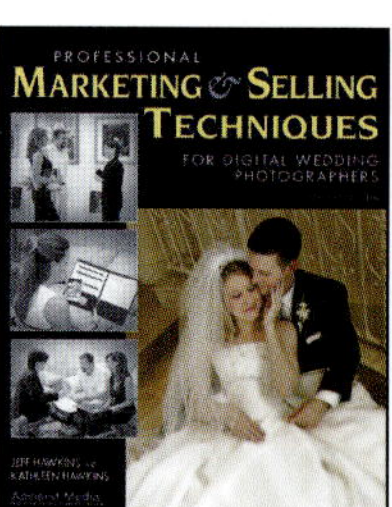

PROFESSIONAL MARKETING & SELLING TECHNIQUES FOR DIGITAL WEDDING PHOTOGRAPHERS, SECOND EDITION

Kathleen Hawkins

Taking great photos isn't enough to ensure success! Become a master marketer and salesperson with these easy techniques. $34.95 list, 8½x11, 128p, 150 color photos, index, order no. 1815.

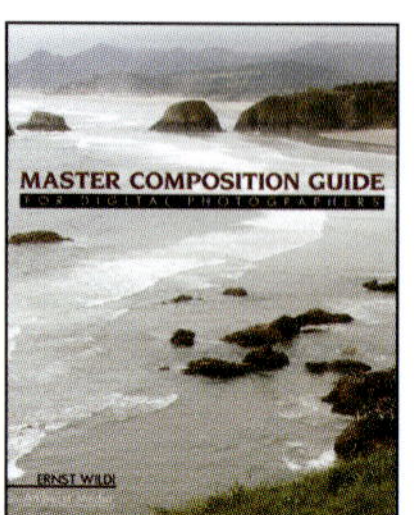

MASTER COMPOSITION GUIDE FOR DIGITAL PHOTOGRAPHERS

Ernst Wildi

Composition can truly make or break an image. Master photographer Ernst Wildi shows you how to analyze your scene or subject and produce the best-possible image. $34.95 list, 8½x11, 128p, 150 color photos, index, order no. 1817.

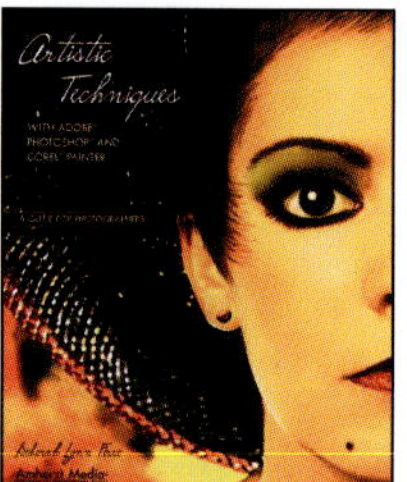

ARTISTIC TECHNIQUES WITH ADOBE® PHOTOSHOP® AND COREL® PAINTER®

Deborah Lynn Ferro

Flex your creative skills and learn how to transform photographs into fine-art masterpieces. Step-by-step techniques make it easy! $34.95 list, 8½x11, 128p, 200 color images, index, order no. 1806.